W9-BMH-835

BUMPING INTO GENIUSES

MY LIFE INSIDE THE
ROCK AND ROLL BUSINESS

Danny Goldberg

GOTHAM
BOOKS

GOTHAM BOOKS
Published by Penguin Group (USA) Inc.
375 Hudson Street, New York, New York 10014, U.S.A.
Penguin Group (Canada), 90 Eglinton Avenue East, Suite 700,
Toronto, Ontario M4P 2Y3,
Canada (a division of Pearson Penguin Canada Inc.);
Penguin Books Ltd, 80 Strand, London WC2R 0RL, England;
Penguin Ireland, 25 St Stephen's Green, Dublin 2,
Ireland (a division of Penguin Books Ltd);
Penguin Group (Australia), 250 Camberwell Road,
Camberwell, Victoria 3124, Australia
(a division of Pearson Australia Group Pty Ltd);
Penguin Books India Pvt Ltd, 11 Community Centre,
Panchsheel Park, New Delhi - 110 017, India;
Penguin Group (NZ), 67 Apollo Drive, Rosedale, North Shore 0632,
New Zealand (a division of Pearson New Zealand Ltd);
Penguin Books (South Africa) (Pty) Ltd, 24 Sturdee Avenue,
Rosebank, Johannesburg 2196, South Africa

Penguin Books Ltd, Registered Offices: 80 Strand, London WC2R 0RL, England

Published by Gotham Books, a member of Penguin Group (USA) Inc.

First printing, September 2008
1   3   5   7   9   10   8   6   4   2

Copyright © 2008 by Danny Goldberg
All rights reserved

Grateful acknowledgment is made to the following for permission to reprint:

Pages 251–52: "Life'll Kill Ya" by Warren Zevon, used with permission by Zevon Music
Page 264: "Dirty Life and Times" by Warren Zevon, used with permission by Zevon Music
Page 278–79: "My Ride's Here" by Warren Zevon, used with permission by Zevon Music

Gotham Books and the skyscraper logo are trademarks of Penguin Group (USA) Inc.

LIBRARY OF CONGRESS CATALOGING-IN-PUBLICATION DATA

Goldberg, Danny, 1950–
Bumping into geniuses: my life inside the rock and roll business / Danny Goldberg.
p. cm.
ISBN 978-1-592-40370-7 (hardcover)
1. Goldberg, Danny, 1950–   2. Sound recording executives and producers—United States.
3. Sound recording industry. I. Title.
ML429.G63A3 2008
781.660973—dc22   2008013671

Printed in the United States of America
Set in Sabon with Rockwell Display
Designed by Elke Sigal

While the author has made every effort to provide accurate telephone numbers and Internet addresses at the time of publication, neither the publisher nor the author assumes any responsibility for errors, or for changes that occur after publication. Further, the publisher does not have any control over and does not assume any responsibility for author or third-party Web sites or their content.

To Rosemary Carroll and our children,
Katie Goldberg and Max Goldberg

And to two great friends who
have encouraged me for many decades,
Michael Des Barres and David Silver

CONTENTS

ACKNOWLEDGMENTS

Thanks to Rosemary for enduring my many mood swings and for her excellent advice. She prevented numerous errors but deserves none of the blame for those that remain.

Thanks to my agent, Steve Wasserman, who never wavered.

At Gotham, thanks to Bill Shinker for taking the plunge; to my editor, Lauren Marino, for her advocacy, guidance, and patience; Brianne Ramagosa; and to copy editor supreme, Craig Schneider.

My assistant, Laura Benanchietti, was indispensable in countless ways. My colleagues at Gold Village Entertainment, Jesse Bauer, Brady Brock, and Cyndi Villano, have also been great sources of support.

Steve Earle's advice during the writing is yet another example of the fact that he manages my career at least as much as I manage his.

Eric Alterman, Sara Davidson, Leigh Haber, Robert Christgau, Michael Des Barres, and David Silver all gave valuable advice.

I am very grateful to Lee Abrams, Susan Blond, Howard Bloom, Michael Des Barres, B. P. Fallon, Steve Earle, Les Garland, Debbie Gold, Patrick Goldstein, Robert Hilburn, Kid Leo, Kenny Laguna, Mitchell Markus, Mario Medius, Krist Novoselic, Steve Paul, Jonny Podell, Steve Popovich, Bonnie Raitt, Vin Scelsa, Bonnie Simmons, Gene Simmons, Patti Smith, Robert Smith, Larry Solters, Mark Spector, Paul Stanley, Burt Stein, Norm Winer, Peter Wolf, and Jordan Zevon for providing me with their recollections and insights, and to Courtney Love for her friendship.

ACKNOWLEDGMENTS

I was aided greatly by the reading of Carrie Borzillo's *Nirvana: A Day by Day Eyewitness Chronicle* and Jim Ladd's *Radio Waves,* and repeated viewing of Martin Scorsese's film *No Direction Home.*

My rock and roll taste was formed at Fieldston High School by friends including Judy Barnett, Bob Bearnot, Mark Brownstone, June Christopher, David Comins, Karen Gilbert, Joel Goodman (BFF), Karen Hawes, Gil Scott Heron, Billy Horowitz, Joanne Kinoy, Judy Kinoy, Peter Kinoy, Dickie Kleinberg, John Krich, Alex Richman, Laura Rosenberg, Susan Solomon, Robin Scott, and John Scott, as well as two non-Fieldston friends, Val Sowall and Tom Lubart. My brother Peter Goldberg turned me on to both the Kinks and the Animals.

Artemis Records existed because Michael Chambers believed in it and in me. Also indispensable to Artemis were Patrick Panzarella, Ray Chambers, and Daniel Glass.

Eternal thanks to my guru and teacher Hilda Charlton and to my sister Rachel Goldberg for the example she sets in resolving conflicts.

And thanks to every artist I ever met, worked with, or was inspired by and to the formless mysterious force that created rock and roll.

BUMPING INTO GENIUSES

SECRETS OF THE ROCK AND ROLL BUSINESS

"There aren't any secrets," Atlantic Records president Jerry Wexler growled at me, as if I were the stupidest person he had ever met. I was nineteen and it was the winter of 1969, more than thirty-five years before Wexler would be immortalized by Richard Schiff's portrayal of him in the movie *Ray*. I was writing a column for the weekly trade magazine *Record World* when Wexler had asked one of his executives, Danny Fields, to gather a group of young journalists who wrote about rock and roll. The real Wexler was far more imposing than the cinematic version. He was broad-shouldered, with a salt-and-pepper beard and sunken eyes that gave him the look of an Old Testament prophet. He had a thick Bronx accent, an intimidating intellect, and the ultimate rock and roll and R&B pedigrees.

Some months earlier, at the storied Greenwich Village nightclub the Village Gate, I had seen a talented R&B singer named Judy Clay dedicate her hit, "Storybook Children," to Wexler, who stood up and waved with an understated noblesse oblige.

I had no idea what a record company president did, but I was stunned that such a soulful singer would publicly acknowledge a mere businessman. I soon discovered that Wexler had also worked with Otis Redding, Aretha Franklin, and Sam and Dave, and had been the person at Atlantic who actually signed Led Zeppelin.

My awe at Wexler's résumé was reinforced by seeing his house in Great Neck, Long Island, which had an entire room filled with gold records and a living room with original Légers. Amid thick marijuana smoke, Wexler played records on his state-of-the-art stereo, alternating an acetate of a forthcoming Delaney and Bonnie album with the Beatles' *Abbey Road*. It was a relief to know that even an insider like Wexler was a Beatles fan. "Those guys sure know what they're doing," he sighed, listening to the end of "Carry That Weight." During a moment between songs, in a lame attempt to enter the conversation, I asked Wexler if he was going to an upcoming conference on the music business. "I never go to those things," he snarled. "The premise is that you can go there and learn secrets. First of all, there aren't any secrets." He paused dramatically and then, with a wolfish grin, concluded, "And second of all, if there were any secrets, we wouldn't tell them."

Over the next several decades I would come to understand what he meant. Although I never came close to equaling Wexler's historical contribution to the music business, I was lucky enough to find myself in many situations that would make rock history. I had a press pass to the Woodstock Festival. I worked for Led Zeppelin from 1973 to 1976, first as their publicist and later as vice president of their record company. I managed Nirvana when *Nevermind* came out and Bonnie Raitt when she won four Grammys. I did PR for Kiss and Electric Light Orchestra. I worked closely with Bruce Springsteen on the *No Nukes* movie. At the peak of Fleetwood Mac's popularity I helped launch Stevie Nicks's solo career. And twenty-four years after meeting Wexler I was given his old job as president of Atlantic Records.

What few secrets there were could not be of any help to anyone else. But there were stories.

I can't be objective about the music business. I know it hurt a lot of people; artists were often lied to, royalties weren't always paid, bad people sometimes got promoted while good ones were fired. Drugs, misogyny, and death stalked rock and roll. A lot of shlock was produced. A lot of pretense masked shallow, materialistic quests for fame and money. It's not like I don't know these things and it's not that I mind writing about them. It's just that the part of the music business I know best, the rock and roll business, also produced and popularized a lot of music that I love. And it gave me and a lot of my friends a place in the world.

One nonsecret of the rock business is the intertwined nature of art and money. No one became a rock star by accident or against their will. Bob Dylan's memoir, *Chronicles,* begins not with a reference to Woody Guthrie or Allen Ginsberg, but with a meeting Dylan had as a young man with music publisher Lou Levy. Levy showed him the studio on the west side of Manhattan where Bill Haley and His Comets had recorded "Rock Around the Clock," which is widely considered the song that made rock and roll music a part of mainstream American culture.

Dylan did inject a folk music aesthetic into the commercial rock culture that existed. Steve Earle, who grew up in Texas in the 1960s, saw folk music as the vehicle that "brought art into rock and roll." The great beatnik poet Allen Ginsberg saw Dylan's song "A Hard Rain's A-Gonna Fall" as "the passing of the torch of Bohemian illumination and self-empowerment." The ideals and aesthetics that informed folk music of the early and mid-1960s would continue to be present in varying degrees in the minds of many successful rock artists for decades to come.

But one of the main points of Dylan going electric was not merely that he was adapting a more complex musical backdrop for his songs but that he was consciously entering a world and a business defined, at the time, by the Beatles. One of the salient points about Dylan's rock single "Like a Rolling Stone" was that it went to number one on the pop charts. If it hadn't been a hit, it wouldn't have mattered anywhere near as much. Members of Jefferson Airplane, the Grateful Dead, the Lovin' Spoonful, and the Byrds all started as folkies. Far from selling out, they were buying into a rock and roll culture and business that, from the very beginning, had been as much or more about money and success as about the nuances of the art. The trade-off was that rock and roll, corrupted as it had to be to win in the marketplace, was a vehicle that could impact millions more people and, yes, make artists lots of money The contradictions between art and commerce were not something that took folk artists by surprise, but were implicit in their decision to enter the world of rock and roll in the first place.

As the rock and roll business developed, most rock stars amassed unprecedented power in relation to the corporations that profited from their work. In addition to exploiting rebellious creative talent, the business itself was repeatedly transformed *by* that talent.

I was one of millions of rock fans who went to high school in the 1960s and one of a thousand or so who figured out a way into the business of rock and roll in the years that followed. I had all of the contradictions of rock and roll. Like most of my colleagues, I soon got caught up in the sometimes grim reality of what did and what did not make money. And like most of them I never stopped being a fan.

In 2007, at a memorial service for Ahmet Ertegun, the founder of Atlantic Records and Wexler's former partner and my former boss, David Geffen repeated one of Ahmet's aphorisms about the rock business. The way to get rich was to keep walking around until you bumped into a genius, and when you did— hold on and don't let go. In the early nineties, when I finally got an executive job at Atlantic, the story had been repeated so many times that it had become an axiom. Of course, no genius was likely to let you hold on very long if you didn't have anything to offer them. One had to know something valuable about aspects of the way the business worked. Some successful rock businessmen started as record producers. Some began as tour managers or concert promoters. Many offered financial expertise. I began in the subculture of rock criticism and publicity but, over the years, developed a reasonable number of clues about radio promotion, the workings of record companies, and the dynamics of touring as well. Like anyone in business I spent a fair amount of time arguing about and keeping track of money, but I was always of the school that was a little more interested in making the pie bigger than in calculating the distribution of the crumbs.

I was in tenth and eleventh grade in 1965 when the rock and roll business was in the middle of a dramatic expansion and reinvention that began with the launch of the Beatles in 1964. Although the Beatles had initially come across like a turbocharged version of the pop pinup idols that had preceded them, they soon spawned an intensification of focus on rock and roll by both artists and fans. In March 1965 Dylan released the first of his albums to include electric guitars, *Bringing It All Back Home,* a coherent and brilliant body of original songs such as "Mr. Tambourine Man" and "Gates of Eden." It made a dramatic contrast to the disposable pop/rock albums that had one or two hits and lots of filler. (Even the Beatles' early albums had contained a number of "cover" versions of old songs to pad out the Beatles' original material.) In July 1965, the Rolling Stones released *Out of Our Heads,* much of it edgy and rebellious for the time (this was the album that had "Satisfaction," and the first ironic commentary on the record business itself, "The Under Assistant West Coast Promotion Man"). Responding to the challenge in December 1965, the Beatles released *Rubber Soul,* which was widely considered their first serious album. These albums and others created and defined a new business. Previously, the primary rock and roll product was the single, which sold for around a dollar. After 1965, the dominant creative and business product of rock and roll was the album, which sold for five to ten times as much. To the new generation of rock fans like me, these albums were worth every penny. Every photo, every word of the liner notes, and every single song was another window into the minds of artists who were perceived by their fans as the coolest and most interesting people in the world.

Because the rock music of the late sixties was so radically different from the pop versions that came before it, most of the A&R executives at record companies who had controlled the production of commercial records were marginalized and a young generation of rock producers, songwriters, guitar players, singers, and the young friends who became their business associates grew rapidly in wealth and clout. The corporations were making so much money from selling albums by the likes of the Doors and Cream that they were more than happy to keep their hands off of the creative process. Although in future years the record companies and radio stations would start to assert more pressure for orthodoxy, the new template had been established. Rock and roll was a business in which the creative elements were mostly controlled by rock and roll auteurs who demanded and increasingly received a much bigger share of the economic pie, and who had much more control over their work than previous generations of performers. Dylan could have been speaking for many artists when he described the leverage he found once he had success. "I had gotten in the door when no one was looking. I was in there now and there was nothing anyone could, from then on, do about it."

Among the biggest and most talented rock stars I would meet when I got into the business, even those with the fiercest sense of integrity balanced their artistry with streaks of pragmatism. In 1980, I worked with Bruce Springsteen in the context of making *No Nukes,* a political concert documentary that featured several live Springsteen performances. While waiting for the editors to cue up an edit one night, Bruce mused about how elusive a Top 40 hit single had been for him. (*Born to Run* was a press phenomenon, and the title song had been a huge album cut on rock radio stations, but Top 40 barely touched it.) I was amazed to hear that Bruce had recently met with Kal Rudman, who ran a radio tip sheet called the *Friday Morning Quarterback,* filled with radio and promo hype. Rudman talked fast with glib high-pressure shtick. Although, like Springsteen, Rudman was based in New Jersey, he was the personification of the old-school pop business hype that was the ultimate contrast to Springsteen's intense, poetic, unpretentious rock and roll persona. (In Rudman's tip sheet, a hit song was called a GO-rilla.) "Kal explained to me," said Springsteen in his urgent, hoarse drawl, "that Top 40 radio is mainly listened to by girls and that my female demographic was low. And I thought about the songs on *Darkness* and I realized that the lyrics really *were* mostly for and about guys," he concluded, shaking his head ruefully. "So on this new album I'm working on—there are some songs for girls."

Just to hear the Boss utter the word *demographic* was a shock to my system, but then again why *wouldn't* he want to appeal to as many people as possible? *The River* album was released several months later, and, in addition to its many poetic gems and macho celebrations that protected Springsteen's identity, the album included the single "Hungry Heart," which featured a sped-up vocal, a romantic lyric, and retro harmonies by the sixties pop duo the Turtles, with the result that Springsteen did, as planned, finally have his first Top 40 hit.

Of course, the fantasy of rock and roll liberation was often dashed by the reality of the business. More than one rock star I knew found the classic parody of a rock documentary *This Is Spinal Tap* depressing because of its painful similarities to real life. Drug and alcohol abuse were far too common. The tragic arc of Elvis Presley's career was a metaphor for the dark side of rock and roll: materialistic, druggy, and predictable. Kurt Cobain, the greatest rock artist I would ever work with, shot himself to death. He was only one of dozens of brilliant rockers who died decades before their time.

The idea of this book is to give some impressionistic views, through my eyes and through the examples of a handful of artists, of the rock and roll business from 1969 through 2004. It is by no means an attempt at a comprehensive overview. For one thing, when I made my first tentative steps onto the stage of the rock business in 1968 I had been too young to really experience the seminal rock and roll in the fifties of Elvis Presley, Chuck Berry, et al. I had been a mere fan during the early-sixties British invasion of the Beatles and Rolling Stones and during the initial years of psychedelic rock.

There were many vital aspects of the business (engineering the sound of albums and selling them at record stores are two that come to mind) that I was to know little or nothing about. Although I tried to live by and impart commonsense principles of business such as the difference between hype and income, between the gross and the net, and about the need to spend less than one makes, my focus was primarily on working with artists to protect their art, market it, and get them paid as much as possible. I am neither an accountant nor a lawyer and have little of interest to share about the way artists spent their money or were screwed out of it after they made it.

Moreover, my perspective is very American. Although I worked closely with several British artists and represented several who toured and triumphed all over the world, the bulk of my experience was in the United States.

Large gaps in my memories are interspersed with vivid scenes that exist in my memory as if on videotape. I have written those scenes with quotations from people as I recall them but the truth is that other than a few interviews I conducted in writing this book, there were neither tapes nor notes. The conversations recounted merely represent my personal recollection of them.

No one artist or group of artists can contain the sprawling

and complex totality of rock and roll, but I believe that the artists I write about here, Led Zeppelin, Kiss, Stevie Nicks, Bonnie Raitt, Sonic Youth, Nirvana, Hole, Warren Zevon, and Steve Earle, among others, represent a broad and powerful portion of the psychic real estate of the rock and roll kingdom. I am not objective about any of them. I love them all.

PART I

WOODSTOCK NATION'S BRIEF STATE OF GRACE, 1969–1976

CHAPTER ONE

ALMOST ALMOST FAMOUS

In order to make it in the rock business it was not sufficient merely to "bump into geniuses." I had to develop enough of a semblance of expertise in order to have some value to artists, or at least be perceived so. The turning point in my career came when I met Led Zeppelin in 1973, but if I had not wormed my way into the clique of New York rock critics I would not have been of any use to them. My first, tentative steps into that part of the rock world were the result of a lucky accident.

Later there would be thoughts of the gross and the net, of royalties, fees, and commissions, of airplay and research, of shipments and returns, of image and credibility, of multiples and capital gains, of quarterly profits and of stock prices, but I knew of none of this when I got my first job in what turned out to be the music business. It was the fall of 1968, and I was eighteen. I needed a job, any job, to get my own apartment. I turned to the classified ads in *The New York Times* and got an entry-level clerical job at a magazine called *Billboard* for ninety dollars a week.

Over the next few years I developed some skills **13**

and a decent work ethic, but I could never have gotten anywhere in the business if I had not been a rock and roll fan first.
I graduated from Fieldston, a New York high school, in 1967, a
great year for rock and roll. Among the albums released during
my senior year were Bob Dylan's *Blonde on Blonde,* the Jimi
Hendrix Experience's *Are You Experienced,* Cream's *Disraeli
Gears,* the self-titled debut album by the Doors, and, two weeks
before graduation, the Beatles' *Sgt. Pepper's Lonely Hearts
Club Band.* To me, rock and roll was part of a larger counterculture that was going to change the world for the better, and I
wanted in.

I absorbed the comedy albums of Lenny Bruce and spent
many late-night hours listening to Bob Fass on WBAI, a left-
leaning noncommercial FM station where music was inter-
mingled with the evolving hippie counterculture. Arlo Guthrie
debuted his fifteen-minute comic antiwar song "Alice's Restaurant" on Fass's show about a year before it came out. Revolutionaries like Abbie Hoffman, Ed Sanders, Paul Krassner, Allen
Ginsberg, and Timothy Leary used the WBAI airwaves to rumi-
nate about a vaguely defined new kind of hip consciousness that
enthralled me.

I had been raised by liberal parents, was inspired by the civil
rights movement, had helped organize some of my high school
friends to march against the war in Vietnam, and was a fan of
the political folk music of the early Dylan, Joan Baez, Buffy
Sainte-Marie, Tom Paxton, and most of all Phil Ochs, whose
sarcastic radical song "Love Me, I'm a Liberal" served my adolescent need to differentiate. Like many folkies, I also developed
a taste for the blues via the virtuosity and soul of Leadbelly, Big
Bill Broonzy, and Sonny Terry and Brownie McGhee.

But I soon grew to embrace rock and roll, in part because of
its ability to reach a wider swath of my generation. Rock was a
way for a nerd like me to connect with regular kids while still
maintaining my own identity. I spent hours listening over and
over to records by the Beatles, the Rolling Stones, the Lovin'

Spoonful, Muddy Waters, Jefferson Airplane, the Chambers Brothers, Janis Joplin, Jimi Hendrix, Donovan, Cream, John Mayall, Steppenwolf, Traffic, Tim Hardin, Sonny Boy Williamson, the Fugs, the Byrds, the Mothers of Invention, Blue Cheer, Country Joe and the Fish, the Doors, the Kinks, the Who, Procol Harum, the Holy Modal Rounders, the Velvet Underground, Otis Redding, the Band, Junior Wells, Pearls Before Swine, and especially Bob Dylan, always Dylan.

If a stud like Mick Jagger could complain that he could get "no satisfaction," it meant that it was okay if I didn't. If John Lennon could sing "In My Life," it was safe to express emotion. If a genius like Bob Dylan could feel betrayed by a friend as expressed in "Positively 4th Street," it meant that I was not loser. If Greenwich Village hipsters like the Lovin' Spoonful could believe that rock and roll had "the magic that can set you free," I was not naive. If rock and roll could somehow express the complex mix of deeply personal, sexual, political, and spiritual feelings banging around my teenage head and simultaneously have a similar resonance with millions of others, I was not alone. To listen to these records was like coming indoors out of the freezing cold and holding my numb fingers near the radiator, feeling at the same time both pain and relief.

After I graduated from high school I enrolled at the University of California at Berkeley. One of my first nights in the Bay Area I went to Winterland to see Big Brother and the Holding Company. A beautiful blond girl in a diaphanous white gown was handing out free samples of "white lightning" LSD. I stopped attending classes almost immediately and went on an eight-month binge, consuming every drug I could get my hands on and eventually getting arrested on various charges when I asked a police officer directions while very stoned. It was shortly before my eighteenth birthday and the onerous drug-war laws to come were not yet in effect. I was released in my parents' custody, moved back to New York, and went to group-therapy sessions, where I reflected on how and why I had put myself into **15** a position of having to spend five nights at Alameda County Juvenile Hall.

I became a club-soda-and-lime guy. I had been scared straight, but I still identified with the hippie community. As it happened, a number of rock stars had seemingly gone through some sort of transformation themselves and embraced Eastern spirituality while downplaying or eliminating drugs. Pete Townshend of the Who became a devotee of the Hindu saint Meher Baba. Donovan's records were drenched with cosmic spirituality. George Harrison became devoted to the Hindu holy man Swami Bhaktivedanta, the leader of the Hare Krishna movement, and recorded an album of chants for the Beatles' Apple Records called *The Radha Krishna Temple*. (One of my high school friends, Josh Green, was part of the chorus.) The first single from Harrison's hugely popular solo album *All Things Must Pass* was a devotional song to Krishna called "My Sweet Lord." George was a vegetarian, so I became a vegetarian. Around the same time, Richard Alpert, who had been Timothy Leary's colleague in proselytizing about the benefits of LSD, went to India, found his guru, Neem Karoli Baba, and returned to the U.S. talking about Hindu devotion instead of drugs—but he did so with a hip wit and cosmic sense of humor that fit perfectly into my hippie head. In 1972 I would meet Ram Dass and he suggested I attend weekly meditations held by Hilda Charlton, who guided me spiritually thereafter.

Although I had gotten a haircut to enhance my chance of getting a job, I walked into *Billboard*'s offices in the fall of 1968 without much expectation of having any connection with people who worked in an office building. I had looked at the job as a necessary evil, but within a day it dawned on me that I was not just working for a generic magazine. (I'd thought it had something to do with ads displayed on highways.) My job was to call dozens of record stores around the country and ask them what was selling and help compile the results, thus providing the raw data for the *Billboard* sales charts, which, I soon learned, influenced radio station airplay, TV bookings, and orders from retailers.

It soon dawned on me that the rock music that meant so much to me was also part of something called the music business. Janis Joplin's group Big Brother and the Holding Company had the bestselling album in the country with *Cheap Thrills,* but there were lots of other kinds of records selling that I knew nothing about: R&B by artists like Little Johnny Taylor and Jerry Butler, country and western by artists like Buck Owens and Sonny James, and a form of pop music called "bubblegum," studio-created "groups" such as the Archies and the 1910 Fruitgum Company.

To those in the business, the greatest predictor of chart success was radio airplay. The people at record companies who "worked" radio and cajoled my bosses to list their records higher on the charts were "promo men" (in those days they were indeed all men). They carried themselves with the swagger of mobsters but, with varying degrees of success, also paid homage to the post-Beatles hippie fashions of the increasingly rock dominated record business. Their haircuts were long but perfectly coiffed.

The chart department was also given the task of predicting which of the new singles would be hits. Once a week we were played a dozen or so songs promoted heavily by the labels. We then voted on whether we expected the single to go Top 20, Top 60, Top 100, or to stiff entirely. One of my jobs was to report the results to an eminent advisor to radio stations named Bill Gavin, who ran a tip sheet in San Francisco that influenced radio airplay in smaller markets. The week we had heard the Plastic Ono Band record "Give Peace a Chance," I told Gavin we had predicted that it was destined for the Top 20. He replied incredulously, "Have you seen the lyrics? No Top Forty radio station is going to play that." I explained to him that it didn't matter whether or not any pop stations played it. It was a John Lennon song, sung by John Lennon. With or without radio every Beatles fan in the country would know about it overnight and want to own it. Gavin was correct that it got almost no Top 40 airplay, and I was right that it would sell. It rose to number fourteen on the Hot 100. In subsequent weeks Gavin became much more solicitous of my opinions. I tasted the heady wine of being perceived to know "the street."

I noticed that in the back pages of *Billboard,* after endless stories about job changes at record companies, radio stations, and chains of record stores, there were one-paragraph reviews of albums and slightly longer reviews of musical performances at clubs and concert halls, some of them by rock bands I liked. I had been an inconsistent student in high school, but I had written passably for the school newspaper, and I knew that I could write about rock and roll more authoritatively than the jaded trade writers whose idea of a good assignment was in direct proportion to the amount of free liquor they could get while "covering" a show.

I was able to land assignments that no one else wanted. I would happily have written for free just to get a byline and to get into the shows, but I was paid the freelance rate of thirty cents per inch that was published. In August they asked me if I wanted to cover a weekend event upstate that none of the regulars had any interest in: the Woodstock Festival.

On the Friday morning before the festival began, I went to Broadway and Forty-fifth Street to the tiny one-room office of Jane Friedman, whose firm, the Wartoke Concern, was doing PR for Woodstock. Along with Vince Aletti, who was on assignment from the short-lived radical New York weekly *The Rat,* Jane and I got into a black stretch limousine and headed north.

Jane was a sixties version of the kind of character Jean Arthur had played in movies a generation earlier: tough, streetwise, but with a heart of gold. Although she couldn't have been more than thirty, Jane had a maternal relationship with many of the young wild-eyed rock writers who were struggling for foreholds in the rapidly changing cultural environment of the time. She kept up a cheerful monologue as the limo wended its way through back roads to avoid the worst of the traffic, passing by nude hippie skinny-dippers. Once we got to the concert site, I was eager to wander around on my own and feel the dimensions of the vast crowd. Because the *Woodstock* movie has been so popular and enduring, it is hard to separate my actual memories from some of the highlights that have become indelibly etched in the highlight reel of the cultural history of the sixties. I know, for example, that I was there when Jimi Hendrix played the national anthem, but I was very tired and the image that stays with me is from the movie, not from my groggy recollection. I do, however, vividly recall the sense of euphoria I felt throughout the three days and nights at the vast and growing size of the hippie community and the omnipresent sweetness of the crowd. The wishful thinking about the nature of flower power, so often betrayed, was, for those brief few days, in perfect synch with reality, as far as I was concerned. Great as the music was, for me it functioned as a backdrop to the transient but ineffable sense of hippie camaraderie.

The band onstage when I arrived was Santana, whom I had never heard of before and who had yet to release their debut record. They played a compelling set of classic head music that literally made them stars overnight. Drawn by their compelling rhythms and Carlos Santana's transcendent extended guitar solos, I made my way up front. The way to get backstage was to have someone already there vouch for you. A beaming young promo guy from Warner Bros. recognized me from *Billboard*'s office and told a husky security guard I was OK. I briefly gawked at Joe Cocker, Stephen Stills, Joan Baez, and others but soon wandered back out again. I was in love with the crowd.

Wartoke had provided us with hotel rooms, and over the next few days I felt a little conspicuous in my clean unmuddied shirt. My focus kept alternating between the music on the stage (Joan Baez, Johnny Winter, and Janis Joplin stand out in my memory) and a sense of bliss at the sheer quantity of seemingly kindred spirits. I didn't feel like a freak in a city of freaks.

The editors at *Billboard* indulged me by running my long rhapsodic review on the front page. I saw myself not as a journalist but as part of the audience, as a spy on its behalf infiltrating the old-school music business. However, hippies didn't read *Billboard,* not in 1969 anyway, and the people who did read trade magazines were more interested in the charts than in musings about the counterculture.

One person who did read it was Sid Parnes, the editor of one of *Billboard*'s competitors, *Record World,* and he offered me a job in which I would write full time. They needed someone to cover the growing rock business. No more charts. With the sense of entitlement of hippie youth, I demanded a weekly column and Sid agreed. It was the sixties.

I wanted to worm my way into the world I really cared about, the community of rock critics. From rock's birth in the mid-fifties until well into the mid-sixties, the closest thing to journalism on the subject of rock and roll was found in fan magazines aimed primarily at teen and preteen girls. As Gloria Stavers, who edited *16 Magazine,* put it, her magazine was "for girls too old for Daddy's lap and not old enough yet for the boy next door." (*16* was not for girls who were actually sixteen but for younger girls who wanted to *act* sixteen.) *16* covered the early Beatles with stories focused on their looks, and their menu of sixties stars revolved around pretty boys such as Herman's Hermits, the Dave Clark Five, and Paul Revere and the Raiders. Because Gloria herself was a fan of the "underground rock" that was emerging in the mid-sixties, she would occasionally sneak in a blurb or photo of Bob Dylan or Jim Morrison, both of whom she knew personally (according to rumors *very* personally).

When Dylan started playing rock and roll, millions of folk fans, college kids, and high school iconoclasts like me suddenly decided it was not necessarily moronic to appreciate rock and roll. The emergence of guitar heroes like Jimi Hendrix made rock culture one in which macho guys were not embarrassed to participate. But most members of this vastly widened audience for rock music would not be caught dead looking at a "pinup" in magazines like *16*.

Robin Leach, later to achieve celebrity as host of *Lifestyles of the Rich and Famous,* briefly published a rock magazine called *Go,* which tied in with Top 40 radio stations around the country. There were a few writers for daily newspapers who occasionally mentioned rock and roll in the same sentence with jazz and beat poetry. Al Aronowitz, a columnist for the *New York Post* (still a liberal paper in the sixties) introduced the Beatles to Bob Dylan and was present when Dylan gave the Liverpudlians their first taste of marijuana. Ralph Gleason played a similar role at the *San Francisco Chronicle,* where his coverage of jazz, avant-garde comedians like Lenny Bruce and Lord Buckley, and beatniks segued seamlessly into coverage of the Haight-Ashbury hippie scene and the rock groups it spawned, such as Jefferson Airplane and the Grateful Dead.

However, the rigid formats of teen magazines, trade magazines, and daily newspapers gave little room for writers to examine and discuss rock music at the very time when this music was becoming the focus of intense analysis among fans. There were "serious" folk magazines such as *Sing Out!* but the aesthetic that informed these publications required contempt for rock music. Paul Nelson had attended the University of Minnesota during Dylan's brief stay there and wrote about folk music for the *Little Sandy Review* and for *Sing Out!* In the Martin Scorsese documentary about Bob Dylan, *No Direction Home,* he is the guy whose Woody Guthrie albums Dylan stole. Nelson stood in front of the stage when Dylan was booed by the crowd for going electric. Shortly thereafter, he resigned from *Sing Out!* when he realized that the folk purists who ran the magazine were going to reject Dylan for his apostasy. Paul's farewell piece concluded, "Those who booed chose suffocation over innovation. I choose Dylan. I choose art. I'll bet my critical reputation, such as it is, that I am right."

The first publication that applied serious critical and intellectual writing to rock and roll was *Crawdaddy!*, which debuted on February 7, 1966. The creation of Paul Williams, a student at Swarthmore College, *Crawdaddy!* was a revelation to me during my latter years of high school. I loved Williams's painfully earnest prose, such as his review of Donovan's album *Sunshine Superman,* in which he gushed, "Donovan looks at the world with a sort of hip innocence, paints his pictures with a dab of irony, and a dash of awe, and somehow never neglects the delicate in the decadence around him." Just as the French film critics of the 1950s had given would-be intellectuals "permission" to be unrestrained in their enthusiasm for movies, so did rock critics legitimize the passions of millions of sixties rock nerds.

Williams attracted a group of rock writers who would, in future years, help define the Zeitgeist of rock critics. One of the first and most prolific to join him was Paul Nelson. Another *Crawdaddy!* star was Jon Landau, who, after several years as one of the most intellectually respected rock critics, wrote a review of Bruce Springsteen for the *Boston Phoenix* in which he proclaimed Springsteen "the future of rock and roll," and not long thereafter became Springsteen's producer and personal manager.

Paul Williams was no businessman and had no sense of how to make his cultural creation a profitable one. Jann Wenner, living in San Francisco with a front-row seat to the blossoming of the hippie/rock scene, borrowed $7,500 from his wife's family and convinced Ralph Gleason to be a partner in a new magazine. When *Rolling Stone* first published on November 9, 1967, it was immediately better funded and better connected than *Crawdaddy!*

Rolling Stone portentously informed its readers that it would be dedicated "not just to the music but to everything it represents." With more focus on news and more savvy about marketing,

Rolling Stone soon eclipsed *Crawdaddy!*, in part because it hired away many of *Crawdaddy!*'s best writers, whose aesthetic increasingly required a cynical, questioning attitude about rock and roll, especially records that were widely hyped by record companies or the pop media (*Life* magazine was already covering artists like Airplane and the Doors in pieces written by the cynical but clever Albert Goldman).

To address the growing audience for rock criticism, several new writers got perches in mainstream media, such as Robert Christgau at *Esquire,* later to be at *The Village Voice,* Richard Goldstein at *The New York Times,* and Ellen Willis at *The New Yorker.* (Rick Hertzberg, who would later become a speechwriter for President Jimmy Carter and then a brilliant political journalist for *The New Republic* and *The New Yorker,* began as the backup rock writer for Willis.) I devoured what they wrote and their voices would be echoing in my head when I began writing for *Record World.*

One of my first columns for *Record World* was about an MC5 show at an outdoor venue in Queens called the Pavilion, which was where the 1964 World's Fair had been located. The band was filled with great rock energy, but I knew I was going to write a rave before I heard the first note. The MC5 were lauded by all of the rock critics I admired.

The day after my column ran, I got a phone call that would have a huge impact on my career. I was invited to lunch by Danny Fields of Atlantic Records because he had liked the MC5 column. A former journalist and editor, Danny's first record company job had been at Elektra Records, which had originally been a folk label. After the Doors exploded Elektra into the rock world, the label hired Danny to be their "company freak" (this was his actual title) with the mission of liaising with the likes of Jim Morrison. Danny was one of the few openly gay men in the music business in the late sixties and he had introduced the Velvet Underground to Andy Warhol, giving him a permanent caché in the downtown art scene.

Danny had signed the MC5 to Elektra and orchestrated their hip ascendance by persuading Richard Goldstein and Jon Landau to write about them early for *Rolling Stone* and *The New York Times,* and later had Elektra hire Landau to advise the band on how to take their anarchic and political energy and focus it on the commercial rock market. Shortly thereafter, Danny signed another Detroit act, the Stooges, to Elektra as well. Yet there were real-world limits to the power of freaks. When a Detroit department store called Hudson's refused to stock the first MC5 album, *Kick Out the Jams,* the band took an ad in a local underground paper that said "Fuck Hudson's" and included the Elektra logo. Elektra dropped the band and fired Danny. Jerry Wexler promptly hired Danny to work at Atlantic, signing the MC5 with the understanding that Landau would produce their next album.

Before meeting Danny I had written about music in private obscurity. Trade magazine journalists, at that time, were not typically part of the inner or outer circles of rock and roll. Through Danny I met most of the New York rock writers. Danny had a way of expressing enthusiasm for his favorites, whether they were rock bands or people, in a way that made it seem like it would be a personal betrayal (and a moronic one at that) to disagree with him. The apex of his influence would come a few years later, when he discovered and managed the Ramones.

In addition to discovering artists, Danny also was responsible for accelerating the careers of many writers and executives (or "inventing" us, as he would sardonically describe it). The clique who revolved around him could often be found at Max's Kansas City, which had a restaurant downstairs and a small stage upstairs. Max's was a storied hangout for New York artists, many of whom had traded paintings to Max's owner, Mickey Ruskin, in return for forgiveness of their bar and food bills. Andy Warhol and many of his self-styled "superstars" were Max's regulars, as were an exotic mixture of drag queens, visiting celebrities, and edgy socialites. Danny (and Warhol when he came) hung out in the "back room" of the first floor.

The very first night I went there with Danny we sat with Gloria Stavers of *16 Magazine* fame. Gloria, a native of North Carolina, had come to New York in the 1950s to be a fashion model. In addition to her reputation as the most successful fan-magazine editor, she was a classic beauty whose romantic conquests had included Mickey Mantle, Jim Morrison, and the love of her life, Lenny Bruce. Although by 1969 her influence on rock culture had waned, she remained a regal and respected figure in the rock world. Gloria was a compulsive note-taker and dictatorial control freak who somehow balanced her instincts about which guys would appeal to her pubescent readers with a growing interest in Eastern spirituality. (Ram Dass often stayed at her apartment when he visited New York.)

The same night at Max's we were soon joined by Lillian Roxon, an Australian journalist who covered American culture for *The Sydney Morning Herald* and who would shortly become the weekend rock columnist for the *New York Daily News*. Then in her late thirties, Lillian was short and overweight, with short blond hair that fell frequently over her exotic, sexy face. I soon learned that behind her veneer of urbane sophistication and sarcasm was a vulnerable and sentimental enthusiast of pop culture. Although she easily took offense if she felt she was not shown the appropriate respect, Lillian was otherwise a generous and loyal friend, who was particularly welcoming to newcomers to the scene such as myself.

Lillian had recently decided that people who wrote about rock and roll were themselves a special group and she took it upon herself to play a maternal role with many young critics, actually writing about several of us for the *Herald*. A few weeks later she wrote a column in Australia about young writers, with a sentence each about me, Lenny Kaye—a long-haired aesthete who wrote for the fledgling rock weekly *Changes*—and Ronnie Finkelstein, editor of the glossy rock magazine *Circus*. I kept a crumpled Xerox of the piece in my jacket pocket for months, periodically staring at my name in print to keep my spirits up. Years later Lenny told me that he had similarly ascribed magical powers to Lillian's public validation.

The final seat at the crowded table was filled by Steve Paul, who had run the legendary rock club the Scene, where Hendrix had often jammed, and who was then managing the careers of Johnny Winter and his brother Edgar. In a single night, my circle of acquaintances and my professional life had changed forever. Having been blessed by Danny I now strode confidently into the back room, which became the center of both my professional and social life.

I did not meet many actual stars during my late-night forays into Max's back room, but several artists of the future worked the room as assiduously as I did. Jonathan Richman, whose group the Modern Lovers would be an innovative alternative rock band, worked briefly as a busboy. David Johansen, the lead singer of the New York Dolls, prowled the room with the self-assurance of a small-town celebrity. But by far the most incandescent unknown artiste was Patti Smith, who, when I first met her there, had a day job as a clerk at the elegant Scribner Book Store on Fifth Avenue, near what was then called Publishers' Row in Midtown. "What book do you want me to steal for you?" she asked, as if this was a normal service she provided to all of her new friends. I asked for a hardcover edition of the *I Ching*, which she soon dutifully produced. In exchange I made her a copy of Dylan's then unreleased "basement tapes." She was an ardent rock fan and shared my obsession with Dylan. She recalled that as a teenager she had visited her local record store in New Jersey day after day in anticipation of the release of *Blonde on Blonde*.

Patti was then living with Robert Mapplethorpe in a small loft down the block from the Chelsea Hotel on West Twenty-third Street. I was not very sophisticated about art and it never occurred to me that the soft-spoken Mapplethorpe's photographs would someday be worth millions of dollars, but I knew, even then, that Patti was a genius.

In addition to her obsession with rock and roll Patti was deeply steeped in literature. She effortlessly quoted the poems of Verlaine, Baudelaire, and Rimbaud, and excitedly turned me on to Bertolt Brecht's *Manual of Piety* and the work of revolutionary Russian poet Vladimir Mayakovsky. She exulted in her discovery of Blaise Cendrars. ("I woke this morning," she gushed excitedly one night, "and said to the air—'Blaze on, Blaise!' ")

Patti was not the first rock star to study poetry. Just as folk music, blues, and Eastern spirituality had added currents of energy to rock and roll, so had the beatniks. Members of the Grateful Dead had bonded over their enthusiasm for the novels of Jack Kerouac (as would the members of Nirvana thirty years later). William Burroughs was a hero to many rockers. But it was Allen Ginsberg whose talent and soul was the largest source of fusion between beatniks and rockers. Dylan had paid homage to Ginsberg by placing him in the opening-credits sequence of the film *Don't Look Back*. The Beatles had derived their very name from the beatniks. In the mid-nineties I released Ginsberg's last recording, "Ballad of the Skeletons." He had persuaded Paul McCartney to overdub a bass part and I needed Allen to call the Beatle to make sure we got the legal right to use his name. Afterward Allen came into my office giggling and told me that after cheerfully agreeing, McCartney had boasted to Ginsberg, "You know, I read *Howl* before John did."

Patti was acutely aware of the beatnik tradition and later became close friends with Burroughs and Ginsberg. Although she was a prolific artist and tried her hand at acting in underground theater, her core identity in 1969–1970 was that of a poet. She always had a new poem, almost all of it stunningly original. (The line "Jesus died for somebody's sins, but not mine" originated in a poem written at this time and was reworked for the first song on the *Horses* album several years later.)

Of course, there was no way to make a living writing poetry, even in the late sixties. I recommended her for a job at *Rock* magazine. She later wrote some memorable pieces for *Cream.* Patti also worked briefly as Steve Paul's assistant, dutifully taking notes to keep track of his schedule and his manic bon mots.

It was obvious that Patti was creatively several dimensions above a mere Max's character. (Years later she would tell me, "It was not my world. I moved through it.") For one thing, Bobby Neuwirth was frequently hanging out with Patti, and Neuwirth was widely recognized for having a jeweler's eye for genius. Although Bobby always struggled with his dual careers as a painter and folksinger, he had a Yoda-like sense of beat hipness that crossed the boundaries between several art forms. Bobby had been a mentor and alter ego to the likes of Kris Kristofferson, Janis Joplin, and, of course, Dylan at early stages of their careers. (Neuwirth is ubiquitous in the Dylan documentary *Don't Look Back.*) I had always been intimidated by Neuwirth's world-weary hip sophistication and cutting wit, but when he hung out with Patti, he adapted the persona of a jocular sidekick. He knew who she was and who she would become.

It seemed like one day Patti and I were talking like geeky fans about the supposed virtues of Dylan's *Self Portrait* album and the next Patti was staying with playwright Sam Shepard at the Plaza Hotel. She invited me to come visit them, excited to show me the interior of a room in the hotel where the fictional Eloise had lived. A few weeks later I attended a preview at the American Place Theatre of a play she had written with Shepard called *Cowboy Mouth,* a two-character drama in which she and Shepard played thinly disguised versions of themselves. One of the props was a stuffed crow that Patti had named Raymond and had been carrying around for months. I was mesmerized. This play was a vehicle for so many facets of Patti's quirky charismatic brilliance that it would, I was sure, make her a star overnight. But for some reason (I thought it was because Shepard was so overshadowed by Patti) Shepard abruptly canceled the rest of the previews and the play never opened.

Patti was not long deterred. It turned out she could sing. Soon thereafter rock writer Lenny Kaye, who was also an excellent guitar player, put in the patient hours and weeks of work to give Patti the framework for her to launch her brilliant and influential career in the art form that was her true love: rock music. Jane Friedman, the press agent who had taken me to Woodstock, became Patti's manager and when her first album, *Horses*, was released in 1974, the rest would be history.

Although there were people in other parts of the country writing about rock and roll, the sheer quantity of rock press concentrated in Max's could make a big impact. With a clientele that continued to include many figures from the literary and art worlds, Max's cultivated an aesthetic that was far more cynical and dark than the optimism that had prevailed in the hippie era. In the early seventies David Bowie made himself a fixture there. He hired several hangers-on from there and accelerated his trajectory to superstardom. Lou Reed's hit song "Walk on the Wild Side" was the ultimate Max's record, produced by Bowie in 1972, with lyrics featuring various back-room characters.

We all were sure that what we thought about rock and roll mattered and many a night included earnest arguments about who did and who did not have authentic talent and energy. Several of my Max's friends got into the habit of taping their phone conversations in order to have a record of the feverish daily dialogue about what was happening. Robert Smith, who wrote for a later version of *Crawdaddy!* in the early 1970s and who later became a successful record executive, recalled, "It seemed, for a time, that to write about rock and roll was to carry on your shoulders an aesthetic and set of values about the entire counterculture."

Lisa and Richard Robinson wrote about rock and roll for a variety of magazines and syndicated services and for a time published *Rock Scene,* a definitive chronicle of the seventies New York glitter rock era when Bowie was king. Their apartment on the Upper West Side often served as an informal salon for visiting musicians and rock writers. In one moment of delusive hubris a group of us decided we should call ourselves the "collective conscience" to advise record companies and other major media on how to maintain the integrity of the rock culture. Danny leaked the idea into a few columns and a phone was installed in the apartment of former yippie leader and Columbia Records corporate freak Jim Fouratt, but the phone literally never rang.

With the business exploding it seemed like there was a party for a rock band every night, with free food provided by the record companies. Hanging out at such affairs as well as at Max's became my social life. However I failed to become an important rock writer, not solely because of my literary limitations (although I never could hold a candle to masters like Nelson, Christgau, and Landau). The truth was that I revered rock musicians and felt guilty when I criticized them. One of my early *Billboard* reviews was of a concert by the Rascals, whose pop/rock hits like "Good Lovin,'" "I've Been Lonely Too Long," and "People Got to Be Free" were among my favorite guilty pleasures. A hybrid between first-stage, Beatles-style rock and roll and Motown R&B, the Rascals' signature sound came from their two lead vocalists, songwriters and singers Felix Cavaliere and Eddie Brigati. By 1969, when I saw them, great guitar heroes such as Hendrix and Clapton had exploded the boundaries of what rock guitarists could express. Gene Cornish, the Rascals' guitarist, was pedestrian by comparison and so, in the context of an otherwise enthusiastic review, I made a dismissive comment about Cornish's playing, referring to it as "twanging." An irate Cornish called me, saying that he was offended by my critique. I could barely believe that I was even talking to someone whose photo I had seen on albums that I loved. I felt terrible that I had hurt his feelings. I looked up to rock artists, even ones that twanged the guitar.

After a Janis Joplin show at Madison Square Garden I was so emotionally moved by her vulnerable monologues about her boyfriends (she had just been loved and left by New York Jets quarterback Joe Namath) and her acoustic performance of "Me and Bobby McGee" that I giddily wrote, "Janis is alive. Happiness is possible for everybody." It was heartfelt but not the sort of prose likely to get me much respect in Max's.

My proudest moments were when my rave reviews were quoted in ads such as those for the debut album by Loudon Wainwright III and for Van Morrison's *Moondance*. The Morrison rave got the attention of his manager, Mary Martin, who arranged for me to interview Morrison for *Jazz and Pop*. I took a bus ride up to Woodstock, where Morrison was living with his wife, Janet Planet. I was surprised by the thickness of his Irish accent. He explained to me that he was able to sing in an American "voice" by emulating the pronunciation of Ray Charles and other American R&B singers he had listened to incessantly since his teenage years in Belfast. Although Morrison's *Astral Weeks* album had been rich with quintessentially cosmic lyrics, Morrison seemed mystified by hippie culture. He became animated only when talking about music. In awe of his talents, I was stunned to realize that Van was as insecure as mere mortals. After I finished the interview, Janet suggested that he play me "Domino," the lead single from his forthcoming album. "But if someone doesn't like it I'll cry," he whined before playing it. Not surprisingly, that did not turn out to be a problem. "Domino" was a classic.

One day I saw a guy who had worked with me in the *Billboard* chart department sitting in the backseat of a cab at a stoplight. When he asked what I was up to I manically recited a list of freelance work I was doing. "You mean you are still in this shitty-assed business?" he sneered bitterly as the taxi pulled away. I felt an immediate pang of dread. The very idea of being

31

out of the business terrified me. My tenuous association with rock and roll had given me an identity, a purpose, and a way of paying the rent. I literally could not imagine another realm in which I could work without being plunged into self-loathing and darkness. The fear of being deprived of a place in the business would continue to be an animating force within me for decades to come.

In 1970, I had a brief tenure as managing editor of *Circus* magazine. *Circus*'s publisher, Gerry Rothberg, was a product of the magazine business, and I always had the feeling that the affable and stylishly dressed Rothberg would have been just as happy publishing a magazine about motorcycles or fishing. *Circus*, uniquely among rock magazines of the time, published color pictures of rock stars. Rothberg didn't pay very much, but he had a history of hiring legitimate rock writers as editors and trusting their judgment about content.

At age twenty-one I was a rock and roll generation removed from fourteen-year-olds. Obsession with age was a continual theme of the rock culture at a very early stage. Landau's famous 1974 review of Springsteen in the Boston weekly *The Real Paper* began, "I'm 27 today, feeling old—on a night when I need to feel young, he made me feel like I was hearing music for the very first time." I became fascinated with the populist midwestern success of Grand Funk Railroad, who, without any critical support whatsoever, had become the box office champions of early seventies rock festivals. After I wrote a favorable cover story, Dave Marsh, editor of *Cream* and a fierce exponent of a critical rock sensibility, called me enraged and said I had been "hyped." *Cream* was published in Detroit and championed the political rock of the MC5. Grand Funk was from Flint, Michigan, and had bombastic songs about girls. I didn't see why a rock fan couldn't like both, but to Marsh this indicated a lack of seriousness.

Not long after this I got my first offer to publicize an artist. Michael Lang, the most quotable and photogenic of the Woodstock promoters, had parlayed his celebrity into funding for a label called Just Sunshine, which released Karen Dalton's album *In My Own Time*. Dalton was a protégée of the brilliant melancholy singer-songwriter Fred Neil, and she had recorded a folk album filled with aching blues vocals and even more aching sad poetry, just my cup of tea. She was also unbearably shy, so the only way to get her music any attention was by getting the album reviewed. In return for a thousand dollars I mailed copies to several of my rock writer friends and when none of them "got" it, I wrote a review myself, which became the first piece of mine published in *Rolling Stone*.

The issues I was dealing with at twenty-one were the same ones I was to wrestle with for the next several decades. There were the ever-alternating feelings of power and powerlessness. At times it seemed like all doors were open to me. At others the frustration of being unable to actually *make* an artist successful was maddening. Neither Loudon Wainwright III, nor the MC5, nor the New York Dolls, ever connected with mass audiences. On a parallel track, I wanted to somehow keep faith with the emotions that had attracted me to rock and roll and the hippie counterculture in the first place and at the same time figure out how to make as much money as possible. This mirrored the agendas of most artists I would work with, to maintain their artistic control and integrity and also to reach as many people as they could and get rewarded for success. Like many musicians I met, I wanted desperately to stay in the game, ardently to do well at it, and determinedly not to disappoint the sixteen-year-old version of myself that had been the unconscious but passionate architect of my career. To have the career that my adult self wanted, I soon realized that the world of the press, while a great place to launch an artist and an indispensable piece of any true superstar's realm, was not, in and of itself, sufficient to win me mastery of the rapidly changing rock business. For example, there was this thing called radio.

CHAPTER TWO

UNDERGROUND RADIO

Although we denizens of Max's were loath to admit it, a half-million people had not been drawn to the Woodstock Festival solely because of rock critics and word of mouth. A couple of years earlier "underground" rock radio had arrived on FM stations around America. At first they played the same albums the rock critics had been writing about, adding exponentially to the audience but hewing to the same aesthetic. But these radio people, it turned out, actually thought that *they* were the ones who were "making" things happen. Shortly after Woodstock, rock radio's primacy became clear when Led Zeppelin, whom most rock journalists marginalized or hated, became instantly beloved by the huge rock audience who were introduced to them by the underground jocks. The other side of the coin would be even more sobering for rock writers. Many critical darlings such as the MC5 and Patti Smith would find limited support from most rock DJs and programmers and thus an audience only a fraction of Zeppelin's.

Like *Rolling Stone* underground rock radio **35**

was born in San Francisco. In the late sixties and early seventies rockers from San Francisco all had a smug sense of hip superiority, but who could blame them? Allen Ginsberg had first read *Howl* in the city in 1955. San Francisco encompassed the Haight-Ashbury hippie neighborhood, Golden Gate Park where the "first human be-in" had taken place, and Bill Graham's Fillmore, where bands like the Grateful Dead and Jefferson Airplane and Big Brother and the Holding Company crystallized their careers.

Top 40 had helped launch the Beatles and the rest of the British invasion in 1964, but to teenagers, 1967 was not three years but three lifetimes later. Top 40's endless repetition of hit songs and the hyper patter of its DJs were, to the hippie generation, hopelessly passé.

The "underground" radio format was created by a former Top 40 DJ named Tom Donahue, whom I first heard on KMPX in Berkeley in the fall of 1967, several months after he had the epiphany that there was an audience for an eclectic flow of rock albums, blues, and jazz, with an occasional classical record thrown into the mix. KMPX played multiple songs from albums, not just the singles. The DJs were emotional about the music and they spoke informally, as if they had just smoked a joint, which many of them had. Local San Francisco musicians like Jerry Garcia or visiting royalty like Mick Jagger would often show up unannounced to talk on the air.

In early 1968, after a dispute with the owners of KMPX, Donahue and the entire staff took their format to a station owned by Metromedia and rechristened it KSAN. For many years my contact at KSAN was Bonnie Simmons, who joined the station's staff as record librarian in 1970. "I was originally turned down for the job because Tony Pigg, the music director at the time, was convinced that the librarian should be a Virgo and I was a Sagittarius," Simmons recalled. (Pigg, Simmons tartly reminded me, later became the voice of *Live with Regis and Kathie Lee*.) Bonnie listened to the dozens of albums that came in each week, categorizing them and marking which tracks had dirty lyrics.

Donahue convinced local businesses such as boutiques, hair salons, and sex shops to advertise by having the station create entertaining commercials customized for KSAN that the rock audience would accept. Bonnie loved to play one for the music store Record City that had a musical bed of weird rhythmic horns set against a pseudobeatnik poem read by an earnest DJ:

I put pan pipes from Peru to blue Krishna lips on slopes of Spanish roses. Caravans from Nepal couldn't carry all the perishable mental Persian silks I spun in one Chinese puzzle late Berkeley afternoon. Solar night tucks Record City in along endless beds of streets, waiting for the midnight dawn when merchant ships sail down Telegraph Avenue canals. The heart of your mind is open. Record City, 2340 Telegraph Avenue, aglitter in silver double images.

When Donahue died in 1975, Bonnie, then twenty-four years old, became program director for KSAN, a position she held for the next decade. "We actually knew who our listeners were; we *were* our listeners. Early on there was an oil spill in Stinson Beach and thousands of birds were dying on the beach. We set up a switchboard, which was all of three phone lines, and asked people to go and wash birds. They had to drive over a mountain from San Francisco to get there and five thousand showed up the first morning."

The Metromedia chain soon adapted the "underground" format in New York (WNEW), Philadelphia (WMMR), and Los Angeles (KMET). In his book *Radio Waves* KMET rock DJ Jim Ladd would rhapsodically recall, "Tom Donahue was the man who stole the keys to the glass booth and opened it up to an entirely new generation of radio pioneers, long-haired, barefoot, tie-dyed dreamers, who came to their tiny run-down and woefully ill-equipped stations filled with the rhythm of adventure and the melody of revolution." Following the example set by Metromedia, owners of underperforming FM stations around the country adapted variations of the new format.

My first personal exposure to people who worked at these radio stations was at a weird, one-time gathering called the Alternative Media Conference, which took place at Goddard College in Vermont in June 1970. I got invited via Danny Fields, who, in his spare time, had been doing part-time DJ work at WFMU, which was owned by Upsala College in New Jersey. Larry Yurdin, one of WFMU's programmers, had organized the conference with a utopian notion of creating connectivity among underground radio people, rock writers, musicians, political radicals, and hippie visionaries. A few years later it would prove impossible to explain to those who weren't there what the connection was between the yippies, mysticism, and the crass commercial task of getting rock records on the radio (or, from the station's point of view, selling advertising), but in the moment it all seemed to make sense.

A private plane from San Francisco to Vermont transported several KSAN DJs, as well as members of the legendary commune the Hog Farm, who arrived at the Goddard campus midway through an acid trip that had begun while they were literally in flight. "People had these big smiles and you could just smell the acid coming out of their skin," remembered Peter Wolf of the J. Geils Band.

I found myself pulled in contradictory directions, enraptured by most of the political and spiritual messianic notions of the fragile hippie culture and yet also pragmatically drawn by the cluster of rock and roll businesses inventing themselves seemingly before our very eyes.

The cosmic side of the culture was represented by WBAI's Bob Fass, *The Realist* editor Paul Krassner, and Baba Ram Dass, who lectured the assembled media freaks. The music business imperative was embodied by Mario Medius, a promo man for

Atlantic, who called himself "the Big M." Mario was nothing like the slick pop promo men I had met at *Billboard*. He was the first of a new breed, an *underground* promo man. I had seen him at press parties for artists on Atlantic Records, a hyperkinetic black guy whispering in the ear of artists or working his way through the room. He bore himself with a level of intensity that indicated he was not simply there to have a good time or opine about the day's performance. He was doing business.

Originally hired to call retailers, Mario loved music and couldn't wait to get out of the sales department, where records were referred to not by the name of the artist or album title but by number. He convinced Atlantic to create the "underground" promo job, although Ahmet had cautioned him that "those guys are freaks," meaning they weren't influenced by old-school favors or payola. The Big M was up to the task, promptly getting the freaks to play Brian Auger's version of Donovan's "Season of the Witch." He soon became a legendary part of Atlantic's rock mystique. I asked him how he got such spectacular results and he laughed and said, "Man, I'd go by the station, sit up with them all day, smoke weed with them, and beg them to play the record." On one occasion a late-night DJ passed out and Medius did the last hour of his air shift shamelessly playing a series of Atlantic album tracks.

In the year before the conference the record that made Mario an indispensable player in the rock business was Led Zeppelin's self-titled debut album. "I got it as a test pressing in a white jacket," Mario recalled. (Promo records were placed in plain unmarked white sleeves before the album artwork was done.) "The blues was my background and the record really excited me by the way it brought the blues up to date." This was still a time when each DJ picked their own music and the Big M quickly got copies to the key FM jocks. No station was too small for Mario's attentions. Vin Scelsa, who was the program director of WFMU, recalled, "The Big M was the first record-company guy to pay attention to us. He came out with

39

the Zeppelin album and brought an inflatable plastic zeppelin. Several of us liked the record and played it. He returned the next day with cartons of the entire Atlantic catalog in the trunk of his Cadillac, enough for everyone at the station."

The key market to breaking Zeppelin wide open was Boston. Although much smaller in population than New York, Boston was more influential because of the tremendous concentration of trend-setting college students who lived there. Moreover, WBCN in Boston had developed the reputation among stations around the country of being hip tastemakers. Program director Al Perry was a purist who was, in Mario's words, "a blues cat who hated rock bands." His first impression of Led Zeppelin was that they were the latest in a line of British bands who were corrupting the genre. The Big M, one of the very few blacks in the rock culture of the sixties, played the race card, insisting, "I *am* the blues. I was born in Mississippi. I was raised in Chicago. I was in the back of the bus." Perry relented and played "Whole Lotta Love," which soon became one of the most popular songs with WBCN listeners and soon thereafter with all of rock America.

As a result of his success with Led Zeppelin, the Big M was able to prevail upon Atlantic to sign the J. Geils Band. He had been in Boston with Dr. John, whose song "Right Place Wrong Time" was spreading onto underground stations. Mario recalled, "J. Geils were the opening act. I was in the dressing room while they were playing the last song of their set, 'Serve You Right to Suffer.' I thought it was some black cats from Chicago." Medius turned around and walked into the club. As Peter Wolf, the band's singer, passed him, Mario asked, "Where are the brothers at?" Peter laughed and introduced himself.

Wolf had grown up in the Bronx as Peter Blankfield. His love affair with rock and roll began via his sister Nancy, who was a dancer on Alan Freed's rock and roll TV show *The Big Beat*. After graduating from high school Peter attended the School of the Museum of Fine Arts. A fanatic blues fan, Wolf embraced visiting blues singers such as Muddy Waters, who sometimes stayed at his apartment in Boston. Peter hung out with an assortment of young counterculture cognoscenti in Boston, including Jon Landau, then a student at Brandeis, and future film director David Lynch, who was briefly his roommate. When WBCN launched the underground format in Boston, Wolf was enlisted to do a late-night blues show, *Wolfa Goofa Mama Toofa*. Van Morrison told me that he had heard Wolf's show on a trip to Boston and he, too, thought Wolf was black until he showed up for an interview.

At the Alternative Media Conference the J. Geils Band performed material from their soon-to-be-released debut album for the sixteen hundred DJs and other assorted media freaks and once-and-future political radicals who gathered at the conference. "It was like an elite Woodstock," Wolf remembered fondly, "and after that we were considered cool all across the country, not just in Boston."

The AMC also featured a "Gay Liberation Workshop," a screening of lefty activist Saul Landau's film *Fidel*, and a lecture called "Understanding Rock Poetry" by A. J. Weberman, a self-styled Bob Dylan fan who called himself a "Dylanologist" and had gone to the extreme of trolling Dylan's garbage for clues he felt would get him closer to Dylan's "meaning."

Conference cuisine consisted of brown rice and tofu. Panel discussions were not about selling advertising, new technology, or demographics but on topics such as "Spiritual Responsibility of the Alternative Media" and "Free Enterprise and the Cultural Revolution." I attended one on underground cartoons to hear Harvey Kurtzman, who had been one of *Mad* magazine's most innovative editors. Just as Kurtzman was beginning to describe his take on the Woodstock culture his work had helped to spawn, a couple disrobed and started having sex on the floor. Several attendees started clapping their hands in rhythm with the couple's movements. In response two feminists angrily yelled at the lecherous attendees to stop clapping. Kurtzman and the

41

other panelists looked perplexed and the crowd that had come to hear them quickly dispersed.

Ultimately the connections between the activists and those in the rock business, including the musicians, were somewhat less than met the eye. In part this was because of the self-preoccupation of the rock culture, but also because of the incoherence of the self-styled "revolutionaries" of the time. Although most rock artists were against the Vietnam War and racial discrimination and sexism, attempts by radical groups to "direct" the anarchic energy of rock and roll had usually backfired. In 1967 there had been a meeting before the "Be-In" in San Francisco, in which Berkeley radicals such as Jerry Rubin tried to convince members of the Grateful Dead and Jefferson Airplane to add "demands" to the cosmic hippie gathering. The musicians had dismissively laughed at such a linear notion. At the Woodstock Festival, Abbie Hoffman had jumped onstage during a set by the Who to talk to the audience about the Vietnam War, only to be physically kicked off by guitarist Pete Townshend.

The political dimensions of the counterculture that had appealed to me had been those rooted in nonviolent thinkers such as Martin Luther King and antiwar Quakers. I wasn't into guns or bombs as political tools, left wing or otherwise. Moreover, I had always been baffled by that word *revolution*, when used literally. How could a few dozen or even a few thousand freaks and/or Black Panthers physically defeat the American government? How could such behavior persuade electoral majorities?

The rhetoric of the radicals who spoke at the Alternative Media Conference had a shrill, apocalyptic tone that implied that anyone who didn't join with the speaker and his or her friends was some sort of a political sellout, and this was a time when the Weathermen were gaining currency in the underground press with open advocacy of violence. But the Weathermen had very few followers in the rock world. As Paul Krassner dryly observed, "They took their name from the Dylan lyric that said, 'You don't need a weatherman to know which way the wind blows,' but ironically their whole purpose was to try to tell people which way the wind was blowing." To me Neil Young's "Ohio" or John Lennon's antiwar activities and songs had much more moral and practical resonance than the shrill pamphlets or speeches in the oddly dated language that the Weathermen and their ilk employed. When I wrote about it for *Crawdaddy!*, I did my best to put a positive spin on the Alternative Media Conference, but as with much of my so-called journalism of the time I had a personal agenda. I ended the piece with a quote from Mayakovsky about art and revolution in an attempt to impress Patti Smith.

Despite the conference's incoherence and the absence of any kind of follow-up to it, the shared aspirations of commerce and counterculture were not forgotten by many individuals who were there. Thirty-seven years later I spoke of it to Norm Winer, who, having been program director of WXRT in Chicago for the previous two decades, was still an enormously influential person in both the broadcasting and music industries. He remembered it with surprising clarity. "I think about it all the time. All roads led to there and all roads came from there."

ROCK AND ROLL
GROWN-UPS

In the late sixties and early seventies the grown-ups who made the real money from rock and roll were not baby boomers. They were older than me and most of the rock writers. On the record company side, they were guys who'd had their feet planted in the music business earlier, in folk, jazz, pop, or fifties rock, and had the insight to embrace long-haired hippie rock before their competitors. They embodied an odd hybrid of fifties hipster and sixties hippie culture, but they were smart, intimidating guys who would fiercely hold on to their power.

For a time, the record companies seemed to be the center of the universe. Peter Wolf told of the moment when Jon Landau took him to Jerry Wexler's office for the final discussion about the terms of the deal for the J. Geils Band. He was devastated to hear that they planned to release the group on their Atco imprint, which they were using for rock bands such as Buffalo Springfield and Vanilla Fudge. Wexler went through an elaborate contrived monologue in which he pretended that conceding on the subject was a great sacrifice. As a result of   **45** his eventual "victory" on this point, the rock singer accepted all of Atlantic's onerous economic terms. That's how much prestige the name Atlantic conferred in the late sixties.

In 1967 Ertegun had sold Atlantic Records to a company called the Kinney National Company, which also owned Warner Bros. films and records. Kinney, which would soon change its name to Warner Communications, was run by Steve Ross, who, based on Ahmet's advice, retained Warner Bros. Records execs Joe Smith and Mo Ostin. Mo and Joe quickly signed the Grateful Dead and the Jimi Hendrix Experience and transformed Warners, which had been known for Frank Sinatra, into a citadel of rock hipness and credibility on the West Coast. In 1970 they bought Elektra, a folk label that had been founded in the fifties by Jac Holzman and had become a rock label after the signing of the Doors. (It was Holzman who had brought Danny Fields to Elektra.) This trio of Warner Music labels would have the largest market share in the American record business for the next quarter of a century, based primarily on rock music.

The other hot rock company was Columbia Records, a division of CBS, which had been noted for Broadway show albums but had a unique secret weapon, the Artists and Repertoire vision of the visionary patrician John Hammond, who in his younger years had signed the likes of Billie Holiday and Duke Ellington and who would later sign Bob Dylan and Bruce Springsteen. In 1967 Clive Davis, the thirty-five-year-old president of Columbia Records (which included Epic Records), went to the Monterey Festival and signed Janis Joplin and Sly and the Family Stone.

There were three independent companies that were magnets for rock bands. A&M had been formed in 1962 around the instrumental recordings of its cofounder Herb Alpert and was reinvented as a rock label when Alpert's partner Jerry Moss signed Humble Pie. Island Records had been created in 1959 by Chris Blackwell to record Jamaican music and branched out into rock with the signing of Traffic. Chrysalis Records was formed in

1969 by Chris Wright and Terry Ellis, who had signed Jethro Tull and Procol Harum via an arrangement with Island.

The second-tier corporate companies for rock and roll included RCA (often nicknamed the Record Cemetery of America), which had Elvis and somehow had signed Jefferson Airplane. MCA (the Music Cemetery of America) had inherited the Who from their British affiliate, and Capitol had similarly inherited the Beatles. Among indies, Vanguard had Joan Baez and would remain primarily a folk and classical label, with the notable exception of Country Joe and the Fish. Fantasy, which had Creedence Clearwater Revival, otherwise stayed focused on jazz.

Artists usually, but not always, got a financial advance on signing a contract and/or delivering a finished record. They also, in theory, got royalties from sales, which were calculated in percentage points based on the retail price of an album. Over the years artists' attorneys negotiated better and better terms. In the early sixties royalties could be as low as 3 percent. By the early seventies a typical new artist contract was 10 percent. By the end of the nineties artist royalties ranged from 14 percent to 20 percent.

However, a point was not really a point. Over the years the record companies had developed boilerplate clauses in contracts that reduced the value of a point. Between so-called packaging deductions, returns reserve, discounts, and a clause created in the vinyl age for breakage, a point was really a half a point. (In the early eighties, when the compact disc was introduced, record companies were able to pay royalties based on 75 percent of the new, higher retail album price that was the result of temporarily higher manufacturing prices. When CD manufacturing prices declined, artists and their representatives bitterly complained and the 75-percent rate on CDs was restored to 100 percent).

So in the mid-eighties, when CDs sold for $10, a new artist who got a 12-percent royalty would be credited with around **47**

$0.60 per sale. Foreign sales in those days paid at 50 percent of the U.S. rate. By the late nineties the international/U.S. ratio was much higher. So if a 12-percent artist got $50,000 to sign and spent $275,000 to record and sold one million copies in the U.S. and one million outside of the U.S., they would have a gross royalty of $900,000. Record producers, the guys who oversaw the arrangements and engineering during recording, typically got 3 percent, which in this example would be worth $225,000. After deduction of the advance and recording costs this would leave $350,000 in artist royalties paid to the band. Assuming a four-member group who paid a manager, lawyers, and business manager a total of 25 percent, this would mean around $72,000 per member.

Many albums didn't sell as well as the above example and many spent more money on recording costs, and some companies had dishonest accounting practices. Thus many artists never saw royalty checks.

Artists who wrote their own songs had another income stream from album sales, a so-called mechanical royalty, which was paid to songwriters and their music publishers. The mechanical rate rose over the years from around $0.40 an album in the seventies to $1 an album in 2007. If one songwriter wrote all of their own songs and owned their own copyrights, the above-cited example at a $0.50 worldwide mechanical rate would have generated $1 million in mechanicals for the writer. Of course, many artists recorded some covers of songs they didn't write or cowrote songs, which reduced the mechanicals they would receive. And some writers had signed contracts with music publishing companies that took from 25 to 50 percent of the total songwriting income. But the bottom line was that the total songwriting royalties often exceeded total artist royalties. On albums that sold a few hundred thousand copies, the only royalties available were from songwriting.

Some bands divided all of the songwriting income evenly, but in most bands the actual writers got paid out of songwriting royalties and nonwriting members got none. Songwriters also had yet another income stream from "performance" income, pooled by collection societies called ASCAP and BMI, which collected money from radio broadcasters. Many bands would break up because of the tremendous disparity of income between the writers and nonwriters.

Although I had passing acquaintance with executives from most of the "good" record companies, my identity as a second-rate rock writer did not excite them. However, as a result of my work for Karen Dalton, I got a job as head of PR with what was certainly the worst corporate record company in the business, Famous Music Corp., which was part of Gulf and Western, the conglomerate that also owned Paramount Pictures. The president of Famous was Tony Martell, a first-rate marketing executive who was in over his head when it came to picking talent. His solution was to make a series of "label deals" with an odd collection of music business characters.

One such label was run by Charlie Green, who earlier in his career had had an ill-defined connection to Sonny and Cher and Buffalo Springfield. By the time I met him, Green's sole selling point was the possession of a Cadillac limousine whose seats were covered by mink fur. Green employed a large African-American driver named Wonderful, whom he endlessly berated in his thick Brooklyn accent with the unwitty phrase "Wonderful, you're terrible." Another label, Family Productions, was run by Artie Ripp, a Runyonesque New Yorker who had created and lost control of Buddah Records. Ripp claimed that the name and logo for Buddah had come to him in a vision he had on a psychedelic trip. Ahmet Ertegun had quipped that the cosmic author of the vision apparently did not know how to spell.

Ripp's deal with Famous gave him $25,000 for each album and half the profits after recoupment. Ripp then cut a deal with Ampex Tapes, which had come to the conclusion that reel-to-reel tapes were going to be the format that would succeed vinyl **49** records. Ampex paid $50,000 for each album that was delivered. (When reel-to-reel consumer demand failed to materialize, Ampex would go into bankruptcy.)

Ripp delivered "any box of tape I could find lying around my office" to Famous. Many Family "albums" cost Ripp literally nothing to record, and he kept the full $25,000 from Famous, who recouped from the Ampex advance and then paid him $12,500 as his half of the profit, allowing Ripp to net $37,500 per album even if it didn't sell a single copy. The key was to make sure that no marketing money was spent. At one point we got boxes of an album called *Brown Dirt* and I wanted to do a press mailing. Ripp screamed at me, "Why would I want anyone in the press to hear it? You know why I called it *Brown Dirt*? Because that's what dried shit is."

Ripp had signed one real artist, the former lead singer of an ill-fated Long Island rock band the Hassles, Billy Joel. But Joel's debut album, *Cold Spring Harbor,* was mastered at the wrong speed, making Joel's voice sound higher than it should, and Ripp refused to spend the several thousand dollars it would cost to replace the faulty inventory. Since I was working for a company that, in his mind, had screwed him, Billy was in a perpetually sullen mood when I called him to set up interviews, but the twenty-two-year-old prodigy gritted his teeth and went through with them.

WLIR, the underground station in Long Island, broadcast one of Joel's concerts that included the then unreleased song "Captain Jack," an anthem about teenage male angst that used the word *masturbate*. This was, in the context of the times, extremely risqué and gained Joel a regional following in the Northeast. Thus emboldened, Joel refused to record another record for Ripp and moved to L.A., where he played in a piano bar until his lawyers negotiated a deal in which CBS bought the contract from Ripp, who retained a royalty override and made millions from Joel's subsequent success.

My favorite artist in the Famous constellation was Mitch

Ryder, whose band Detroit was signed directly to the Paramount label. Ryder was a great singer in a style that was called "blue-eyed soul" and was known for the hit single "Devil with a Blue Dress" with his previous band the Detroit Wheels. Ryder was an incredible live performer and had a compelling charisma that made me want to do anything I could to help. I loved listening to his rambling, free-associating raps. I felt, in his presence, that I was close to the mysterious flame of rock and roll genius. However, Ryder had no talent for having talent. His live show was much better than his record. He was undisciplined and quick to anger. He never achieved commercial success commensurate with his talent.

Ryder was managed by John Sinclair, the legendary founder of the White Panther party. Sinclair had previously managed the MC5 and then had gotten arrested for the possession of two joints of marijuana. Handed the onerous sentence of ten years in prison, Sinclair became the focus of a national movement. In December 1971 John Lennon and Yoko Ono had performed at a benefit in Ann Arbor to free Sinclair. Miraculously, Sinclair was freed by a Michigan appeals court three days later. He had served two and a half years. Shortly after he got out of jail he began managing Ryder and told me, "I think that the country is really turning around. A lot more guys have long hair than when I went into jail." Sinclair would soon get acclimated. He would write several books and host a long-running countercultural radio show that was still available on the Internet in 2008.

The most successful rock writer to engage record companies was Landau, who produced records for the MC5 and Livingston Taylor before having a commercial breakthrough as a producer of Bruce Springsteen's *Born to Run* and Jackson Browne's *The Pretender.*

Landau's fellow *Crawdaddy!* alumnus, Paul Nelson, traveled the corridors of business with considerably less ease and success. In 1970 Paul took a job as a Mercury Records PR guy, **51** but he stubbornly refused to hype artists he didn't like. Paul's primary strategy was to take everyone he knew out to lunch. I was working at *Circus* at the time and I got to know him over the course of many lunches at La Strada, at which he would invariably order two Coca-Colas and a hamburger, which he ate without a bun while chain-smoking Nat Sherman cigarettes. Paul was painfully shy and rarely made eye contact. He seemed to have no interests except for records, movies, and hard-boiled detective novels. He spoke in a soft midwestern twang and liked to tell stories of going to college in Minnesota with Bob Dylan, tales that I was more than eager to hear.

Paul lived in perpetual fear of Mercury president Irwin Steinberg, an old-school record man whose roots with the company went as far back as Patti Page and Lesley Gore. Steinberg had survived by paying careful attention to costs. The romance of late sixties rock was lost on him. On one occasion Steinberg instructed Nelson to tell a band that they were dropped after they had driven across the country to meet him. To add insult to injury, Nelson was supposed to charge the band five dollars apiece for press kits that the band needed to help them attract club bookings. Nelson let them take a couple of hundred of the press kits for free, an act of rebellion that did not endear him to the boss.

Nelson had a brief moment of corporate glory because he was the only guy at Mercury whom Rod Stewart liked. Paul parlayed his clout into getting Mercury to sign the New York Dolls, who were the darlings of the Max's rock critics. We all felt that the Dolls were "our" version of the Rolling Stones, the cutting edge of a new joyous reinvention of rock. The Dolls were Paul's first and last signing. When their first album flopped commercially despite rave reviews, Paul was fired, never to work inside the music business again.

After being dropped by Mercury, the Dolls' lead singer David Johansen had found that his cult followers at Max's, such as myself, had been unable to get the band another deal. One night at Max's, David's girlfriend, Cyrinda Foxe, said something nice about me and David uncharacteristically snapped, "Danny is always nice except if you ask him to actually do anything to help your career." It wasn't for lack of trying. The fact was that rock critics were big fish in a very small pond and had extremely limited influence over the "real" music business. I had fared no better at Famous Music than Nelson had at Mercury. My cocky rock-critic attitude was irritating to the old-school guys who ran the company and I was soon shown the door. I scrambled for other ways in.

Steve Paul was the richest guy I knew in the music business. By dint of managing the careers of Johnny Winter and the Edgar Winter Group he had bought a big house on a lake in Stamford, Connecticut, and we all saw him as "our" tycoon. The first gold album I ever got was from Steve because of a glowing review I'd written for *Rolling Stone* of Edgar's album *They Only Come Out at Night*. When I was in Steve's office he always seemed to be on the phone with the booking agency for Johnny and Edgar, Premier Talent.

For an artist on their way up, the opportunity to be the opening act in front of the right headliner's audience was as important to building an audience as the media. And of course touring was also a big business in its own right. There were many artists, such as the J. Geils Band, the Allmans, and most famously the Grateful Dead, who made much more money on the road than they ever did from records. Those who controlled the opening-act slots had clout. No one had more of such power than Premier Talent, the all-rock booking agency that had been created by Frank Barsalona.

Barsalona had booked the Beatles and the Rolling Stones tours for the show-biz agency GAC and started Premier in 1964 based on the insight that although most old-school promoters viewed rock and roll as "lower than rodeo," there was a growing new baby boom audience that viewed it as art. Barsalona was an Italian-American, had thinning blond hair, and wore silk shirts, but there was nothing thuggish in his affect. When people referred to him as the godfather of touring they were referring to the strength of his client list and his highly disciplined sense of favors done and favors owed. Frank spoke in a soft, controlled high-pitched voice that implied a level of real-world sophistication. He had unerring judgment about what song an act should close a show with in order to elicit an encore and he schooled many a lead guitarist on what kind of wine to order.

Among concert promoters themselves, Bill Graham was first among equals. I had an apartment on St. Mark's Place two blocks away from the Fillmore East, so Graham loomed particularly large to me. A Hungarian Holocaust survivor whose real name was Wolfgang Grajonca, Graham had a Slavic face, a sensual grin, and a booming New York voice. He was a charismatic and intimidating figure who somehow upheld the grown-up concept of authority when it came to getting paid but was also indisputably hip, a guy who could get high with the musicians whose shows he promoted. He was as close as a businessman could get to being a rock star himself.

Graham had been living in San Francisco in the mid-sixties. Among the self-selected hippie impresarios in the Bay Area, he was the one who also had conventional business chops. In the context of utopian hippie ideals Graham was considered a mercenary who made money off of the counterculture, but compared to the promoters who came before and after him, Graham was a soft touch. He was frequently to promote benefit concerts for no charge and for many months gave over the use of the Fillmore East to a local radical group called the Motherfuckers, cutting them off only after they trashed the place.

Prior to Graham, rock and roll shows typically consisted of a dozen artists who each did two or three songs. Jonny Podell, who booked many artists, including the Allman Brothers Band, into Graham's venues, explained, "Bill created a rock emporium. I remember going to a rock festival in Atlanta at which John Fogerty of Creedence was complaining bitterly about how shitty the sound was. Bill Graham fixed all that. He made the presentation side an art while also making a lot money. When you went to the Fillmore, you got great sound and lights, a light show, and a program booklet you could keep. His people would serve you coffee while you waited on line to buy tickets. You could buy posters that later became worth thousands." Graham also provided a party atmosphere backstage that included high-quality catering. When a band went over with the audience, he would personally go to the dressing room to cajole them into doing an encore.

Mark Spector was an NYU student when he took a job at the Fillmore East just prior to its opening in March 1968. "What we thought of as the music business was small. I remember the night that Steve Paul read a short article in *Rolling Stone* about Johnny Winter and said he was going to fly to Texas to meet him." Paul signed the albino blues guitar virtuoso as a management client and several weeks later got Graham to put him as an opener to B. B. King and Terry Reid. Soon afterward Clive Davis signed Winter to Columbia. Premier became Winter's booking agency.

"There wasn't a model on which what we were doing was based," Spector recalls. "There was a sense that everything was happening for the first time, that this thing that would eventually be called the rock-concert business was being invented on a daily basis, from technology that supported it to the way it was marketed and presented. The model of a two- or three-act show where you work your way up the ladder was a model that stood the test of time for quite a few years." Many bands' careers were launched by Graham's decision to make them the opening act at the Fillmore or Fillmore East. "Graham was the guy they all looked at," recalls Podell. "If he liked J. Geils or Tower of Power or Humble Pie, they were booked everywhere."

Bill particularly appreciated the acts that worked their asses

55

off, who would play for three hours like the Allman Brothers and the Grateful Dead, and he took it personally when artists, in his view, failed to give enough to the audience. On New Year's Eve, 1969, the last night of the 1960s, Jimi Hendrix was debuting a new ensemble, the Band of Gypsys, and Graham thought that the first show lacked energy. He went into Hendrix's dressing room and, according to Spector, "read him the riot act" for letting the audience down. Any other businessperson who dared to say such a thing would have been physically thrown out of the dressing room, but because the messenger was Bill Graham, Hendrix meekly apologized. "He played the second set like he was a different person," Spector recalled with awe.

Graham created a brand that had a value of its own and he was ruthless about getting paid for it. In the late sixties, when tickets cost an average of five dollars, Graham required artists to play two shows each on Friday and Saturday night. A four-show weekend could gross $50,000. He paid artists $7,500 for the headliner, $5,000 for the special guest, and $2,500 for the opening act. The headliners would also get a bonus if concerts sold out. "Bill wanted to get paid as an artist as well," Podell said ruefully. Podell would later work with George Harrison and Crosby, Stills, Nash and Young as well as the Allmans and said, "Every artist I worked with was fine making less money to play for Bill Graham."

I still had a soft spot for folkie singer-songwriters. Besides the Fillmore East my favorite place to see music was the Gaslight on McDougal Street in Greenwich Village. I spent many hours listening to Gaslight owner Sam Hood wistfully tell stories of Bob Dylan's early years. Although he never had a gift for making money himself, Sam was an important tastemaker, nurturing such vital singer-songwriters as Loudon Wainwright III, John Prine, Steve Goodman, Tim Hardin, Fred Neil, and Paul Siebel as well as such future superstars as James Taylor, Carly Simon, Linda Ronstadt, Cat Stevens, and Kris Kristofferson.

The businesspeople I admired the most were the managers,

because they were the closest to the artists. Managers were independent operators in small companies, not part of big corporations, and they were iconoclasts by nature. They alone had the total overview of the business, supervising the relationships with record producers, backup musicians, road managers, booking agents, concert promoters, publicists, record companies, lawyers, accountants, and, in many cases, girlfriends and dope dealers as well.

For a time in the early seventies I worked for the legendary Albert Grossman, who managed Bob Dylan, Janis Joplin, and the Band, among others, and who was immortalized by his prominent role in *Don't Look Back,* the documentary about Dylan's 1965 tour of Great Britain. Grossman was the subject of Dylan's song "Dear Landlord," which ended with the timeless phrase "if you don't underestimate me, I won't underestimate you." Grossman had also created Bearsville Records, the first boutique label built around a manager. Management, Albert explained, was a service business and did not aggregate assets that could be sold, as did music publishers or record companies. This is why the financially savviest managers, such as David Geffen, Chris Blackwell, Lou Adler, Grossman, and Allman Brothers manager Phil Walden, eventually created labels.

At his peak Grossman had moved to Woodstock, built a studio, and created an insular world in which he was both king and rebel. Grossman looked like Benjamin Franklin. He was tall and had a large stomach and a long white ponytail and big round glasses. Albert was a master of implying that there was wisdom that he alone possessed, often communicated by grunts and shrugs. A gourmand who would travel thousands of miles for a five-star meal, Albert was also a self-styled expert on art, architecture, and all facets of hip culture. For the first few years I knew him I was so intimidated that I nodded in ardent agreement with everything he said, lest I would be consigned to the ranks of the pathetically unhip. But even Albert Grossman was

57

dependent on artists for his power. After Dylan left him and Janis Joplin died, his larger-than-life image and the influence that came with it began to fade. My job in his office was in the music publishing division, in which I was supposed to go through the catalog of songs he controlled and try to get artists to record them. I was in over my head; I produced marginal results and was fired. Desperate to stay in the business, I begged everyone who would take my call to give me any leads and took to praying ardently for a decent job.

Gloria Stavers had recommended me to Lee Solters, whose firm, Solters, Sabinson and Roskin (SSR) was the leading PR firm for Broadway shows and who also represented mainstream celebrities such as Barbra Streisand and Frank Sinatra as well as their most reliable client, Ringling Bros. and Barnum & Bailey Circus. Lee hired me, ponytail, baggy jeans, and all, to be SSR's resident expert on rock and roll and the rock press.

Lee looked and talked like a character in a movie from the 1930s. He was short and broad shouldered, wore thick glasses, and usually had an exasperated look on his face, which was broken occasionally by rueful laughter. He had started as a press agent in the early forties and had gotten to know Walter Winchell well enough that he was later made a consultant on the classic Burt Lancaster film noir about New York flackery, *Sweet Smell of Success*. SSR's office looked like an old-fashioned newspaper city room. Dozens of press agents worked at dingy desks. On each desk sat a manual typewriter, a box of file cards with "contacts'" names on them, and piles of typing and carbon paper. One quiet corner of the large open space was reserved for a mild-mannered man with a photo of Bela Lugosi over his desk whose sole function was to write jokes that would be attributed to SSR clients and then serviced to syndicated showbiz columnists such as Earl Wilson and Jack O'Brien.

SSR's office was populated with cynical middle-aged press agents who were oblivious to rock and roll and the hip culture. The rock and roll pundits in my Rolodex meant literally nothing to any of them. But these hardened old pros were generous to me, explaining how to write "items," guiding me through the press lists, teaching me how to deal with the wire services, and subtly training my mind to the craft of real-life public relations—giving me the professional tools to survive the end of the hippie era.

When Zeppelin's American lawyer, Steve Weiss, approached Solters to solve the band's PR problem, Lee asked me to accompany him to Paris to meet Led Zeppelin and their manager, Peter Grant. "You'll have to do most of the talking," he said. "I'm from the Guy Lombardo generation."

CHAPTER FOUR

LED ZEPPELIN, "MILD BARBARIANS"

When we met Led Zeppelin in the spring of 1973, they were the biggest rock band in the world by any grown-up standards. Their previous album, the band's fourth, had sold eight million copies worldwide, even though it lacked a title and didn't even have the name of the band on the cover, merely four runic symbols representing the band's members, lead singer Robert Plant, guitarist Jimmy Page, bassist and keyboardist John Paul Jones, and drummer John Bonham. That album included the song "Stairway to Heaven," which was the most played song on album rock radio stations the year it came out and would remain the most requested rock song in the United States for decades.

Sales of the first four Zeppelin albums were so consistent and massive that they represented more than one-fourth of the annual sales of the entire quarter-century-old Atlantic Records catalog. Although they had been originally signed by Jerry Wexler, his curmudgeonly musical purism was less attractive to Zeppelin than the charm and glamour of Atlantic's founder, Ahmet Ertegun, who became **61** a fixture at major-market Zeppelin concerts and available for periodic renegotiations in which he would plaintively tell Grant, "Peter, you're taking me to the cleaners." (This proved to be a more sophisticated version of Wexler's con of Peter Wolf. Atlantic still made a fortune from them.)

Uneasy kings of the rock and roll mountain, Zeppelin turned their attention to the one realm in which they lacked stature and prestige: the press. During the first few months in which I worked for them, Nick Kent of the *New Musical Express* would write, "Zeppelin and the press remain uncomfortable in each other's company. A classic example of the sort of mutual disregard which seems to exist between the two occurred in 1972 during Led Zeppelin's annual mammoth American tour—which was again phenomenally successful but which lost out in the publicity stakes to the Rolling Stones' destruction of America that same year." (The Stones were drenched in the eternal essence of sixties Zeitgeist and thus had permanent credibility in the rock-critic subculture. As if that weren't enough, the Stones' entourage in 1972 had included such media magnets as Truman Capote and Princess Lee Radziwill, and landed them the cover of *Newsweek*.)

Page candidly told Kent, "We didn't have a press agent at the time. The press has always been into images rather than music. Anyway, for this tour, we thought we'd bring in some of the press just so the media would be informed of our goings-on." Which was his way of saying that they had hired me.

It seems inconceivable to younger people who put Zeppelin in the upper levels of the rock pantheon that in 1973, in the collective mind of the critical clique, Led Zeppelin was not only not cool, they were distinctly uncool. Actual rock and roll stardom was created by fourteen- to sixteen-year-olds. But the prevailing journalistic arbiters of cool were in their twenties when Led Zeppelin emerged in 1969–70. Led Zeppelin was the first big group to make that slice of baby boomers feel mortal. "Their audience is so young," one anguished twenty-something rock writer said to me one night at Max's, after having seen Zeppelin in concert—as if that were a bad thing for a rock band.

To get some perspective before meeting them, I called Diane Gardiner, who handled press for Jefferson Airplane. Years earlier she had played the role of rock specialist for the movie PR firm Rogers, Cowan and Brenner, where she had been assigned Zeppelin's debut album in 1969. Diane was a classic hybrid of rock chick and professional publicist, with twinkling eyes and a persona that combined Haight-Ashbury hippie culture with a 1940s style of a young Barbara Stanwyck, whom she resembled. She was also close friends with Jim Morrison and Pamela Courson and she'd had a long affair with Chuck Berry. (She took up with Berry after going backstage after a Bay Area concert and saying dramatically to him, "I throw myself on the altar of your art.")

Notwithstanding these rock bona-fides, Diane had been unable to get much press for Led Zeppelin in those early years. Hypersensitive to early bad reviews, the members of the band exacerbated their image problem by demonizing journalists. There had been an incident with a *Life* magazine writer named Ellen Sander, who was rudely insulted by the band after a few days on the road. They developed a reputation for throwing televisions out of hotel windows and there was a widely circulated story, immortalized in a song on one of Frank Zappa's albums, that members of Led Zeppelin had stuffed pieces of dead sharks into orifices of some groupies in Seattle. "They were so young when I had them," Diane sighed, "I bet they'll be much better now"—concluding with worldly affection, "They really do have a sweet side."

By the time of the fourth album, Robert had been goaded by his father to get some more visibility, and the band hired the elfin Irish PR maestro B. P. Fallon, who had orchestrated the emergence of T-Rex and had a commitment to the hippie ethos. B.P. saw everything in terms of "vibes." At dinnertime he would say "eating vibe." At four in the morning he would say good-night with the words "Sleeping vibe." For all of his good

63

vibes toward the media, B.P. found he could rarely get Zeppelin to do more than an occasional interview. "It just wasn't time yet." But echoing Gardiner, he told me, "Now I think the vibe is right." Easy for them to say.

Before meeting the band, Lee and I had an audience with their legendary manager, Peter Grant. Peter had the ultimate chip on the ultimate shoulder. He was a street-smart cockney who weighed over three hundred pounds, having begun his career in the rock business as a driver and bodyguard for Don Arden, the notorious tough-guy manager of the Small Faces and the Animals. Grant had previously been a professional wrestler in England. Feared for his willingness to use physical intimidation, Peter was also considered the shrewdest of his generation of British rock managers. He understood, more than any of his peers, that artists had grown more powerful. He took Led Zeppelin away from Premier Talent in 1971 and booked the band directly without an agent, thus recovering 10 percent of Zeppelin's sizable concert grosses for the band. This shocked the nouveau establishment of rock promoters and agents. Many of them never forgave him, and Peter couldn't have cared less.

Peter insisted on a much higher percentage of the profits for his band, forever changing the economics of the touring business. The biggest rock attractions, such as Grand Funk Railroad, were getting 50 percent of the gross, which usually amounted to around 75 percent of the net profits. (And promoters often fudged on expenses taken off the top.) Grant insisted that Zeppelin receive 90 percent of the net profits and insisted on personally approving any expenses. He realized that in most instances advertising was not necessary for a Led Zeppelin show because a few mentions on the local rock radio station were sufficient to cause a sellout. "You know why I asked promoters for ninety percent?" Peter asked me rhetorically after I'd worked for him for a while. "Because I'd do it. I'd take ten percent of Led Zeppelin. That's a lot of money for no risk." Soon, every major headliner demanded and received a 90/10 deal.

In earlier times managers had positioned themselves as the ultimate schmoozers, currying favor with record companies, the media, and those in the concert business in order to best represent their clients. Peter Grant cared solely about his artists. Everyone else could go fuck themselves if they didn't do what Led Zeppelin wanted. Grant developed an almost mystical image in England as the champion of rock artists. I had dinner with Ray Davies of the Kinks shortly before Zeppelin's reunion concert in 2007. Davies had been through four decades of rock business charlatans and saw the business through canny, jaundiced eyes, but he spoke with grudging respect for Grant, who had died a decade earlier. "It can't *really* be a Led Zeppelin concert without Peter Grant," he mused.

When we met him, Grant's stature was enhanced by the contrast of his scruffy beard, silver-and-turquoise rings on several fingers, and oversized blue jeans with the old-world elegance of the Hotel George V, where the band was staying prior to an appearance the next night at the Palais des Sports.

Peter said that he thought that contempt for the rock press had worked in the band's favor in the early years but that by 1973 it was time to go the other way—although he wanted to continue their practice of avoiding any TV appearances. The sound on television speakers just couldn't do the band justice, he said, but he wanted them to be much more proactive with the rest of the media. I told him that Led Zeppelin had the reputation of being barbarians on the road. Peter laughed soundlessly and answered in the gentlest version of his deep cockney growl, "Yeah, but we're just mild barbarians."

The next day, all four band members sat diligently in Peter's suite. Despite the fact that Jimmy Page was the musical and business leader of the band, it was Robert Plant who did most of the talking, and he was very clear about what they wanted. Robert was twenty-five years old, in the full flower of youth, his classically handsome face unlined, his blond curls tumbling long past his shoulders—so recently a boy, yet infused with the

65

worldliness developed by several years of actual rock stardom. Robert literally beamed with optimism and joy and a sense of rock and roll entitlement that was contagious. Peter asked me to explain what he bemusedly called "the barbarian thing," and Robert airily reassured me, "Look, we were very young when we first started. We're over all of that now."

The members of Zeppelin all had nicknames by which they were known to each other and their intimates. Robert Plant was "Percy," Page, "Pagey," Jones, "Jonesy," and Bonham, "Bonzo." Peter Grant was always almost always referred to as "G."

"Look at all the publicity the Stones got on their last tour!" Robert said, as if this was the most absurd journalistic error imaginable. He wanted mainstream fame, and while the rest of the band were not as forceful in asking for it, they certainly wouldn't mind having it either. "What you are saying," drummer John Bonham said to me earnestly at the end of the meeting, "is that you're going to get us known to people who don't know about us yet."

Despite their affability Zeppelin continued to view the rock press with suspicion. Bonzo spat contempt as he referred to reviewers who had disparaged his famously long drum solos. "Look, if Buddy Rich says I'm shit, then I'm shit, but what the fuck do those wankers know?" Page's choirboy looks and educated articulation masqueraded a deeply paranoid side. He spoke with bitterness about the bad reviews, wondering darkly if some of the critics were not clandestinely in league with Jeff Beck, who had been one of Page's successors as lead guitarist of the Yardbirds, and with whom he had some ill-defined rivalry. His dislike of the press was sufficiently well-known that the New Musical Express's Kent wrote that when I made Zeppelin accessible in 1973, "most of the journalists present seemed so shocked that one of them said: 'My first question to you, Mr. Page, is—why are you giving me this interview in the first place?'"

At twenty-two I was also a little old to be a pure fan of Led Zeppelin. But at one of the first Zeppelin shows I saw, I watched a teenage boy's jaw literally drop at the sight of a laser beam hitting the mirror ball as Robert sang the last line of "Stairway to Heaven." At first it was through such mesmerized kids that I vicariously connected with Zeppelin's music. Over the course of several more shows, as I listened to their extraordinary rhythm section, to Jimmy Page's heroic solos and Robert's searing vocals, I become hooked myself. Moreover, I soon realized that in the process of getting Zeppelin the image in the press that they now coveted, I could establish my own identity in the music business as well. I became obsessed.

I knew that other than my closest friends, I would get nowhere with the sixties rock critics. Lillian Roxon trudged out to Kennedy Airport to meet the plane with me when Led Zeppelin arrived and dutifully wrote a full-page piece for the *New York Daily News* (on the condition that she got the first interview— even PR friendships has its rules). When she saw them in Madison Square Garden, Lillian grumbled, "I guess Robert Plant would be impressive to people if they had never seen Roger Daltrey." Having become a devoted Zeppelin partisan I thought the comparison utterly wrongheaded, but I bit my tongue. Mercifully, Lillian restricted her coverage of Zeppelin to news and quotes.

Rolling Stone had never written a positive word about the band. The week that Zeppelin's fifth album, *Houses of the Holy,* came out the magazine had rushed into print a poor review calling the album a "limp blimp." Although I felt that the reviewer's snobbish prejudice had blinded him to a brilliant new group of songs, I could not think of anyone in the Max's clique who would have both the stature and the inclination to transform Led Zeppelin's image among critics.

Lee Solters had impressed upon me that there was a limit to the amount of favors one could get but there was no limit to the number of good stories that could be pitched. I needed a story. The first two concerts of the 1973 tour were at Atlanta Stadium and Tampa Stadium, both baseball parks. Tampa held 56,800 people, which made the crowd slightly larger than that of the Beatles' Shea Stadium show of 1965. Of course, the contrast with Shea Stadium was a reflection of the size of the stadiums, not the relative popularity of the groups. There had been numerous rock festivals that had attracted far bigger crowds, but I figured that those crowds had been drawn by multiartist packages rather than single headliners. (The word *concert* was the key.) I typed up a press release in my hotel room with the headline that Led Zeppelin had "broken the Beatles' record." I took a taxi to the local UPI bureau in Tampa, where it was a slow news night. The story of the "broken Beatles' record" was picked up by hundreds of newspapers. For the rest of the year, every article about Led Zeppelin contained the fact that they had broken the Beatles' single-night concert attendance record, and the London *Daily Express* actually headlined a puff piece about them being "Bigger Than the Beatles."

I was sitting with the band in their dressing room in Atlanta, looking out the window watching the throngs of kids walk in, when John Paul Jones sarcastically quipped, "Come on, kiddies, and bring us your money." Robert looked at him, genuinely shocked, and admonished him without a trace of cynicism, "Jonesy! Those are our fans." Zeppelin played a three-hour set without an opening act, and at some point during the middle Peter pointed to a window that overlooked a highway in which cars were speeding by. "Look at that," he said to me with childlike excitement. "In here people are screaming and jumping around and having the time of their life, and out there those people in those cars don't have the slightest idea what is going on." I later told of this moment to Stephen Davis, who used it in his best-seller about the band, *Hammer of the Gods,* but in Stephen's version Peter was making this observation to exhort me to make the band more famous. My actual interpretation was quite different. I felt that in the euphoria of the moment he was simply tripping out on the notion of parallel realities occurring so close to each other. Rock concerts at their best generated a tribal reality for the fans, in which they shared moments of all-consuming joy and later felt they shared a secret that non-fans could never understand. It was a momentary break from Peter's fierce business identity to that of his inner hippie. I was totally into it.

Notwithstanding such occasionally sweet moments the general atmosphere was one of tension, exacerbated by the huge quantities of cocaine (which, based on some cockney formulation, they referred to as "Charlie"). Both Peter and Bonham thought it amusing to grab civilians such as myself by the balls and ask, "How's your knob?" Sitting next to Peter in the back of a limo was a terrifying experience anytime the car made a sharp right turn and his three-hundred-pound bulk squashed me in an unspoken, and undoubtedly intentional, reminder of our relative power. Although I was never to personally witness any violence, the threat of it always seemed to be just one bad mood away. Peter relished his image as a tough guy and reinforced it whenever possible. He loved to tell a story of having met with a hotel manager to settle up on damages after the band had thrown several TVs out of windows. "This must be very upsetting for you," Peter had commiserated, but the hotel manager had replied that he understood how an artist might be driven to rage by the sterility of some of the rooms. He himself felt that way sometimes. Grant asked the hotelier if he himself had literally had an impulse to throw TVs out the window. When the answer was affirmative Peter grandly peeled off another five hundred dollars in cash and told the guy, "Have one on me."

But these colorful road episodes, despite their perverse glamour, were secondary to rock and roll. And rock and roll, to Peter Grant, was defined by whatever mattered to the band. His devotion to them was reciprocated. "What can you say about a man who is both a father and a brother?" Robert rhetorically **69** asked in response to a writer vainly hoping to find a dissenting view.

The morning after the Atlanta show Peter, in a moment of naive grandiosity, decided that he wanted someone to say that it was the biggest thing that had happened to the city since the filming of *Gone With the Wind*. I was terrified of disappointing him, so I did not confront him about the contrived nature of his request. I begged Lisa Robinson for a favor, giving her an invented quote from Mayor Sam Massell of Atlanta, who had attended the concert. I figured, accurately, that it was too trivial a concoction for the mayor to deny. Although she had her doubts, Lisa dutifully "quoted" the mayor in a puff piece she wrote for the British weekly *Disc and Music Echo,* which got me off the hook and immediately endeared her to Peter.

I felt wistful about these gimmicks because I soon learned that, notwithstanding their unrestrained interest in the by-products of rock stardom, the members of the band took their music enormously seriously. Jimmy and Robert personally signed off on every aspect of the sound, lights, and special effects on tours. A sprained finger for Jimmy Page or a stuffed nose for Plant was considered a crisis of epic proportions.

Both Robert and Jimmy balanced their keen sense of macho rock power, sexuality, and traditional blues with a strong emotional connection to the poetic, folkie side of rock and roll. Robert loved the Incredible String Band and Jimmy adored the Fairport Convention, whose lead singer, Sandy Denny, had sung background vocals on *Led Zeppelin III*. They both idolized Joni Mitchell, whom they had never met, and they had semiserious arguments about which one of them she would be more likely to fancy.

John Paul Jones was, in addition to being an excellent bass player, a brilliant arranger who had, in his pre-Zeppelin days, orchestrated complex sections of Donovan's hits "Atlantis" and "Barabajagal." On *Houses of the Holy* his keyboard/synthesizer arrangements on songs such as "No Quarter" were critical to the evolution of the band's sound. During concert performances of "No Quarter," the stage was blanketed in a cascade of fog generated by dry ice. Jonesey was almost completely disengaged from the PR aspect of the band, occasionally making bitter jokes about being one of the "other guys" who did not get the attention that Jimmy and Robert did, but for the most part he was so quiet in band meetings as to seem invisible. But the fact that he was shy did not mean he wasn't paying attention. Many around Led Zeppelin did cocaine, but I did not, having grown away from drugs under the influence of various yogis. Early in my time with the band a fierce roadie offered me a line and I had a moment of anxiety, wondering if I should snort it so as not to come across as remote or judgmental. Jonesy suddenly materialized and gently chided the roadie, "He won't be wanting any of that," and smiled knowingly at me as he passed by.

Regardless of what kind of business they did, or how the crowd reacted, the band was ruthlessly critical of their own performances, flagellating themselves after shows they considered subpar. Bonham was the most obsessive. He would show up for sound checks an hour before the other guys to customize his drum sound to each venue. While Peter, Jimmy, and Jonesy sought refreshment in the dressing rooms each night during Bonzo's thirty-minute drum solo "Moby Dick," Robert usually stood on the side of the stage watching his boyhood friend reinvent rock drumming on a nightly basis.

For me, the 1973 Led Zeppelin tour was my introduction to the adrenaline of a big-time rock tour, the fleet of limos going in and out of the venues, the escape from frenetic fans, the omnipresence of groupies, the scale of the speakers and lighting rigs, and the intoxicating feeling of insiderness as I doled out tickets, photo passes, and the occasional backstage laminate. My favorite perk was the ability to stand just inside the security barrier on the side of the stage and peer into the faces of the frenetic audience, intoxicated by (among other things) the sheer intensity of the music and showmanship of the band. Inevitably

71

parts of the show became predictable to me, but I always loved the rush that accompanied the cathartic roar of the audience when they heard the drum intro, guitar riff, and opening lines screamed by Robert, "It's been a long time since I rock and rolled," in the opening song. I never got tired of the improvisation and psychedelic shtick during "Dazed and Confused." Like most of the people around them I internalized defiant reverence for the band. After my first month on the road with them I had come to feel that anyone who didn't appreciate Led Zeppelin was an idiot.

PR strategy could sometimes bump up against other agendas. Shortly after the first stories about the broken attendance records came out, I got a call from Zeppelin's U.S. lawyer, Steve Weiss. Weiss was then in his mid-forties, with longish salt-and-pepper hair. He was short but had a wiry physique maintained by frequent tennis. He was the type of rock business character of the time who encouraged the perception that he was mob-connected. I ended up spending quite a bit of time with Weiss over the years and would conclude that he himself was a pretty straightforward and legitimate attorney. But he relished the image of a tough guy. He always referred to the members of Zeppelin as "the boys," and he owned a purple Rolls-Royce in which he had his chauffeur place freshly cut flowers in two small interior cut-glass vases each day.

Weiss was known for having a volcanic temper, and I winced when I realized his call was not to congratulate me but to complain. Some of the newspaper articles, he observed, had included a reference to the gross revenue of Zeppelin's concerts. "We never reveal financial information," he sternly said, "just the attendance figures." I was flummoxed. Reporters *always* asked about money. In any case the concerts in question had a single ticket price of $5.50. Thus it did not take much enterprise for a writer to multiply an attendance of 56,800 at Tampa and get the gross of $312,400. Weiss implied that the large numbers invited the scrutiny of the IRS. I solemnly promised that such information would never come from me again. Later it occurred to me that the IRS had agents who were perfectly capable of doing multiplication and that Weiss's real concern might have been that members of the band might question where all the money went.

For the second half of the 1973 tour Zeppelin leased a private plane that was called *The Starship*. As part of the deal, the owners of the plane spray-painted the band's name on the side of the jet. At that time a private plane with velvet couches was a real novelty to writers who covered popular music, and we were able to get a number of stories that focused on the grandiosity of the band—although I often needed road manager Richard Cole to help me discourage Bonham from berating the writers when he had too much to drink. There was a hideous moment on *The Starship* when, for no apparent reason, Bonzo had taken the thick glasses off the face of a midwestern promo guy named Danny Markus and stomped on them. All of us, including Markus, froze into the pretense that nothing of consequence had happened. But we all knew it was a particularly ugly example of the way some performers lost common civility when intoxicated with extended periods of adulation.

Richard Cole had the gold teeth and bravado of a pirate, and he had been Zeppelin's tour manager since their career started. He was the one who had to deal with complaints from the band about hotel rooms, wives, drugs, or groupies. A cockney street fighter like Grant, Richard had a wicked sense of humor, which he often had to rely on to cajole members of the band out of the variety of bad moods that road life could bring. Richard was also responsible for getting them to every gig on time. He therefore had little patience for small talk, but once he realized that I worked for the band and not for the record company, he became a valuable ally in locating band members at critical times such as when interviews were scheduled.

After each concert I barraged music editors with press re- **73** leases about the size of the band's audience. My mantra was that whether critics liked them or not, Led Zeppelin was the people's band, the favorite of real rock fans, and, I would note pointedly, *young* rock fans. It was no coincidence that the most favorable major newspaper piece about the 1973 Led Zeppelin tour was written for the *L.A. Times,* whose music editor, Robert Hillburn, bought into the idea that there was a generational shift occurring in rock and roll. Hillburn assigned Cameron Crowe, then a fifteen-year-old Orange County high school student who had published a few pieces for rock magazines. "I was more into singer-writers than into heavy rock bands, but I had a sociological interest in the band's popularity and I thought that Cameron could explain it to our readers a lot better than I could," recalled Hillburn.

Cameron's youthful enthusiasm relaxed the band into giving him better quotes than they did to older, more cynical reporters. After the story came out, Jimmy admiringly said to me, "Well, I have a nickname for him: Cameron Crowbar."

In the wake of the "bigger than the Beatles" story *Rolling Stone* asked for an interview with the band. Jimmy told me to turn it down because of the "limp blimp" review. Then Jann Wenner himself called, assuring me that the article would not be written by that previous reviewer, and said he saw it as a cover piece. Jimmy was unmoved. No fucking way. As a typical PR guy in thrall to the media, I would normally have been dismayed by the band's defiance, but I understood their point. Knowing it was a battle I couldn't win, I made it part of my pitch to the rest of the press: Led Zeppelin was so big and so self-contained that they had actually turned down a cover story in *Rolling Stone.*

One afternoon in Chicago on the 1973 Zeppelin tour a very stern Peter Grant summoned me to his suite, a fairly unusual and nerve-wracking occurrence. My stomach knotted up when I found all four members of the band seated on the couches in the living room, while the omnipresent Richard Cole stood menacingly. Peter raised his considerable bulk up from his armchair and handed me that day's *Chicago Sun-Times* with a review and a photo that showed Robert singing and Jimmy playing the guitar standing next to him. "The boys have something they want to talk to you about," he growled.

Jimmy Page, who was usually a silent, almost spectral, presence when I was in the room, spoke up sternly in his high-pitched, educated London accent, "We're sick and tired of seeing photos in the papers that don't include Bonzo and Jonesy. This is a four-person band and I don't want this happening anymore. It's not on." Jimmy went on in this vein at considerable length while Robert nodded solemnly. Jonesy stared at the floor in acute embarrassment, but Bonzo glowered. It was clear that one of the drummer's tantrums had precipitated the meeting. He was notoriously sensitive to real or imagined slights, capable of trashing hotel suites if he thought they were smaller than those of Jimmy or Robert.

Trying to avoid a stammer, I nervously reminded them that we had no control over which photos the daily papers ran. Maybe, Peter suggested, we shouldn't allow any more photographers at concerts. This caused panic in my PR soul. Denying access to the media almost always resulted in bad press.

I had invited Neal Preston, a young up-and-coming photographer, to take photos on the road. Neal got access other photographers didn't get in return for the band's right to disapprove any photos they didn't like, as well as the right to use any of them for PR or marketing purposes. Page was the one with the keenest interest in the selection process, and I had spent many an hour with Jimmy looking at slides while he eliminated the ones that showed the least sign of protruding belly or incipient crow's feet. Neal always dutifully destroyed the offensive photos, reinforcing the band's trust. He was then free to sell the approved photos, and several months afterward, when I saw him driving a Mercedes in Hollywood, he cheerfully told me that the Zeppelin photos had paid for it. (Thirty years later

Neal, who refused any payment from me for the photo of me and Robert printed in this book, was still selling Zeppelin prints to collectors for five hundred dollars a pop.)

I promised the band that Neal would spend his entire time that night shooting pictures that included all four members. This wouldn't eliminate the tendency of some news dailies to use old photos, but it would give us the tool to circulate full band photos to magazines that took handouts from us. To dramatize that I had the requisite macho commitment to solving the crisis, I assured them I would fire Neal if he did not comply. (Neal was the most affable of people and I knew there was no chance he would have any problem with such a request.) To my surprise and relief this solution was accepted by Peter and Bonzo and the meeting abruptly broke up.

That night, the last of three shows at the Chicago Stadium, Neal came up to me a half hour into the set, uncommonly agitated. Shouting over the high-decibel sound, he explained that there were bright white lights on Jimmy and Robert and dim colored lights on Bonzo and Jonesy, which made it impossible to shoot the kinds of pictures I had asked for. I found Richard Cole and reminded him of the agenda of our earlier meeting and explained Neal's dilemma. Richard walked me behind the curtain at the back of the stage to meet with one of the roadies I was unfamiliar with, the man who evidently was in charge of all lighting. I requested that, for at least one song, there be brighter lights on Bonzo and Jonesy. The lighting guy looked at me as if I were insane. He explained to me that "the bright lights are on Jimmy and Robert. That's always been the way it's always been, that's the way it is, and that's the way Jimmy wants it," and walked off. I looked to Richard to exert some authority, but to my amazement he was already walking away. It dawned on me that the conversation in Peter's room had been a charade. Bonzo had obviously had some sort of a freakout and Peter defused it by having the meeting, knowing full well that my suggestion was a nonstarter, hoping I would figure out something along the way to make Bonzo feel more appreciated—but not at the expense of the image of the band that he and Jimmy had long before carefully crafted. The next day Bonzo had seemingly forgotten about tour photos and was joyfully repeating bits of a profane underground tape that Peter had given him, made by comedians Peter Cook and Dudley Moore.

Sometimes what mattered to me was not what mattered to Peter or the band. I was obsessed with the idea that if there was enough repetition of the band's 'bigness" the gatekeepers of pop fame would finally anoint them mainstream superstars. Despite my barrage of statistics-laden press releases, I was politely but firmly rebuffed by the music editors of *Time* and *Newsweek*. I was at the brink of frustration when I finally hit what, in my mind, was paydirt: not a national magazine feature, but a significant mainstream newspaper story. I hyped a writer for *The Miami Herald* into doing a cover story for the newspaper's Sunday magazine section, which would also be syndicated by the Knight Ridder chain to dozens of Sunday magazine supplements across the country. This was real middle-American fame.

I did not accompany the band to their Miami gig and was horrified to hear that, at the last minute, they canceled the interview. "They didn't want to do it," Richard Cole barked over the phone as I sat at my desk in the dingy cluttered office at SSR. I would later become close friends with Richard but at this point we were just getting to know each other and had different agendas. Richard's job was to keep the band in as good a mood as possible; mine was to get the band publicity. Although Zeppelin had hired *us*, the psychology of the relationship often turned into one in which I would try to "persuade" the band members to do interviews. "Who gives a shit about *The Miami Herald*?" Richard barked, "The band will do something else for you next week." *For me.* I tried to explain that there very likely would not be a similar "mainstream" opportunity, and indeed there wasn't. Years later I was still torturing myself. If I had been more aggressive, maybe I could have gotten the band to do the *Herald* interview. If that story had run, maybe it would have triggered *Time* or *Newsweek*. But such results were much more my agenda than that of the band.

Lee Solters shared my nagging sense that we hadn't quite delivered the superstar press coverage to Zeppelin and was worried about the firm's reputation. He told me to write a press release saying that Zeppelin had wanted to play Shea Stadium but that the concert had been vetoed by the New York Mets because they were worried that the rock fans would ruin the grass. Since I had been privy to various discussions about the band's touring plans, I knew that Lee was making the story up and I self-righteously refused to write such a release. With a look of exasperation Lee snapped, "Fine—then I'll do it," and a few hours later a release was circulated "From Lee Solters" that revealed the "news" about the nonexistent cancellation of the nonexistent Shea Stadium concert. The next day, the *New York Daily News,* which at the time had the largest circulation of any U.S. newspaper, ran the story on page three. Lee looked at me smugly and said, "See?" as if I had been an idiot not to recognize the brilliance of his idea. I was terrified that either the band or one of my snobbish rock writer friends would see the story and complain about the corny PR chestnut. However, we dodged the bullet and there was no fallout of any kind.

The Madison Square Garden shows, which were filmed for the movie *The Song Remains the Same,* were the very last shows of the 1973 tour. I was standing backstage when I noticed Peter speaking in an agitated tone to Ahmet. I soon found out what the problem was. Peter had held on to more than two hundred thousand dollars in cash, put it in a safety deposit box at the Drake Hotel, and the box had been broken into and all the cash robbed. The next morning I was summoned to Peter's hotel room to help him deal with TV crews and reporters, who were gathered in the lobby. I asked him if he wanted me to call Atlantic's PR department and he snapped that he didn't want the fucking label there, he wanted *me* to organize the press conference. (Peter was cold sober and handled their questions calmly and gracefully.) Prior to that day Peter had not issued a single compliment to me during the tour and I felt that I was perpetually disappointing him in some way. Yet he wanted me in this moment of crisis. I must have done something right. I got some perverse gratification when the *New York Daily News* ran a boldfaced page-one headline saying, LED ZEP ROBBED. Lee looked at me approvingly in the morning and said, "You see—if we hadn't done all that work they would have said 'rock band' robbed."

What Led Zeppelin really cared about was how the tour was covered in England, where their friends and family lived. They freaked if a British music weekly ran a photo from the Rainbow in Hollywood showing the members of the band with their arms around the local L.A. groupies. I couldn't stop photographers in public places, but I was able to create some positive British press. I had originally given access to Lisa Robinson as a favor to *her* so she could impress her British editor of *Disc and Music Echo,* which typically had less access to superstars than its weekly London competitors *Melody Maker* and *New Musical Express.* However, it turned out that I was a great beneficiary of Lisa's stories. Unlike the typically adversarial and bitchy British rock writers, Lisa wrote positive stories, including whatever clever quotes the guys came up with. In future years she always got first crack at the band when they came to the States.

Near the end of 1973 I flew to England to meet with Peter. His house was around an hour outside of London and was literally surrounded by a moat. Led Zeppelin was being given their own label by Atlantic and "I need you to be my ambassador," he said. Peter would remain based in London and he wanted me in New York, where Atlantic was based. In addition to doing PR for the artists I would be his day-to-day liaison to the promotion and sales departments at Atlantic. Since Peter was also managing the first few artists that would be on the label, he also wanted me to help plan the tours with the booking agents and promoters. I knew at once that this was a huge opportunity to broaden my identity and skill set in the business. I explained that in America conventional titles really helped and he agreed to call me vice president.

The idea of a rock band being given their own label started with the Beatles and Apple Records, followed by Jefferson Airplane's Grunt Records, Deep Purple's Purple Records, and Rolling Stones Records. These labels, as well as Zeppelin's, were in reality imprints funded by the artist's existing label, which, in the case of Led Zeppelin, was Atlantic Records. A typical label deal would pay around twenty points to the label, out of which they would pay their artists. For example, if Zeppelin paid one of their artists twelve points, this would leave an eight-point profit. Typically the parent company made financial advances for overhead, which, in the case of Zeppelin's label, paid for my salary. In some cases the label owner was given puts, a number of albums that the label could force to be released and funded by the parent company, and in other cases each artist deal had to be approved by the parent company. The theory behind giving superstars their own labels was that superstars often spotted talent before A&R people did, and that in a contested situation, the persuasive powers of a rock star would be formidable.

As in other aspects of the business artists eventually developed more clout, so that major-funded label deals in future decades were usually joint ventures that gave the label owner an equity interest in their label that could be sold at a multiple of profits.

Peter Grant and Led Zeppelin were not interested in being entrepreneurs. They just wanted to leverage their stardom into another income stream. And they relished the prospect of giving a few of their friends record deals. But unlike the Beatles and the Stones, Led Zeppelin wanted their label to be more than a showcase of their taste. They wanted to actually break artists.

The first project, Maggie Bell's debut album, *Queen of the Night,* was actually released on Atlantic Records because Jimmy hadn't yet thought of a name for the label. Maggie was a Scottish blues/rock singer with a powerful and soulful voice reminiscent of Janis Joplin's. She had been lead singer of the band Stone the Crows, which had broken up when her boyfriend, and the band's lead guitarist, Les Harvey, was electrocuted during a rainstorm in the middle of a concert in Wales the year before. *Queen of the Night* was produced by Jerry Wexler, who surrounded Maggie's voice with premiere R&B session players. Peter somehow made his peace with Premier Talent, who booked her as an opening act to various of their headliners, such as Foghat, Peter Frampton, and Black Oak Arkansas among others. Maggie was unpretentious and lots of fun on the road. She and Mark London, who comanaged her career with Grant, loved to get stoned and endlessly repeat bits from Carl Reiner and Mel Brooks's comedy album *The 2000 Year Old Man.*

The press reaction to Maggie was incredible. She was a great singer with a British pedigree and there was a feeling that rock and roll could use a big woman star. I did a routine mailing with a form letter to several dozen music writers and was pleasantly surprised when Maureen Orth of *Newsweek* called to schedule an interview. *The New York Times,* the *Los Angeles Times,* and even *Time* magazine did pieces as well, all laudatory. Maggie was booked on *Midnight Special* and *Don Kirshner's Rock Concert,* the two television outlets for rock and roll in those days.

Wexler's idea for the first single was Ringo Starr's song "Oh My My," a plan that was torpedoed when Capitol Records unexpectedly chose the former Beatle's own version of the song to be his third single. "We're screwed," Wexler said dolefully, and he was right. The rock stations played Maggie's version of J. J. Cale's song "After Midnight" but it was a turntable hit, which means that it sounded good on the radio but didn't motivate sales. *Queen of the Night* was supported by the music business but never found an audience. It was too much of an R&B record for rock fans to embrace but not enough of an R&B record to sell on its own terms.

Jimmy finally came up with the name "Swan Song" for the label, a perfect Zeppelin formulation that included both music and death. A swan's dying cry was one of the most beautiful sounds in the world, he told me earnestly.

Bad Company's self-titled first album became the first official release on Swan Song. They were also booked by Premier (mostly on the Edgar Winter tour, courtesy of Steve Paul). They also were launched with decent airplay on the same rock stations that had played Maggie and they got decent reviews, although not the personality profiles that Maggie had received. Lead singer Paul Rodgers was shy and mostly surly and lead guitarist Mick Ralphs was friendly but dull. But Bad Company had one thing Maggie didn't have: hit songs that they wrote themselves, starting with "Can't Get Enough of Your Love," which, in addition to being a rock radio hit, also became a number-one pop single. The album went to number one and sold over two million copies. The media and the business were important in terms of opening doors, but it was the mysterious chemistry or lack thereof between music and fans that made the business run. Bad Company's success was a huge boost to my reputation, but I never could figure out exactly what I did right.

The members of Zeppelin got on all right with Bad Company and Maggie Bell, but they were really Peter's choices. The Swan Song artists that Jimmy and Robert had real emotion invested in were the Pretty Things, an overlooked seminal mid-seventies British rock band, and Detective, an L.A.-based hard rock band fronted by Michael Des Barres, who previously had been the lead singer of the British glam band Silverhead.

For the launch of Swan Song in Los Angeles, we asked Ahmet to throw Led Zeppelin a party. Atlantic rented a ballroom at the Hotel Bel-Air and Jimmy and Robert sent a list of celebrities they wanted invited. Ahmet complained to me in his most derisive aristocratic tone, "Jane Fonda. Warren Beatty. Cary Grant. How the fuck am I going to get people like that to come? Zeppelin sells a lot of records, but they are *not* the Rolling Stones." I told him that this was just a wish list but begged him come up with *somebody* from Hollywood. He delivered Groucho Marx, who was then eighty-four years old but who still was capable of uttering dyspeptic witticisms, which he dispensed to a parade of supplicants. Groucho gave Bad Company bass player Boz Burrell an autograph signed underneath a silhouette of his hand, which Groucho painstakingly had drawn. Erin Fleming, the woman who lived with Marx during the last years of his life, looked around at the crowd of groupies, roadies, and music business types and said sourly to me, "Boy, Ahmet really owes me for this one."

A writer for the British weekly *Sounds* named Andy McConnell politely introduced himself to Bonzo and told him that he thought he was the greatest drummer in the world. McConnell was short and slight of build, Bonham husky and strong. The drummer inexplicably grabbed the writer by the lapels and screamed at him, "I've taken enough shit from you guys in the press and I'm not taking any more." I assumed that at some point in the past, someone from *Sounds* must have taken a shot at Bonham. Like many rock musicians Bonham was unable to internalize the fact that just because one particular writer for a publication had once written something unfriendly about him, all other writers for the magazine were not complicit or even aware of such insults. I spent a lot of the evening calming McConnell down and promising future access and cooperation from the band if he would refrain from referring to the embarrassing outburst in his column.

Around three in the morning I was awakened by an even drunker Bonzo outside my hotel room door, screaming at the top of his lungs, referring to me by one of the nicknames the band had adapted for me, "Goldilocks, I know you're in there.

83

I want you to call that fucking writer from *Sounds* and tell him I want do an interview. I'll give him a fucking interview he'll never forget," he concluded, followed by a menacing laugh. I was torn. On one hand, I had been instructed by Peter to put the band's happiness first on all occasions, to remember that I worked for the band and not for the media or the record company. On the other hand, I knew how sensitive they were to their image in the British press. I kept quiet and after a few minutes heard him trudge down the hall. The next day I nervously explained to Peter my rationale for ignoring the drummer. Peter waved it off. "If you think you get woken up, imagine what I get. You're just the fucking publicist, I'm the manager. If it gets too bad you can do what I do—get two rooms, tell the band you're in one, and actually sleep in another."

Bonzo figured in many of Led Zeppelin's dramas because, while affable when sober and transcendent when playing the drums, he was an angry and mean drunk, referred to at such times by the other band members as "the beast."

In Texas during the 1975 tour Bonham noticed a vintage Corvette parked near the band's hotel. He accosted Richard Cole and insisted that Richard patiently stand by the car until the owner appeared. In telling me the story Richard had tears from laughing as he explained that Bonham said he should tell the guy that "Mr. Bonham would like to buy you a drink." Bonham then instructed Cole that if the owner were not amenable to such a meeting, Richard should "have him arrested," as if this were in the tour manager's power.

Bonham succeeded in persuading the owner to sell him the car by offering five thousand dollars more than it was worth, and then paid thousands more to have the car driven in a truck to Los Angeles, which was home base for the next several weeks of the tour. Everyone was terrified that Bonzo would get into an accident while on tour, so Steve Weiss solemnly convinced him that he was unable to get insurance on short notice that would cover a British driver of a Texas car being driven in California.

Bonham resorted to taking his pals into the garage and revving up the motor without driving it.

Zeppelin mostly hung out with their own entourage, groupies, and other British rock musicians, but Robert had always had a hankering to meet Elvis Presley, whom he had idolized and impersonated from the time he was seven years old. Richard Cole was friends with one of Elvis's bodyguards and took the band to meet The King one night. Robert gleefully recounted that as they were leaving he turned to Elvis and sang, "Treat me like a fool," and Elvis sang back, "treat me mean and cruel."

Zeppelin had forged an identity that took some of the psychedelic imagery of the late sixties bands and added a dark, brooding mysticism. Jimmy Page was a student of the infamous magician Aleister Crowley. I was able, with the help of *Crawdaddy!*'s new publisher, Josh Feigenbaum, to get William Burroughs to interview Jimmy Page for the magazine. Jimmy told me that meeting Burroughs was one of the great experiences of his life. (Two well-known rock bands, Steely Dan and Mott the Hoople, had taken their names from lines in Burroughs's books and in years to come a meeting with Burroughs became a rite of passage for a certain kind of rock and roller such as Al Jourgensen of Ministry, Kurt Cobain—with whom he recorded a single—and, of course, Patti Smith.)

When Zeppelin released the *Physical Graffiti* album and announced plans for a 1975 tour, Jann Wenner called again, offering to do a *Rolling Stone* cover story. He said that they would do it as a question-and-answer piece, meaning that the band's quotes would speak for themselves without the possibility of sarcastic narrative. As a sweetener, Jann said we could pick the writer. I told the band that they had gotten all the mileage they could out of turning down *Rolling Stone* on the last cycle. Jimmy concurred and told me what writer to specify: Cameron Crowe.

Cameron flew to Chicago, where the band had canceled a show due to a sore throat that Robert had. We listened raptly to an advance cassette of Dylan's forthcoming album, *Blood on the Tracks,* and then Jimmy and Robert snuck out unnoticed with Cameron and me to a local movie theater to watch *Young Frankenstein.* A few weeks later Cameron did a second interview with Robert at the Continental Hyatt House in Los Angeles, during which the ebullient lead singer stood on a terrace facing Sunset Strip and exulted jokingly, "I am a golden god." A decade later the line was spoken by a character in Cameron's wonderful homage to seventies rock journalism, *Almost Famous.*

The cinematic character Cameron created for himself placed journalistic truth above his relationship with a fictitious band in *Almost Famous.* In real life, Cameron's cover story thrilled Led Zeppelin. Cameron, who by this time was seventeen, wrote a brief introduction to his interview that spoke for his generation of rock fans. "Over its six-year history, Led Zeppelin has taken some pretty hard knocks from critics of all stripes—this magazine not excepted. During those same years, the band has managed to sell a million units apiece on all five of its albums and the current American tour is expected to be the top grossing event in rock & roll history. Can it be that the critics can't hear?"

Not all was well at Swan Song, however. One afternoon in New York Peter and I saw a screening of Brian De Palma's film *Phantom of the Paradise,* a dramatic/occult fantasy about a rock and roll singer who is manipulated by an evil music executive named Swan, played by Paul Williams, whose company is called Swan Song. At Steve Weiss's request I took notes of every mention of the phrase *Swan Song.* After the screening Peter was much more upset than I'd expected him to be. In one of the final scenes Swan is electrocuted onstage. To Peter this was a horrible reminder of the electrocution of Les Harvey, which, I now realized, had never stopped haunting him. The usually intimidating, giant manager was choked up with giant tears. I assured him that Steve would have a sufficient legal argument to get them to remove the phrase *Swan Song,* but Peter added, "You've got to get them to get rid of that electrocution." Instead of nodding or saying, "We'll do everything we can," I idiotically gave him a "rational" answer, which was that I doubted we had the clout to get them to change a plot point in the film. I was right, but in my need to show how smart I was about such things I came across as unsympathetic and maybe even unsupportive.

Soon thereafter I had a disagreement with Peter regarding the Pretty Things tour following the release of their brilliant and quirky *Silk Torpedo* album. The Pretties had changed members over the years, always fronted by their long-haired, sad-eyed lead singer and writer, Phil May. This iteration played virtuoso rock and roll of the cerebral variety then popularized by Roxy Music. May was an art-school graduate and at the Swan Song party in L.A. the celebrity who set May's eyes aglow was painter David Hockney. May had been listening to elite enthusiasm for many years and he had a fatalistic sense of his own commercial doom that neither I nor subsequent events could dispel.

Some of the more adventuresome rock stations, such as WMMS in Cleveland, gave *Silk Torpedo* decent airplay and the rock press was respectful and generally supportive, but May had not written easily digestible rock hits the way the guys in Bad Company had. Nevertheless a cult audience began embracing them and sales inched toward seventy-five thousand with reorders each week that they were on the road.

Without a hit song the Pretties' quest for viability depended on continual touring. Unfortunately, the release of their first Swan Song album coincided with Bad Company's second, and to my chagrin, Peter decided to jettison Premier Talent and tour Bad Company with the national team who did the Zeppelin tours. Most of the promoters who had played Bad Company as an opening act were thus denied the ability to make money with them as headliners.

I was mortified. The first Bad Company tour had been my entrée into the closed society that revolved around Premier Talent. Peter's career may have been about maximizing the short-term income on Bad Company and Led Zeppelin. Mine, or so I thought, depended on being able to break new acts, a capability that was now diminished.

I told Peter of my worries about how burning bridges with the agency/promoter establishment would make it almost impossible to break acts such as the Pretties. Peter looked at me with a gleam in his eye and said, "But now they will all be that much more nervous about pissing us off and losing the Pretties, won't they? Wheels within wheels, Danny." I thought he was overplaying his hand, but he certainty left no room for further discussion. In the next few months concert opportunities for the Pretty Things dried up and the album died.

At the same time, the vibe around Led Zeppelin became druggier than I had previously seen. I became close friends with Detective's Michael Des Barres and his wife, Pamela, who had counted Jimmy Page among her conquests in her groupie days years earlier. When it came time to take a Swan Song signing photo, I got a limo to pick up Jimmy at the Malibu Colony, where each of the members had rented a house while they wrote songs for what would be their next album, *Presence*. I brought him to my room at the Beverly Hills Hotel, where the members of Detective and Neal Preston were to meet us. Jimmy was nodding out the whole time we were in the car, and when we got to my room he lay down on the couch and immediately fell asleep. When the band got there Michael and I tried repeatedly to wake him, even going to the extreme of throwing cold water on his face, but it was to no avail. Although he was breathing, Jimmy was out cold. After around a half hour I had Neal photograph Detective sitting next to the sleeping Page and then sent him and the band members home.

A few hours later, Jimmy roused himself. There had been rumors that Jimmy was doing heroin and this behavior made me believe them. Not surprisingly, Page had a different explanation. He said he had taken a Valium and must have overreacted to it. He was furious at Michael and me, disbelieving that we had really tried to wake him. He let me circulate the photo but later complained that in doing so I had "made him out to be a twit." In retrospect he was absolutely right. The photo never should have seen the light of day. Detective was lucky to be on Swan Song and it would have been no big deal to schedule another photo session. I had forgotten who I was working for.

Robert was in a gloomy mood as well. He and his wife, Maureen, had gotten into a car accident in Greece and Robert had broken his ankle, requiring several weeks of U.S. dates to be canceled. He hated hobbling around in a cast.

I had yet another awkward moment at a screening of *The Song Remains the Same*. Having been at the performances that were included in the film, I felt that the way it was shot, recorded, and edited made the concert seem much smaller and ordinary than what I had experienced. They shot so little of John Paul Jones that they had to do reshoots. Jonesy had gotten a haircut in the intervening months and wore an embarrassingly fake wig for the close-up inserts. I also thought that the "fantasy" sequences, which were created for each member of the band, were amateurish and embarrassing. I only gave perfunctory congratulations. Later Peter pointedly observed that he felt a lack of enthusiasm from me, which was particularly inappropriate since Ahmet Ertegun had been at the screening. Peter was relying on Ahmet to get Warner Bros. to distribute the film (they did). For decades it was the only filmed document of the band, and it inspired countless rock artists, but in 2003, when a multiple DVD set of various Led Zeppelin concerts over the years was released, it was clear how much more powerful the band's live show was than had been documented in *The Song Remains the Same*.

Peter had agreed to let me manage a singer-songwriter named Mirabai and sign her to Swan Song. I was besotted with her spiritual songs, but the recording was not exciting to any of the members of Zeppelin. Peter got Atlantic to release it and

89

I drove them crazy, vainly hoping that their PR or promotion departments would somehow make the record happen. I had never managed an artist before and I felt my job was to push relentlessly, regardless of how the marketplace responded. In May of 1976 Peter gave me the choice of giving up Mirabai's management or leaving. I don't think he expected me to choose an unknown act. But I was filled with the irrational confidence and self-righteousness of youth. As fierce as he was to outsiders, Peter romanticized his team and didn't like confrontation. "I never thought it would come to this," he said, large tears dripping down his massive face.

The arguments I had with Peter, which seemed so important to me at the time, now fade into relative insignificance. In retrospect I think that my anger at him was almost entirely inappropriate. "You know, all of those friends of yours wouldn't talk to you if you didn't work for Zeppelin," he had ominously said to me not long before. (Peter, I felt, was also talking about himself. Jimmy Page virtually controlled Peter's self-esteem.)

I thought immediately of my friends from the rock critics' world, and many of them did remain friends. But as for promoters and record company people, of course he was right. More to the point, in working for Led Zeppelin for a few years I had gradually convinced myself that I was somehow on their level, that I was somehow part of Zeppelin. This was a psychological disease that many members of rock entourages got (and get), especially those, like me, to whom breathing the air around superstardom was a new experience. Such delusions can be destructive, and I think he was trying to explain that to me before it was too late. Regardless of how I felt about his decisions regarding Bad Company, I worked for him and derived any influence I had from stars whom he managed and had introduced me to. Peter had given me my big shot. He had transformed me from a PR guy to rock executive.

On the other hand, I left at exactly the right time. The drug abuse in the band had gotten out of control and created a more sour, negative vibe than they'd had when I first started working for them. The next few years would be bad ones for Led Zeppelin. In 1977 Peter and one of his roadies were accused of badly beating up a member of Bill Graham's crew at a Zeppelin show in San Francisco, resulting in arrests for assault. Robert's son Karac died in 1977 of a rare infection and John Bonham died in 1980, having suffocated on his own vomit after passing out drunk.

In later years, when I spoke to the three surviving members of the band, they were always warm and gracious, and I got to briefly work with them again as president of Atlantic in 1990 when the Page/Plant album came out. Shortly before he died in 1995, Peter Grant called me out of the blue to congratulate me on some corporate job I'd gotten and to reminisce about the days when he would ask me how my knob was, and I had the chance to thank him for everything he had done for me.

Bumping into Led Zeppelin was the gift that kept on giving. At my first meeting with the members of Kiss to pitch them on being a PR client, Paul Stanley shook my hand to signify that we had a deal and then he said, "OK, now let's talk about what's really important." I wasn't sure what he meant until he added, "What are Jimmy and Robert really like?" In the decades that followed, not a year would go by in which I didn't get some mileage out of telling Led Zeppelin stories.

PART II

CORPORATE ROCK, 1976–1989

CHAPTER FIVE

ROCK PR GETS PROFESSIONALIZED

In 1976, after my departure from Swan Song, I started my own PR firm, which I called Danny Goldberg, Inc. Between my work for Solters and for Swan Song, I gradually developed a professional style of publicizing rock bands. Over time, I became friends with several of the other leading rock PR people of the 1970s and we often traded stories and compared notes.

One of my favorite examples of making something out of nothing had occurred when I was still at Solters, Sabinson and Roskin, and Lee asked me to work on the Moody Blues. The band had no new album at the time. Their only new product was the impending release of a songbook, an anthology of their sheet music, without a single word of accompanying editorial text or imagery. Nonetheless they were about to embark on a four-week American tour for which their promoter, Jerry Weintraub (who also had copromoted most of Zeppelin's shows), wanted media exposure.

In the small British town of Cobham, we found a charming and talented group of musicians who had absolutely no ability to articulate

the mystical subtext of their recorded work. "We're the Cobham mafia," said lyricist and keyboardist Mike Pinder, as if
the mere fact that a group of musicians and engineers from a
small town in England had made it big was the stuff of rock
mythology. Lee, who had represented Frank Sinatra for years
and was quite familiar with the real mafia, could barely keep
a straight face.

The Moody Blues albums had been influenced by psychedel-
ics and were filled with both cosmic imagery and lush multilay-
ered arrangements, which augmented a classic British prog-rock
foundation. One of their most famous early songs was "Timothy Leary's Dead," a tongue-in-cheek tribute to the LSD guru.
(Twenty years later, when Leary was dying, I produced an album
with his musings about the afterlife and the Moodies redid the
vocal under a new title, "Timothy Leary Lives.")

The Moodies had emerged when critics were already looking at acid rock as a bit passé and were starting to embrace the
embryonic beginnings of what would become punk rock, such
as the Stooges. I had a soft spot for the Moodies' trippy porten-
tous albums. Several of their songs were hits on rock radio, and
audiences loved them, but they had absolutely no currency or
instincts for the press. Moreover, Pinder, the mystic, and Justin
Hayward, the lead singer, seemed averse to doing interviews.
That was left mostly to the drummer, Graeme Edge, who was
gregarious, smart, and engaging but who lacked the mystique
to be a big draw to most writers. Thus the assignment was
daunting.

All I could do was to fall back on Solters's basic PR axioms.
One rule was immutable: *More calls are better than fewer calls.*
The desk next to mine at SSR was occupied by Myrna Post,
whose clients were theater and movie producers. Myrna had
the thickest Brooklyn accent I had ever heard and I had snob-
bishly dismissed her as an anachronism, hopelessly incapable of
commanding the intellectual respect of writers. However, I soon
noticed that during the time in which I would make a single

phone call followed by a thoughtful pause, Myrna would have made several. Although she was often rejected, her persistence yielded a surprising number of positive results. (One of her most effective techniques was to beg writers to do a piece "or else I'll lose the client.") I soon realized that *I* was the anachronism, assuming that some exotic form of hipness was sufficient to earn a living in PR. When I emulated her style, not only were the results better, but I felt relief for having shed my pretensions and replaced them with a real work ethic, doggedly setting up interviews with the band by a number of music writers for numerous local newspapers and a few second-tier rock magazines.

Another Solters rule was to write every press release or bio with the assumption that most people would only read the first paragraph and to write the first paragraph as if they would only read the first sentence. The problem I had was that I couldn't think of a single interesting sentence to write about the Moody Blues.

Lee suggested that the group be invited to lecture at the Eastman School of Music, a classical academy at the University of Rochester, New York (and also an SSR client). The previous year Alice Cooper had gotten some ink over the supposed incongruity of a rock artist lecturing at a classical music school, and Lee figured the gimmick could work again. When I pointed out that the members of the Moodies would be incapable of giving a lecture, he impatiently explained, "They wouldn't actually do the lecture—we just *announce* that they're doing a lecture." Beggars couldn't be choosers. I gave "the item" exclusively to Ian Dove, who wrote a weekly pop column for *The New York Times*, and he turned it into a precious paragraph.

I asked Stephen Schwartz, lyricist for the Broadway shows *Pippin* and *Godspell,* and another Solters client, to "write" a review of the Moodies' songbook. Stephen was a couple of decades younger than most Broadway composers. He liked the association. He was happy to be the "author" as long as I wrote the review. Miraculously, both *The New York Times* "Arts and Leisure" section and the *L.A. Times Book Review* were at-

97

tracted by a semicelebrity byline and published the piece. (In 2008 three of Schwartz's songs in the animated film *Enchanted* were nominated for the Academy Award.)

One of my favorite fellow publicists was Susan Blond, who was also a denizen of Max's. Susan was a PR executive for more than a decade for Epic Records, where her charges included Michael Jackson, the Clash, Ozzy Osbourne, Stevie Ray Vaughn, Ted Nugent, and Culture Club. She had gotten to know Andy Warhol pretty well when she worked for his *Interview* magazine.

Susan had dark brown hair and a Jewish nasal voice that was widely believed to have been the inspiration for Bobbi Flekman, the record company PR chick played by Fran Drescher in *This Is Spinal Tap*. Susan had an irrepressible enthusiasm for people, especially writers, and her success owed much to the personal loyalty she built up among them. Unlike the classic Hollywood PR people, Susan never tried to coerce press through intimidation. She was the ultimate schmoozer, so friendly and so much fun that many journalists felt guilty saying no to her.

When she was at a loss for an angle, Susan fell back onto Warhol, who had cast her as a mother who threw her baby out of a window in the film *Bad*. She fondly recalled, "Whenever I would get a new artist I would take them to the Factory to meet Andy, and one great thing about Andy was that he treated an unknown band the same as the biggest star." Epic star Ted Nugent was selling lots of records with his album *Cat Scratch Fever* and her bosses expected her to deliver press, but the critics hated him. Unable to get a single significant reviewer to cover a Nugent show at the Academy of Music, she persuaded Warhol to bring Truman Capote, with whom he was dining later that evening. "I sent a limo for Andy and Truman and they came backstage. Andy asked if he needed to stay for the show and I told him that what I really needed was a picture and then he could leave." Nugent made a sarcastic comment to Capote, saying that he should be tied to the amplifiers; Susan gave it to the columns, and Nugent was in the newspapers. "Andy and Truman didn't mind—they liked being used that way."

Howard Bloom trolled in the same rock PR waters as me and Susan but had a radically different style from either of us. An awkward schmoozer at best, Howard had been a math genius as a young kid, designing a computer that won a Westinghouse Science Award. He exuded bookish intensity, had an obsession with measurable results, and had an utter disregard for what was "cool."

I first encountered Howard when he had succeeded me as managing editor of *Circus* and rebuffed my pitch for a Led Zeppelin cover with his insistence that he was basing his covers on the results of his most current readers' polls. I explained to him that those polls had taken place in between Zeppelin releases. I couldn't believe he wouldn't just take my word for it that his readers would indeed be interested in the new album and tour. He learned. Like a visitor from another planet figuring out a new world, Howard soon adjusted his "analysis" to include previous album sales and concert attendance figures. Later he started his firm the Howard Bloom Organization out of my living room while I was building my own company in the same space. We toyed with the idea of being partners, but Howard wanted to focus solely on PR whereas I wanted to get into management.

Howard's roster of clients grew huge, including Prince and Michael Jackson, but no one touched his soul the way John Mellencamp did. The former science nerd became besotted with the brooding Indiana greaser. Decades after the fact, Howard recalled with a rhapsodic look on his face the first time he heard Mellencamp's song "Hurt So Good" on the radio. "I literally drove my car to the curb on Sunset Strip in Los Angeles and waited until it was over to resume driving."

At this point Mellencamp had zero critical credibility. He was viewed as a contrived and minor pretender to Dylan's throne, and Mellencamp was further burdened by having originally presented himself to the public with the name Johnny Cougar, which was made up by David Bowie's manager, Tony DeFries. According to Howard, DeFries had attempted heavy-handed pressure on writers, which further added to the perception of inauthenticity.

Howard had convinced himself that Mellencamp was, at his core, a midwestern exponent of rock's most personal, and thus most authentic, traditions. "John had been a star in high school in Indiana. He watched Paul Newman movies and he felt that he was like those characters. He had been a star for being a fuckup and for being the leader of the guys who were fuckups. He had funny-colored hair and listened to music that others in Indiana didn't know about. Then he graduated and he was taken off of the small screen of high school and was just a speck on the big screen of life. For two or three years he was totally depressed; he literally didn't have the strength to put his shoes and socks on. He was working for the telephone company. He fell in and out of a bad marriage. This period was the defining experience of his life and this is where all of his songs came from." Having been disempowered by losing his high school identity, Mellencamp became empowered and got his macho swagger back by his musical ability to express his feelings. Howard was convinced that if Mellencamp could learn how to tell his story in a concise and memorable way, he would be accepted as an important rock and roll auteur.

Referring to himself as "a secular shaman," Howard wanted to "find the personality that writes the songs—the one that dances when they're standing onstage—and that is a different person than the one who lives normal life." He worked with Mellencamp to create a narrative based on the most interesting parts of his own life.

In addition to helping Mellencamp hone his rap, Howard needed to find receptive listeners. Howard had a jaundiced eye about the critical elite, comparing them to a herd of sheep who mindlessly followed a handful of tastemakers. Once a "lead sheep" such as Landau decided an artist was good or bad, other critics were intimidated into mimicking his opinion. "If you're a critic and go to dinner and mention the wrong name with the wrong tone of voice—if you mention somebody you are supposed to dislike in a tone that implies you like him—you're out! You've made a fool of yourself. If you take someone you're supposed to like and talk about them in a disparaging way, again you're frozen out—you're not cool." (There would indeed be several examples of rock artists who were dismissed by "serious" critics initially, only to be "discovered" by serious writers in later years, such as the Beach Boys and Creedence Clearwater Revival. The music didn't change—the arbiters of "cool" did.)

To help transform Mellencamp's reputation, Howard decided that his "lead sheep" could be Ken Emerson of *The New York Times*. "I swear," Howard recalled, "when Ken wrote a review of one of John's early albums, he didn't listen to it but must have responded to the perceptual frame about Mellencamp that already existed, that said he had a horrible personality and that his music was even worse." Howard was certain that Emerson's musical sensibility was such that if he listened to Mellencamp's new music with an open mind, he would become converted. Over a series of lunches, Howard persuaded Emerson to give Mellencamp's music a careful listen, to meet the artist, and to see him perform.

Adapting traditional show-biz media training to a rock and roll context, Howard told the usually surly Mellencamp, "If you want to be a star, you need to be like a hooker and make every interviewer feel that they are the best you have ever met." Most writers who walked into Mellencamp's hotel room would ask "stupid questions," but Howard counseled, "No matter what they ask, what they really want is a great story. To be a star you need a story that helps other people understand who the hell they are and gives validation to parts of themselves they thought were insane."

Mellencamp was an apt pupil, as well as a gifted and resourceful artist. Within a year his press image was transformed to that of an authentic rock auteur. It didn't hurt, of course, that Mellencamp had a series of hit songs and was a compelling performer. But lots of artists would have hit songs but limited press mystique. Ken Emerson came to be one of his biggest champions, as did other writers who were initially skeptical. Twenty years later Howard still exulted that at a Mellencamp show at Radio City, journalists Tim White, Ken Emerson, and Vic Garbarini, whom he had been hounding about his client for the previous year, "each separately came over to me and held my arm and said I had been right."

Later in his career, after Bloom had shut down his PR firm, Mellencamp hired Lee Solters's son Larry Solters. After the first few weeks Mellencamp complained to Solters that he wasn't giving him enough time. "You know, Howard Bloom used to spend hours with me on the phone going over every detail." When I was president of Mercury Records, Mellencamp delivered the album *Mr. Happy Go Lucky*. Because the album came out while Mellencamp's popularity was declining, it was not a pleasant experience and I was on the receiving end of many Mellencamp diatribes linking me to a string of supposed idiots and incompetents who had worked on his records over the years. However when he found out that I had been friends with Howard, Mellencamp quietly acknowledged, "I learned a lot about the media and a lot about life from Howard Bloom."

The Eagles were another band with massive commercial success who were dismissed by critics. Larry Solters played the same role for them that I did for Led Zeppelin. He met them in 1976 when they were totally alienated from the press. When the Eagles' first album had been released, "the elitist New York critics were into the New York Dolls and the Ramones, and the media portrayed the Eagles as *inauthentic* rhinestone cowboys. The band was having tremendous success due to radio hits and touring and the critics often took immense pride and pleasure in dismissing their credibility."

Solters realized that most of the newspapers outside of New York were not part of the "East Coast" critical clique. "We often invited writers in cities such as Chicago, Minneapolis, Cleveland, and Detroit backstage before the show and treated them royally. A lot of these guys had never even seen an amplifier up close, not to mention been on an arena stage." It was a crucial detail of Solters's strategy that the writers came backstage *before* the show instead of afterward so that their good feeling and treatment would influence their attitude toward the performance and the band. "We turned it around in middle America." Less subtle tactics sometimes worked with some writers. "Once I gave my tour jacket to the writer from the *Detroit Free Press* and he actually let me write the review myself," Larry recalled with delight.

Solters, with Eagles manager Irving Azoff, also perfected the antischmooze, directly confronting writers who pissed them off. Eagles stars Don Henley and Glenn Frey were self-styled intellectuals and it irritated them that New York journalists held them in such low regard. As they bitterly wrote in *Rolling Stone* some time later, "Music critics didn't like us very much. In fact, it seemed they didn't like anyone in our particular 'genre,' or anyone who made music in L.A., for that matter. You know, all you laid-back, mellow, high-flying, West Coast cowboy angst-meister types. It seems that we were all victims of some kind of petty cultural war between L.A. and New York."

In March 1977, while *Hotel California* was propelling the Eagles to the summit of rock stardom, Elektra/Asylum Records threw them a party in New York, after their concert in Madison Square Garden, at the Penn Plaza Club inside the arena. John Belushi and Faye Dunaway were among the celebrities who attended. The label submitted a list of thirty-nine journalists to receive invites. At the band's behest all but four were rejected.

At the Boston Eagles concert, rock critic Lester Bangs, ac- **103** customed to being coddled by rock bands, drove up in a rented Rolls-Royce. Bangs was denied entrance to the backstage. In Los Angeles, after Patrick Goldstein wrote an item for the *L.A. Times* column "Pop Eye" about a girl getting sick at Don Henley's house, Azoff & Solters sent him a dozen roses spray-painted black and had them delivered to the paper along with a telegram that read, "This will serve to sever our professional relationship in light of your erroneous statements in yesterday's *L.A. Times*. Your reporting has been unprofessional inaccurate and malicious. Please refrain from calling our office or printing our names or our clients names in the future. Best Regards, Irving Azoff and Larry Solters." (Patrick's reputation immediately skyrocketed in the newsroom, where "pissing off someone in power is a badge of honor.")

To try to create an alternative journalistic narrative about the Eagles, Frey got Ed Sanders to chronicle the 1977 tour. Sanders had unassailable hip bona-fides. He was the singer of the beatnik rock band the Fugs and was also one of the founders of the yippies. Frey told Sanders about seeing *Rolling Stone* publisher Jann Wenner at the Penn Plaza party as they walked in: "Wenner turned to us as we were walking in and said, 'I don't do the record reviews. I don't handle that.' And Henley says, 'You oughta. It's your fucking paper, man. You ought to read them. You ought to know who is doing a hatchet job on somebody.'" However, Sanders's book was never completed and he was unable to make much impact with his revisionist view of the Eagles.

It was Cameron Crowe who played the key role in covering the Eagles for *Rolling Stone* during the early years of the band's career when they were alienated from the magazine, similar to the role he played for Led Zeppelin. In 1978 the band made its breakthrough with *Rolling Stone,* and it was the result of both Cameron's support and their relentless determination to confront their journalistic tormentors.

The Eagles had taken to playing softball games against the

staffs of local radio stations. Chuck Young, who at the time penned the *Rolling Stone* column "Random Notes," made a sarcastic reference to some game that they had lost. Frey wrote a letter to the editor accusing Young of having neglected to list the several softball victories the band had won and ended with the challenge "Anytime you pencil-pushing desk jockeys want to put on your spikes, we'll kick your ass too." Recognizing that, at this point, the Eagles were too big to ignore, *Rolling Stone* accepted the challenge, and in May 1978 at USC the game took place. The crowd included Joni Mitchell, Donald Fagen, Chevy Chase, and Mary Kay Place. The Eagles won 15–8, but more importantly they scored a PR trifecta: They showed that they had both a sense of humor and a fierce commitment to their own identity; they bonded with former journalistic adversaries, and they had created a story. "We lucked out," recalled Solters with a satisfied grin, "Not only did we have a great drunken dinner at Dan Tana's afterward with the *Rolling Stone* staff, but we also made the front page of the sports section in newspapers nationwide."

One of my first clients at my PR firm was Don Arden, who had been Peter Grant's first boss in the music business and was the only person who intimidated him. Arden was husky, frequently wore open-necked shirts, which displayed gold jewelry, and was reputedly connected to British gangsters. He walked with a swagger that was supposedly the basis of the Bob Hoskins portrayal of a British crime boss in the film *The Long Good Friday*.

Determined to exude wealth and power, Arden rented a mansion in Beverly Hills formerly owned by Howard Hughes, the living room of which had a retractable roof. Once when he took me along on a shopping trip to Tiffany in Beverly Hills, he walked out and told me dismissively, "Van Cleef and Arpels craps all over this place."

Earlier in his career Arden had managed the Animals and

the Small Faces. When he hired me, his big act was the Electric Light Orchestra (ELO), whom he managed and who was also signed to his label Jet Records. ELO would later be respected as having created pop/rock classics, but at the time they were considered by the rock press to be Beatles-derivative shlockmeisters propelled by overwrought stage shows and the gimmick of including classical string instruments in a rock band. Nonetheless, the rock-buying public loved ELO and their albums sold in the millions. The genius behind ELO's music was Jeff Lynne, who wrote the songs, produced the records, and sang most of the leads. Later in his career Lynne would become widely respected as a collaborator of George Harrison and as the key musical architect of the Traveling Wilburys. Lynne was unfailingly sweet and gracious but he was intensely shy, rarely speaking more than a sentence to me and rarely available for interviews. Drummer Bev Bevan was the primary band spokesman, and although Bev had a credible British rock background and an affable temperament, he was not a superstar by anyone's reckoning, including his own. The best we were able to do for the band was to get secondary features in rock magazines

I avoided Arden's wrath primarily because his daughter Sharon took a liking to me. Sharon made sure I was paid on time, which, given my fragile cash flow at the time, was crucial. I always wondered what Sharon thought when her father started ranting about the negative impact of women on rock groups. "The Small Faces were doing fine," he said, "until Ronnie Lane's mother stuck her nose into things. With ELO, everything is going great, but now I have Jeff Lynne's wife asking a lot of questions." And so forth. Sharon would later marry Ozzy Osbourne and become a star in her own right as Sharon Osbourne. When she took over the management of Ozzy's career from her father, he saw it as another piece of female perfidy and did not speak to Sharon for many years, actually suing his own daughter at one point. Later on, when Arden was older and retired, Sharon reached out to him, patched things up, and Don Arden appeared on a couple of episodes of *The Osbournes*.

But in 1978, Don was at the height of his powers and as ELO's New York appearance at Madison Square Garden loomed, the day of reckoning was at hand. Arden asked me to organize a "big party" that would give him and the band the visibility he coveted. This was a moment in New York when high-profile celebrities were into the famous disco Studio 54, where, unlike Susan Blond, I had no caché.

I suggested a party at Regine's, the famous disco that had been a much bigger deal a few years earlier and thus was happy to take Arden's money. From my point of view the party was a disaster. Very few of the famous people we invited showed up, but in our desperation to "deliver" we had invited too many hangers-on and thus the room was uncomfortably and un-glamorously packed. My assistant was close friends with Peter Frampton's girlfriend. Frampton was at the peak of his celeb-rity, having recently released *Frampton Comes Alive!*, which, at the time, was the bestselling album in history. Frampton was "delivered," but horrified by the crush of the crowd, he left after five minutes. Nevertheless, he did get photographed by the *New York Post*. The caption in the next afternoon's paper men-tioned ELO and the party, but the photo was of Peter alone, and that was the extent of the press we got for the party—with one exception.

The only celebs who showed up were on what Kathy Grif-fin would later call the "D list," and among those was the former heavyweight champion Joe Frazier, who was about to release an ill-fated R&B record under the name Joe Frazier and the Knockouts. When Frazier arrived, I pointed him out to Don Arden. It was unclear whether or not Frazier knew who the garrulous, gruff Englishman was who ebulliently wel-comed him, but he was clearly under instructions from his own press agent to "work the room," so he and Don exchanged macho witticisms for a few minutes as our hired photographer **107** snapped their picture. Such photos were only of interest to trade magazines where we had some clout, and *Billboard* dutifully ran it.

Happily for me, Arden was thrilled with the photo with the champ, and the people he cared about read *Billboard*. It made him look "big." I had dodged a metaphorical bullet. Arden retained my company for another year.

My other big-name post-Zeppelin client was Kiss, who were at the peak of superstardom, selling out stadiums. Kiss had not merely been rejected by critics, their very existence seemed to mock the whole idea of rock as anything other than a purely commercial enterprise. I understood the aesthetics of my friends who were appalled by what they saw as crass co-option of rock and roll by mercenary poseurs, but I always felt that any sober look at the first generation of rock and roll would reveal similar vulgarity in much of the oeuvre of Jerry Lee Lewis, Elvis, et al. (This populist argument didn't work with everyone. Years later Steve Earle would taunt me with his repeated assertion "Neither Lynyrd Skynyrd nor Kiss was ever cool.")

Singer Paul Stanley and bass player Gene Simmons, who created Kiss, had a concept of rock and roll that had no connection whatsoever with either the folk aesthetic that spawned Dylan and the Grateful Dead or the hippie or beatnik cultures that had been so significant in the early days of underground radio. As the band's competent but unspectacular bass player, Gene Simmons didn't even stress instrumental virtuosity, which would become a hallmark of many of their heavy metal successors. Gene told me that he "was never as interested in rock and roll, the music, as much as in rock and roll, the thing." No one understands better than Simmons the dark and subtle relationships between rock and roll and money. He is a guy who signs his name with the letter *S* intersected by two lines to make it into the dollar sign. Kiss's version of rock and roll was defined primarily by male aggression as expressed in hair length, macho sexuality, rebellion against authority, outrageous theatricality, loud volume, and high energy.

When I was writing this book, I asked Gene to explain what he meant by "the thing." He eagerly elaborated, "It's the Elvis syndrome. When you become a rock star, you become bigger than your songs. Wang Chung had number-one songs, Huey Lewis and the News had lots of hits, but they weren't rock stars. The fans didn't care about the people. Rock stardom is charisma with melody. The Beatles themselves were bigger than any of their songs. The Dylan photo with his Jewfro and black shades made him a rock star—bigger than his songs. The music matters—but the messenger is more important."

I cannot be sure whether my connection to Kiss was fueled by a populist streak or simply a grim determination to make as good a living as possible from the business. I soon developed a real respect for their two-dimensional but genuinely well crafted version of rock and roll and was charmed by both the warmth and diabolical cleverness of Gene Simmons. To this day I cannot hear the chorus of "Rock and Roll All Nite" without smiling.

In 1976, when I met them for our first meeting about their press, Gene and Paul explained that when they formed the band in 1973 they had carefully analyzed the rock culture and business of the early seventies and were influenced not only by superstars but also by Slade, a British glam-rock band who never made it big in the U.S. (Quiet Riot would later have a multiplatinum album based on covering Slade's song "Come On Feel the Noise.") "Paul and I saw Slade on a bill with the J. Geils Band and Frampton's Camel. They were the opening act and they didn't play their instruments as well as the other bands, but when we walked out, our ears were ringing with Slade's over-the-top assault. It had a kind of simplicity to it. They were not trying to be profound. It was a celebration of volume. You swam in the volume. They played too loud and were clearly having the time of their lives."

Although bonded to Simmons in their long-running partnership in Kiss, Paul Stanley is far less of the calculating businessman than Gene professes to be. To Paul, Led Zeppelin was and is his role model. Almost forty years after the fact he told me of seeing the band when he was in high school, when Zeppelin played at the Pavilion in Queens. "It was a religious experience. I was speechless. It was not just the music. It was also the sexuality. It was the essence of rock and roll." Paul continued to gush. "They wrote the book and all of us are just trying to write a page. They are the template and the road map that everyone else follows. Robert Plant invented a style of singing. I'm sure Terry Reid, Steve Marriott, and Janis Joplin influenced him—but he took it to the ultimate level. Jimmy Page is more than a guitar player. He is a visionary. He arranged their music as though he were creating a symphony."

The signature that made Kiss famous was their makeup. Gene was a horror-movie aficionado who had studied the life and career of Bela Lugosi. But it is unlikely that they could have been successful in the melding of horror and rock imagery had the groundwork for rock stars in makeup not been laid down by Alice Cooper, whose first album had come out in 1969 and who combined gender confusion in his name and ghoulish makeup with violent images onstage that included chopping off the heads of dolls with guillotines.

In private Gene Simmons had an intense, professorial manner. He was born Chaim Weitz and was raised by his mother, Florence, a Hungarian Holocaust survivor. He had studied at the yeshiva and had briefly taught high school before forming Kiss, and he relished arguing about rock and roll and the business with those who did not share his piercing cynical notion of the location of the true center of the rock and roll business.

Kiss had been ignored or reviled by the critics and gotten very little in the way of rock radio airplay. "We toured. We had our own announcer who would say, 'You wanted the best—you got the best—the hottest band in the world, Kiss!'

We self-proclaimed ourselves the hottest band in the world," Gene proudly admitted. "It was more like professional wrestling than like art."

Simmons recalled, "Alice Cooper had a woman's name and had been on Frank Zappa's label. Led Zeppelin at least had Jimmy Page. We had zero credibility. We were seen as Godzilla. Supposedly smart people know it's big but they don't take it seriously. Year after year we tried to break through the wall." Gene had as much contempt for critics as they had for Kiss. He reminded me of Van Halen lead singer David Lee Roth's remark about the rock press: "The reason critics hate Van Halen and love Elvis Costello is 'cause critics look like Elvis Costello." (Gene had discovered the members of Van Halen when they were still called Daddy Longlegs and produced the demos that got them a record deal.)

One of Kiss's principles was to never give up, so they hired me to try to help with the press. The number-one priority was to get a feature in *Rolling Stone,* which had totally ignored them until that point. Chuck Young accepted my logic that at a certain point the enthusiasm of rock fans trumped all other arguments about the definition of "important" rock and roll, and he got an assignment to interview Gene. At his comfortable but scarcely opulent apartment on Central Park South, Gene was at his articulate best in explaining the niche in populist rock and roll that Kiss was ably filling. As he was completing a monologue connecting sexuality, horror movies, comic books, the sixties, the seventies, money, success, and audiences, Gene was interrupted by the sound of the door to his apartment opening. Into the living room walked Gene's mother, Florence.

"Chaim, I didn't know you had friends over. I just brought you some matzo brie." Gene could not completely hide his discomfort at the interruption of his macho presentation. "Mom," Gene said with the slightest edge in his voice, "this is Chuck Young from *Rolling Stone,*" hoping she would get the hint to leave. "Okay, Chaim," she said cheerfully, Gene cringing at the mention of his real name, which had been unknown to the rock press up until that moment, "I'll put them in the freezer and then leave."

It seemed to me that *Rolling Stone* had a great story. Not only had Chuck gotten a first-rate Gene Simmons interview, he had a unique anecdote with the long-tongued rock monster and his Jewish mother. I eagerly anticipated a breakthrough article, which would put the band in a different artistic, cultural, and human context. Alas, Chuck had no interest in playing that role. His piece was dominated by several paragraphs in which Chuck compared Kiss's music to buffalo farts. He ran a few quotes from Gene, but the tone of the piece was generally a recitation of the commercial success of Kiss with a clear subtext that their fans were not as bright as the average *Rolling Stone* reader. If I had arranged for such an interview with Jimmy Page with similarly disappointing results, there would have been raging recriminations from the band and manager. With great trepidation I called Gene and asked him what he thought of the piece. After a pregnant pause Gene, ever the pragmatist, said calmly, "Well, it's better that they ran it than if they had run nothing at all," and that was the last I heard about it. Paul shared Gene's stoicism about the press. "I live in the house bad reviews built," he said.

Seven years later, in 1983, when they hired me as a management consultant, the shock value of the makeup had long since dissipated. Simmons recalls, "When we first started, our original manager, Bill Aucoin, had the idea that we should never be photographed without our makeup. He compared it to the way that Hollywood movie stars of the thirties and forties never went to the store without their glamorous makeup on. We would keep the mystique all the time." But a decade later, two of the original members, Ace Frehley and Peter Criss, had left the band and Kiss ticket sales in the United States were flagging. As the years had gone by, I knew that Paul Stanley had gotten frustrated by the anonymity. He wanted recognition as a mainstream rock lead singer. I felt that the band should reinvent themselves without the makeup.

Paul had already been pushing for the change. "We were in steep decline and survival is based on reinventing yourself. It was do or die. We had lost our hunger and sense of why we loved being Kiss. Each of us fell to our own vices that came along with fame—money, drugs, women. We forgot why we started Kiss. I had wanted us to take it off for the album *Creatures of the Night*. I thought that was one of our better albums, and when that failed I realized that people were listening with their eyes. For Gene it was a harder decision to make, 'cause he personally was so reliant on the makeup. Over the years his character had almost become synonymous with the band. For him to give that up meant he had to go out virtually naked."

Simmons relented but he felt that the first photo session didn't work. "Then, for one photo I stuck my tongue out and that made it feel like Kiss." The band unmasked at a live press conference aired on MTV. "That's when people found out that Paul was the best-looking guy in the band," Gene recalls. "A friend of mine thought I looked like a shish kebab salesman because I don't have those Bon Jovi looks."

The first no-makeup album, *Lick It Up,* sold triple what their previous opus had. They made a major comeback as a mainstream hard-rock "hair" band and had another decade of sold-out tours, but Gene noticed that the sales of toys and other merchandise went down. "Without the makeup we were just a band."

As the cycle of the nonmakeup version of Kiss was waning, Gene created the idea of "Kiss conventions" at which members of the band would talk about their history surrounded by hundreds of pieces of Kiss memorabilia that Gene had lovingly saved over the years. Tickets to get in were a hundred dollars. At one point Steven Tyler of Aerosmith called Gene and asked if he thought his band could do the same thing. "I told him that they couldn't because they had no stuff. Was he going to put his scarf on a mike stand? We had dolls and games."

113

There were some Kiss fans at MTV who covered one of the conventions for *MTV News* and who talked the band into doing an *Unplugged* broadcast. By then it was 1997, and I had recently been installed as president of Mercury Records. One of my first tasks was to talk MTV into allowing us to release the *Kiss Unplugged* as an album. Although I succeeded, it was obvious to me that MTV viewed this as a "favor" and that the band had lost all relevance to the people who actually ran the network. So I prevailed upon Gene and Paul to put their makeup back *on*. Of course, they had been thinking about it anyway. And as the years had passed, Frehley and Criss had come to regret their impetuous departure from the group and were eager for a return to the spotlight. Thus the "news" angle was not only the return to makeup but the reuniting of the "original" band. In keeping with Gene's notion that everything about Kiss had to be big ("for Kiss, size does count"), the announcement was made on the USS *Intrepid*, a retired battleship docked on Manhattan's West Side. Conan O'Brien introduced the band to a handful of Kiss fanatics and a dozen photographers.

We arranged for the band to make a "surprise" appearance on the Grammy Awards as presenters. Tupac Shakur introduced them. Wanting some validation the next day, I called Lisa Robinson, then writing about rock and roll for the *New York Post,* and a rock journalist who had known the band since their beginnings. "As they came off the stage," Lisa told me, "Gene walked over to me, towering over me in those huge platform boots, and whispered in my ear—'do you think the Ramones could do this?'" Lisa paused for effect. "Can you believe that he still is jealous of the press they got all these years later?"

I asked Gene if he remembered that line and he said, "Yes. The rock press was always attracted to the Talking Heads, Television, the Ramones, the New York Dolls, the Sex Pistols— bands who couldn't sell out a stadium or even an arena. There is a side to that media completely devoid of connection to the people who make up most of the rock audience, a holier-than-thou Jon Landau disease, as if they are telling kids that they and they alone know what's important. We are still not in the Rock and Roll Hall of Fame, but there are three thousand licensed Kiss products, a Kiss toothbrush that plays '(I Want to) Rock and Roll All Nite' when you put it in your mouth, and everything from Kiss caskets to Kiss condoms. There are no Radiohead condoms."

CHAPTER SIX

INMATES LOSE
CONTROL OF ASYLUM

Kiss's flair for iconography was unique. The far more common pathway to the mass rock audience of the 1970s and early '80s involved rock radio, which changed quite dramatically. The hippie-drenched culture of the "underground" format began to morph into the conventional corporate broadcasting culture within a year of the alternative media conference.

The prevailing view of the mainstream rock culture of the 1970s and '80s was summarized in a Wikipedia entry in 2007:

> *Corporate rock is an often pejorative term used primarily by music critics to describe rock music, particularly music from arena rock bands, which are alleged to be purely commercial, formulaic, or lacking in creativity or authenticity. According to these critics, the primary goal of the corporate rock artist or band in making music is profit and radio airplay rather than artistic creativity. . . . Styx is often given as a prime example of corporate rock.*

117

For several years in the early 1980s I managed the career of Styx lead singer and songwriter Dennis DeYoung, who had a chip on his shoulder and for good reason. He was almost painfully earnest as a writer, singer, and producer, but he knew that the self-appointed rock cognoscenti in New York and London had no respect for his work.

The implication of the phrase *corporate rock* was that the stigmatized artists were pliable tools in the hands of their record companies. This was not fair to DeYoung, who did not have a single friend at A&M Records. Styx records were all recorded in Chicago, and they were a prickly group of outsiders who had few relationships in the business.

In 1982 I had tried to manage the band at the peak of their career, when they had released four consecutive albums that went triple platinum, a feat that even Led Zeppelin had failed to accomplish. I cannot deny that my interest was largely fueled by images of the millions of dollars I could make by commissioning their income, but when I did the requisite homework I was genuinely moved by their most recent album, *Paradise Theatre,* which revolved around a sentimental rendering of a fictional theater from the 1920s as a metaphor for America's changes in the 1970s and '80s. An earlier album, *The Grand Illusion,* was an elegant tirade against materialism and featured one of rock's classic cosmic anthems, "Come Sail Away." This was scarcely fodder for the kind of sex-drugs-and-rock-and-roll, lowest-common-denominator, crass rock commercialism that a group like Kiss cheerfully trafficked in.

Styx rejected me in favor of Irving Azoff, but when the band broke up, DeYoung asked me to manage his solo career, which was launched with an album he wrote and produced called *Desert Moon.* Dennis knew that his kind of rock and roll would never be accepted by rock critics, and so our conversations about marketing quickly centered on rock radio.

The "corporatization" that rock critics picked up on was **118** not in the hearts and minds of artists such as Styx but in the transformation of much of rock radio. During the brief "underground" phase the rock stations, artists, rock writers, and record companies were partners in launching a new business and a new culture. By the mid-seventies it was clear that while rock radio stations had overlapping interests with the rest of the rock world, they were in an entirely different business. Their ultimate purpose was to sell advertising, the rates for which were determined by Arbitron ratings. For a long time stations had judged a song's popularity based on the amount of phone calls it generated, but over time they came to realize that these "active" listeners did not necessarily represent the taste of the mass listening audience, most members of which were "passive" in the sense that they would never make such calls. By the mid-seventies many programmers had decided that research based on calling passive listeners was the best predictor of programming that would get good ratings. What began to matter to programmers was not finding out which songs inspired passion, but which were irritating enough to nonfans to cause them to turn the dial.

This was the context in which, with a few notable exceptions, underground rock radio had been replaced by tightly formatted FM rock stations, which now referred to their format as "album-oriented rock" or AOR. The most successful of these stations became cash cows for their owners by programming content that was, for the most part, dictated by consultants. The most powerful of these was another native of Chicago, Lee Abrams.

Although I was not a fan of the kind of radio Lee Abrams created, I knew I needed to get to know him and found him to be an enormously likable rogue. As a young baby-boom rock fan and radio nerd, Abrams had perceived a huge audience of "vulnerable Top 40 listeners," who rocked out when the Rolling Stones' "Jumpin' Jack Flash" came on but hated it when a Donna Fargo country pop song followed. "These listeners wanted to hear Cream and Hendrix," but they still wanted

119

to hear music in a conventional format, not in the free-form stoned outflow. "The typical underground jock would refuse to play Jethro Tull because that was uncool, but he'd play twenty-minute drum solos." Abrams's first big idea was to focus on well-known rock "superstars" and to play album cuts in addition to the singles that Top 40 played. The familiarity that bonded listeners to the station would no longer merely be hit songs but hit *artists*. The music would be all rock and roll, but mostly *popular* rock and roll, with a much shorter list of approved artists, so that listeners felt secure that they would be hearing something they knew or liked a majority of the time. Beaming with satisfaction decades later, Lee said that with his format "you had comfort and depth at same time." In 1972, when Abrams was nineteen years old, he convinced the owner of WDRQ in Raleigh, North Carolina, to try his format and within three months the rating went from a 1.0 to an 11.0. By 1979 he was consulting over one hundred stations, reaching more than 80 percent of the top hundred markets, and his success spawned competitors like Jeff Pollack, who consulted for dozens more of the remaining rock stations using similar programming theories.

These guys (yeah, they were all guys) didn't look at themselves as purveyors of shlock but as the honest brokers of the demands of the rock audience. Abrams recalled a meeting he had with the staff of *Rolling Stone* in the eighties. "They kept talking about how great these obscure punk bands like Gang of Four were and how much commercial rock bands like Styx sucked. And at one point I said to them, 'You know, if you would just go and spend a week in St. Louis, you would look at this all very differently.' "

But the real tension wasn't geographical, it was that radio stations were aiming at different audiences than rock magazines, artists, managers, or record companies were. We were selling artists and their work to intense fans who bought albums, concert tickets, and t-shirts. They wanted the widest possible audience, so they downplayed the significance of the superfans and were much more concerned about the far larger group of casual fans who listened to rock music not as the soundtrack to their lives but as background music. Abrams divided the radio audience into "cult," the hard-core fans, and "fringe," casual, passive listeners. The "cult" were the people who bought records and tickets, but the "fringe" was the larger group whose listening habits made the difference between good and bad ratings.

The other division between rockers and broadcasters was demographics. We cared about anyone who would buy a record, regardless of how young they were. Radio stations only cared about the demographic group that advertisers wanted to reach. "I remember being at an NAB convention in 1978," recalled Abrams, "when an expert on advertising told everyone that by 1982 there wouldn't be any teenagers left." Obviously this was an exaggeration, but the point was that advertisers wanted big numbers of consumers and the big baby-boom generation were now adults. In earlier years ratings of eighteen-to-twenty-four-year-olds were vital to radio-station economic health. Going forward the focus was to be on twenty-five-to-thirty-four. This older audience wanted more "recurrents," old songs by favorites like the Stones, and were often turned off by edgier, more intense rock music.

Broadcasters prized familiarity; we prized originality. They cared about avoiding negatives; we were concerned about intensity of positives. But rockers' access to a mass audience was through these damn mass-market rock stations. A record had to be acceptable to older passive rock fans in order to get its music heard by younger, more active ones, which was why so many hard rock bands had to resort to ballads in order to "cross over" into the radio world while giving hard rock concerts to their real fans. (The biggest hit that Styx ever had was Dennis's love ballad "Babe.")

The talisman that motivated the programmers was "re-   **121** search," which was ostensibly "objective" and thus trumped personal opinion, whether generated by taste or payola. But research made creative people and their cohorts nervous. Research could only measure the past, not the future; it was a way of looking at musical culture through a rearview mirror. Creativity was about anticipating the future. But for Lee Abrams and the hundred stations he influenced, research was reality.

The power of the superstars format was brought home to the record business with the release of the self-titled Boston album in 1976. Its slick rock and roll was perfect for the format: proficient enough lead guitar to clearly brand it as rock and smooth enough not to irritate any of the "fringe." The album sold ten million copies in its first eighteen months of release, the most successful debut album in history. Over the next decade a series of critically ignored or reviled rock radio stars emerged: Foreigner, Kansas, and Styx, among others, who expressed a midwestern rock sensibility and who owed their success to the superstars format.

My perspective on the business was that of an advocate for artists I worked with. I hated the idea that rock and roll was a commodity, the purpose of which was to gather audiences to sell to advertisers. But I knew that within the boundaries of programming that would deliver ratings, there were a number of discretionary calls that guys like Abrams could make, and that was the zone where those of us in the business could make a difference, where "promotion" occurred.

Many promo guys made sure to bring cocaine with them when they visited programmers. "We didn't trade drugs for airplay, but it was a door opener. A guy with great blow was let right in—they definitely had access," Abrams acknowledges.

I was sometimes able to work with artists to exploit the other dirty little secret of most rock programmers: Although they worshipped at the altar of ratings, in their heart of hearts many of them were also fans. Notwithstanding his reverence for research, Abrams did get to know certain artists personally. The British band Yes was a quintessential superstar act. Because their popularity came exclusively from rock radio (they didn't create crossover Top 40 singles), Yes helped define the AOR format. "Rock critics hated them; the Lou Reed crowd couldn't stand them," Abrams recalls gleefully. The members of the band schmoozed him well enough that a quarter of a century later Abrams was still in touch with their guitarist, Steve Howe.

Similarly, the Alan Parsons Project hired Abrams to write liner notes and actually used his voice doing a parody of generic old-school radio shtick as part of a montage in the song "Let's Talk About Me."

Dennis DeYoung knew that he needed Abrams's support and he had a plan. Abrams was a lifelong fan of the Chicago White Sox, whose manager, Tony LaRussa, was a big Styx fan. One afternoon Dennis drove Lee and myself out to Comiskey Park and took a photo with LaRussa and future Hall of Famer Carlton Fisk. "Desert Moon" got plenty of superstar airplay right out of the box, the only hit song to come from any of the solo albums by Styx members.

Years later I asked Lee why his stations had been so resistant to the punk-rock music the critics loved, and he responded with research talk. "Our audiences liked long hair; punks had short hair. Our audience loved great guitar players; most punk musicians seemed like they had gotten a guitar a few months before. Our audience still liked the sixties ideas of peace and love; punk lyrics were about shooting the queen."

Another stress point for mass-appeal rock radio was its resistance to black artists. The reality on the ground at radio was that most radio formats remained unofficially but culturally segregated. The occasional black *rock* artist such as Hendrix, Earth, Wind and Fire, or later Lenny Kravitz were readily accepted by rock audiences, but according to the rock radio guys most black artists played a version of R&B and R&B tended to attract women more than men and thus found more of a home on Top 40 radio then it did on rock. (The ad salesmen at stations always impressed upon their programmers that since the other music formats skewed female, the "job" of a rock station was to deliver men.)

In the late seventies disco music became the rage of pop radio, appealing to millions of young people who liked its differentiation from what was now a decade of established rock sounds.

Rock audiences (mostly white males) felt left out of the disco culture. Abrams explained, "Our listener was about blue jeans, theirs was about clubs that you couldn't get into if you didn't dress up; ours liked sweaty guitar players, their music featured synthesizers."

Abrams was accurately summarizing the rationale that research revealed to him, but he didn't seem to take into account that there was some latent racism in a segment of the straight white male rock audience that skewed the numbers and that a popular phrase like *Disco sucks* was perceived not merely as a comment on music but on the music's fans as well.

Fortunately for the rock culture Abrams and his ilk did not control all of rock radio. There remained a few idiosyncratic programmers who had the skill to get decent ratings without structured formatting. Bonnie Simmons kept KSAN eclectic for another decade. Scott Muni did the same at WNEW-FM in New York, and the renegade station that had the most impact on the careers of edgier rock artists was WMMS in Cleveland, which I first visited in 1974 when I worked for Swan Song.

The key guy at WMMS was "Kid Leo" (real name: Lawrence J. Travagliante). He had joined the station in 1973 as a weekend jock and soon became their afternoon "drive-time" guy (two to six in the afternoon) and music director. "Cleveland had the worst sports teams, our economy was in shambles, and the Cuyahoga River was so polluted it actually caught on fire," Leo recalled. "The one thing we clung on to was rock and roll." (Alan Freed had coined the phrase *rock and roll* in the fifties while working at a Top 40 station in Cleveland.) Somehow or other Leo and the other jocks at WMMS figured out a way to balance their own personal passion for new music with enough familiar music and a messianic sense of rock and roll passion to get ratings so spectacular that the station's owners left them more or less alone.

Cleveland thus became the launching pad for many artists whose music was too edgy or quirky to flourish in the Abrams format. WMMS launched David Bowie and Bruce Springsteen and was an oasis in an otherwise resistant rock radio environment for artists such as Roxy Music and the New York Dolls.

I always tried to go when artists I worked with visited Cleveland because it was such a big part of the Zeitgeist. Rock people usually stayed at a mediocre hotel called Swingos, which was depicted in *Almost Famous*. Almost every band played their first gig there at a thousand-seat ballroom called the Agora. At the first Bad Company show in Cleveland I was walking around at the back of the Agora and a teenage boy, noticing my backstage pass, asked if I worked with the band. When I nodded he told me he was sure they were gonna be big. "We're a breakout market," he said, as if he were a slick marketer instead of a stoned, pimply-faced teenager. When I told the story to Leo he laughed knowingly and said, "Rock and roll is all we had and the kids knew it."

Leo was a sports freak who sported a retro greasy ducktail haircut, but he had an encyclopedic knowledge of music. He read every rock magazine, British and American, and listened to every record. Talk of research and demographics fell on deaf ears at WMMS. Leo was a throwback to the underground jocks in the sense that it was mostly about whether or not he liked the music, although he had a fierce competitive streak and was loyal to his friends. Promotion people catered slavishly to WMMS's incessant demands for exclusivity in Cleveland for artist visits, concert promotions, et cetera. It was worth it. These guys had no inhibition about being the first station to play a record. Whatever they wanted, they got.

Years later I managed Ian Hunter, the lead singer of Mott the Hoople, whose version of Bowie's "All the Young Dudes" was a bigger hit in Cleveland than anywhere else. Ian told me, "We'd been playing half-empty clubs and we would get to Cleveland and the Agora would be mobbed." One night Hunter dedicated a song to Kid Leo, the first time an artist had ever mentioned his name. It was the moment, Leo said, that made him feel "it's all worth it." Hunter rerecorded his song "London Rocks" with the lyric "Cleveland Rocks" for his solo album *You're Never Alone With a Schizophrenic*. It was a blatant suck-up to WMMS and it worked. "Cleveland Rocks" was subsequently used as the theme song for *The Drew Carey Show*. The songwriting royalties from the TV exposure allowed Ian to buy his house in Connecticut.

No description of radio's relationship to the music business would be complete without a reference to the world of independent promotion people and their influence, and the limits thereof on Top 40 radio.

I always felt that their importance was exaggerated. The shadowy world of favors were important in "bringing a record home," but no amount of money could make a stiff into a hit. I figured my job was to work with the artists via touring, press, and/or rock radio to develop a core fan base. When they developed sufficient traction with rock fans, they would earn the priority attention of the head of pop promotion at their label, and the promotions department would take it from there. Some big rock artists such as Styx also had songs that could work at Top 40 and some, like Led Zeppelin, didn't.

I was always in favor of getting the record company to

spend more money on indies. I wanted the artists I cared about to get more airplay and more success. I never had any moral qualms about how promotion people did their job. I preferred a system in which people who believed in an artist could get them played on the radio regardless of what research said.

CHAPTER SEVEN

STEVIE NICKS: TURNING RAINBOWS INTO MUSIC AND MUSIC INTO GOLD

I knew that Peter Grant was right that rock stars held the real power in the business, but it took me some time to make it work for me. My ambitions were such that it wasn't enough just to be thought of as a good PR person, since rock PR rarely led to career opportunities other than more rock PR. By the spring of 1979 it had been three years since I had left Swan Song, I was soon to turn twenty-nine with thirty looming ominously on the horizon, and I was consumed with the fear that my success with Zeppelin had been a fluke. The money that came in from PR fees didn't always pay my monthly bills. I took a series of loans from my parents that added up over time to thirteen thousand dollars and I didn't have any plan except to just stay in the game. I was saved by Stevie Nicks.

I met Stevie when she was dating Paul Fishkin, who was president of Albert Grossman's Bearsville Records and one of my best friends. Bearsville's first hit had been "We Gotta Get You a Woman" by Todd Rundgren, who had grown up with Paul in **129**

Philadelphia and had written the song about him. Paul's adolescent shyness had long since left by the time I had met him during my brief stint working for Grossman's music publishing company. He had long curly black hair and a bushy black mustache and was a bit of a dandy, dressed in the expensive and well-tailored velvet-and-leather hippie clothing prevalent at the time. Paul always seemed to have an attractive woman on his arm but also had a gregarious affability that made him one of the guys.

Paul had developed an expertise in pop and rock radio promotion and was so instrumental in getting the blues-rock group Foghat to million-selling (platinum) sales status that Grossman gave him a 20-percent interest in the Bearsville label and the title of president. (Title inflation meant that the "president" was the number-two person in most record companies, typically reporting to the "chairman.") Not long thereafter Paul retained my company to do the PR for all of Bearsville's artists.

Paul had met Stevie at a Warners sales convention and a romance had promptly blossomed. Fleetwood Mac's album *Rumours* was the best-selling album in America at the time. (It would remain number one for thirty-nine weeks, a feat that has never been duplicated.) Stevie had written and sung "Dreams," the biggest hit on *Rumours*, a haunting, beautiful, and bitter song about her highly publicized breakup with Fleetwood Mac guitarist Lindsey Buckingham. Lindsey had reciprocated by writing the biting "Go Your Own Way" about Stevie.

Paparazzi had no interest in rock stars in the 1970s, but Stevie was a glamorous and highly recognizable figure in the rock subculture. She had a vivid stage "look" defined by billowing chiffon skirts, shawls, top hats (or, later in her career, feathered berets), layers of lace, and her long curly blond hair. Only five feet one in her stocking feet, she habitually wore six-inch suede platform boots and walked with the confident, erect posture of a beauty queen.

The first time I met Stevie was when she came as Paul's date to a press party I staged for Foghat at the New York Public Library at Lincoln Center. In those days she had a perfect hourglass figure dressed in a slightly subdued version of her velvet-clad stage persona. Stevie was at her defining moment as a rock icon and I was momentarily intimidated by her glamour but was soon put at ease by her warm, self-deprecating manner.

The party was the culmination of the best PR stunt I ever pulled off. Foghat's success was based on the rock radio hits "Fool for the City" and "Slow Ride" and extensive touring orchestrated by Premier Talent. The band had been virtually invisible in the rock press. Their signature sound was an energetic and entertaining version of British blues that was unapologetically derivative of Cream and Zeppelin. Even if a journalist liked them, there was nothing interesting to say. I discovered that the singer, Lonesome Dave Peverett, was a true blues aficionado, and he bought my idea of a tribute-to-the-blues concert in which Foghat would play with some of the blues masters who had inspired them. The blues guys, long out of fashion in the post-Fillmore era, were easy to get. The concert was at the Palladium in New York, and Foghat jammed with Muddy Waters, John Lee Hooker, Otis Blackwell, Johnny Winter, and Honeyboy Edwards. The show was covered approvingly in *The New York Times* and *Rolling Stone*. We filmed it and got four songs broadcast on the syndicated TV show *Don Kirshner's Rock Concert*. Profits from the concert were used to buy a collection of blues albums for the Lincoln Center library, the unveiling of which was the rationale for the party, which would get Foghat a second PR hit.

I had dinner with Paul and Stevie the following night. She wanted my advice on how to get Margie Kent, the woman who designed most of her clothes, into *Vogue* magazine. I wondered why she didn't ask the PR person for Fleetwood Mac, or the Warner Records PR department to help, and I was astonished to hear that Stevie had extremely limited clout in the context of **131** the group, which was managed by its drummer and cofounder, Mick Fleetwood. The band had formed in 1967, another British blues outfit, and had been through a series of lead guitarists when Lindsey Buckingham was invited to join in 1976. Buckingham was then living with Stevie. They had made a Buckingham/Nicks album, which sold almost nothing, and they were broke. Stevie was working as a waitress at the Clementine Restaurant in L.A. when they got the offer to join Fleetwood Mac. Although I, and millions of other rock fans, saw her as the principal star of Fleetwood Mac because of her hit songs "Rhiannon" and "Dreams," she was treated as "a space cadet" or "chick singer." She was devastated that one of her favorite songs, "Silver Springs," had been excluded from the *Rumours* album, presumably to limit the amount of songwriting income she would receive. Stevie explained how she had created an alternative group of advisors. In addition to Margie, her circle included Robin Snider, who gave her lessons to strengthen Stevie's vocal chords against the rigors of the road, and Herbie Worthington, who took dozens of photos of her and was sufficiently talented that the group had hired him to do the *Fleetwood Mac* and *Rumours* covers.

Paul had advised me that this was not a time to pitch a PR client but to create, instead, a friendship. It was a complex and delicate situation, talking to an individual member of the world's biggest rock group, but he had a strong sense that there was business there as long as I was cool about it. Paul himself did not want to be perceived as a businessperson but as a boyfriend, so this left the door open to me to investigate. I offered to do what I could to help and was rewarded with her home phone number, and I contrived a trip to Los Angeles almost immediately.

At this time Stevie was living in a pink house on El Contento Drive in Hollywood that had been built for the silent screen star Vilma Banke in the 1920s. The house was always filled with

132   members of her entourage, first among equals of whom was

Robin Snider. Robin's influence derived from the fact that she had gone to high school with Stevie and was her oldest and most trusted friend. In their early twenties Stevie and Robin had worked as waitresses in numerous restaurants together. Robin was a natural blonde with classic good looks that reminded me of a younger version of the actress Lee Remick. She was the only girl in Stevie's circle who was in a stable relationship, engaged to a tall, handsome album promotion person from Warner Records named Kim Anderson. (Kim had been the local guy in St. Louis, and as far as I could tell he was promoted to a national job solely on the basis of his access to Fleetwood Mac.) Robin was interested in learning more about the business side. For a time she worked for my PR company, assigned to get press for the legendary Brill Building songwriter Barry Mann. She was tenacious enough to get decent results, but she soon tired of the repetitive nature of pitching stories and the rejection that went with the territory and returned to life as Stevie's full time aide-de-camp. I always felt Robin was responsible for much of my subsequent success in getting Stevie to bet on me.

The center of action in Stevie's house was either in the kitchen, where she liked to make tacos, or the living room, which had a Bösendorfer piano, one the first luxuries she had bought when she made money from Fleetwood Mac. I almost stopped breathing the first time I saw her hunched over the piano, singing trancelike a mournful arrangement of "Rhiannon" quite different from the recorded version. Many artists are less impressive in person than indicated by the carefully produced versions of their vocals that record production affords. Stevie was more magnetic, more compelling, and more charismatic. I was besotted. (In the way a fan is besotted. I was not the kind of guy Stevie was interested in romantically and I knew it.) It turned out that Stevie had written fragments of songs based on the Welsh cosmology, in which Rhiannon was a goddess. Over the course of time we talked about the possibility of the songs forming the basis for a movie.

I didn't know anyone at *Vogue,* but I had a friend who did fashion PR who was sufficiently taken with Stevie to make an effort. He was unsuccessful. *Vogue* cared nothing about Stevie Nicks or her clothes, but the effort bought me time to get to create a deal between us, empowering me to "produce" a movie based on the songs, in the unlikely event I could get one off the ground. Although no money exchanged hands, I remember the euphoria I felt when I got the signed letter of agreement. Stevie Nicks had publicly said I was someone she was in business with!

To give some credibility to the "project" I was dispatched to Tucson to meet with Evangeline Walton, the seventy-five-year-old author of a series of paperback popularizations of the Rhiannon myth. Walton had a rare disorder that had made her skin a vivid shade of purple. She had no illusions about the value of her books and agreed to assign them to us for no cash unless a film was actually produced. ("Don't worry, dear," Evangeline said when I explained the tenuous nature of Stevie's plans, "all true artists are a little neurotic.")

Stevie proceeded to write more Rhiannon-themed songs, of which she made piano/vocal demos to be part of our presentation. I was mesmerized by her intuitive writing process. She would sit at the piano and zone out for hours and come out with a song. Stevie's mysticism was entirely self-taught. Not for her were studies of Rimbaud, Blake, or Ginsberg, nor even the Bible. She was an autodidactic mystic who viewed the universe through the eyes of a middle American.

All stars have big egos, but Stevie's was unique in my experience. In order to feel "vibey" she wanted those of us around her to feel that way too. Stevie wanted praise and reassurance, especially in response to her songs. But she put considerable energy into making the people around her feel important.

Thus, according to Stevie, Herbie Worthington wasn't just a photographer, he was a genius. She wanted as many friends as possible in the studio to listen to her new songs or listen to her new ideas, and in return she made everyone around her feel that somehow we were *part of* what she did. Stevie peered at whomever she was talking to with an uncommon intensity (in part because her contact lenses did not totally compensate for her farsightedness). She spoke in an intense quiet cadence that conveyed the idea that whatever topic she was obsessed with at the moment was of transcendent importance. But she was also extravagantly generous in her praise of others, laughed heartily at others' jokes, and created the illusion that everyone in her entourage was somehow her equal.

Stevie had asked a local jeweler to create several dozen crescent moons out of eighteen-carat gold, which she presented to her close friends with a solemnity like that of an initiation. I was deeply touched the night she gave me one and although I had not ever worn jewelry before and haven't since, I bought a chain and wore it around my neck for several years.

The first home video recorders had recently come on the market and we spent many a night watching fantasy films like *Dumbo* and *Beauty and the Beast* and brainstorming about *Rhiannon*. Notwithstanding the fact that between us we had zero experience in writing or making movies, Stevie was a big enough star that many power brokers in the movie business wanted to hear the *Rhiannon* movie pitch.

My role was to set up the meetings and to chime in occasionally to give structure to her rap. We visited legendary producer Ray Stark at his Columbia Pictures office, but he wanted to jettison the Welsh mythology and use the songs as the backdrop for a remake of an old Kim Novak movie he owned the rights to called *Bell, Book and Candle*. Jon Peters, then living with Barbra Streisand, was in no mood to give power to another strong-minded woman, and Stevie, already feeling powerless relative to Fleetwood, didn't want to be a trophy rock celebrity in a Peters Hollywood film. Don Simpson, then a production VP at Paramount and soon to become the legendary producer of *Flashdance,* visited El Contento and stayed late and free-associated with Stevie and me in a way that made us utterly comfortable. But hanging out was one thing and the commercial movie business was another, and Simpson passed. We met with the great British producer David Puttnam, who impressed us with the beauty of Ridley Scott's *The Duellists,* but after a brief flirtation with a deal, Puttnam and Scott went on to greener pastures. We had a similar near miss with Australian director Gillian Armstrong, whose feminist period piece *My Brilliant Career* similarly enthralled Stevie.

I was nervous that I had used a lot of Stevie's time with no tangible results, but perseverance paid off when David Field at United Artists bought our treatment, subject to my partnering with Rob Cohen, who had produced several films for Motown and was at the time finishing *The Wiz.* There wasn't much money involved. I think I got around ten thousand dollars and Stevie around fifty thousand for the option, but getting paid anything at all on her own and not as a member of Fleetwood Mac was a milestone for Stevie. That I had delivered it differentiated me from pure hangers-on.

Paul Mayersberg, the man who had written the David Bowie vehicle *The Man Who Fell to Earth,* was hired as a screenwriter. Although the film was never made, the process took the better part of a year, during which time I further consolidated my relationship with Stevie. I still have a cassette somewhere of the Rhiannon songs Steve wrote, and hope that they see the light of day. They contain some of her best poetic lyrics. Around the same time, Stevie played me a children's song called "The Goldfish and the Ladybug," which she imagined could be an animated TV special. I was able to get a development deal at the ABC network after she met with their two most senior executives, Fred Pierce and Tony Thomopoulos, but it, too, would eventually run aground based on the chasm between Stevie's rich imagination and the commercial limitations of the business.

All these meetings required me to spend an increasing percentage of my time in Los Angeles. My two main assistants at my PR company in New York were appalled by my apparent obsession with Stevie. Over the next few months both of them resigned, worried that I had either lost my mind or was abandoning them. I hated losing them, but I knew how rare an opportunity it was to bond with someone as commercially talented as Stevie. While my New York friends were trekking down to CBGB enjoying and, in some instances, creating a new current of punk rock music that would reverberate for decades, I was cheerfully working my way into the heart of the L.A. rock business.

I had kept a place in Los Angeles ever since I left Swan Song, first in a spare room in Michael and Pamela Des Barres's apartment in Hollywood and later a series of places of my own. Although it was not the sole center of the music business (New York, Nashville, and London were at least equally important), it was the home of Warner Bros. Records, Elektra Records (which had moved there from New York), and A&M Records, three of the premiere labels for rock and roll. L.A. was also a source of rock and roll creativity, having spawned the Doors, the Beach Boys, the Mamas and the Papas, and the Byrds and, more recently, the Eagles, Linda Ronstadt, and Jackson Browne. And L.A. was home to such music business icons as David Geffen, Dick Clark, Lou Adler, Phil Spector, and Berry Gordy.

For reasons I have never been able to understand, L.A. always had a wider variety of good rock stations than New York did and by the late seventies L.A.'s radio tip sheet, *Radio and Records*, had influence on broadcasters that superseded that of *Billboard*. For many years the definition of a radio hit would be to be deemed a "breaker" in *R&R*, based on a mathematical formula the editors cooked up to compute radio airplay. Pop radio indie promotion rates were based on *R&R*'s weighting of stations: three thousand dollars per record added for a big station called a P1, two thousand for a secondary called a P2, and one thousand for the smaller P3s.

137

Southern California was also home to the most commercially talented session musicians of the late seventies, guitarists Waddy Wachtel and Ry Cooder, bass player Leland Sklar, drummers Russ Kunkel and Jim Keltner, among others whose playing animated records by Bob Dylan, Neil Young, and literally dozens of successful and classic records. Stevie sang background vocals on a hit song called "Gold" by John Stewart, written about these hit makers. It referred to Kanan Road, which connected Malibu, where Stewart lived, to the San Fernando Valley, where many recording studios were located: *"Drivin' over Kanan, / singin' to my soul, / There's people out there turning music into gold."*

Because of Fleetwood Mac's quirky history Stevie was signed to Warner Bros. only as a member of Fleetwood Mac, not for solo projects. Typically, when a record company signed a band, they also had "leaving member" clauses, which gave them options on solo projects by the members. Fleetwood Mac had signed to Warners in 1967, and the band had settled into the mediocre sales of a respected but journeyman British blues band that had a habit of changing guitar players every couple of years. Thus, the label had not signed the latest in series of what they viewed as commercially irrelevant backup musicians when Lindsey and Stevie joined Fleetwood Mac in 1974 to perform on the band's ninth album. The "real" members of the band were perceived to be the founders, bassist John McVie, his ex-wife Christine, who sang and played keyboards, and charismatic drummer Mick Fleetwood, who also managed the band with an iron hand. With the mysterious magic by which certain songs overcome layers of record company assumptions, "Rhiannon," which Stevie both sang and wrote, helped grow Fleetwood Mac's sales from a plateau of one hundred and fifty thousand, where they had resided for years, to over four million.

Because of Stevie's flamboyant appearance she was often underestimated as a songwriter. Very few lyricists would be capable of transforming such a little-known Welsh myth into a popular song. By the time Warner Bros. figured out they had a new star, she had no incentive to precipitously sign over her solo rights, and since they had no reason to believe that she had plans to record on her own, they had left well enough alone.

When Stevie broke off her relationship with Paul to have a passionate and initially clandestine relationship with Mick Fleetwood, Fishkin was heartbroken, but he was enough of a careerist to see the same opportunity I did. Now that they were no longer an item, there was no reason not to talk to her about forming a small record label revolving around her future solo work. Stevie would be feeling a little guilty about having dumped Paul so unceremoniously. And she respected Paul as a "record man" who knew promotion and sales, and had confidence in me as a PR guy deeply committed to her solo talent. In retrospect I'm not sure how I had the balls to suggest it to her, but when I presented the idea of the three of us starting a label together she went for it.

The business proposition was that she would receive the same royalty and advance that she would get in the marketplace, plus own 10 percent of our company. (Her 10 percent was economic only. Decision making was equal between Fishkin and myself.) One of the key selling points of this new venture was that it would also be a vehicle for Stevie's friends. In addition to her presence on the John Stewart hit, Stevie and Lindsey had done guest vocals on "Magnet and Steel," a single by their old friend Walter Egan that was also a Top 10 hit, and she had sung a duet with Kenny Loggins on his song "Whenever I Call You Friend," which was also a smash. We felt that there was a kind of creative mafia attracted to her that could spawn a real record label.

Even at the peak of her romantic excitement about Mick Fleetwood, Stevie knew that this was the same guy who had refused to include "Silver Springs" on the *Rumours* album. Moreover, she knew that her own romantic history consisted of short relationships and she obviously wanted to preserve an artistic and professional lifeline for herself that would survive any future breakup.

We created a short-form agreement for two albums and prepared to shop for a deal for a joint venture, patterning a business plan on the Bearsville/Warners deal, which Fishkin knew so well. In addition to Stevie's signature and the giant shadow of Fleetwood Mac's continued sales, we had piano demos of songs she had written for the Rhiannon movie as well as a number of more produced song demos of material that had been rejected by Fleetwood Mac, in addition to a stunning duet she had written for Waylon Jennings and Jessi Colter of a song called "Leather and Lace." Fortunately for us, Jennings had passed on it. Stevie's demo featured an astonishing vocal by Don Henley (another one of Stevie's exes) doing the male part of the duet.

Stevie understood that in order to get top dollar we might need to talk to various people, but we promised her that we would go to Mo Ostin of Warner Bros. first. She felt a personal affection for Mo and his wife, Evelyn, and also appreciated the fact that her success as a member of Fleetwood Mac had all occurred with Warner Bros. (The customized license plate on Stevie's Volkswagen was BBUNNI in honor of the Warner Bros. famous animated mascot.)

Mo Ostin was the most revered record executive in Los Angeles. I was in awe of him but hardly knew him. Mo didn't get to New York often and, unlike Wexler, had little interest in current or former rock critics. A year earlier I had sat in one of the Warners conference rooms while Jim Steinman played the piano and Meat Loaf sang songs from the unreleased *Bat Out of Hell* to Mo and his equally legendary head of A&R, Lenny Waronker. Bearsville had paid for the album, which had been produced by Todd Rundgren, but Bearsville's deal required Warner's approval to release records and Mo and Lenny had been underwhelmed by the record. The in-office performance didn't change their minds. Consequently Fishkin had to sell the album to another label and Bearsville missed out on the huge profits from the twenty million copies that the album went on to sell. Paul felt that Albert Grossman had not really gone to the wall for the Meat Loaf album, which was one of the reasons he wanted to start his own company with me.

The rationale for the Bearsville deal had been to be in business with Albert Grossman, whom Mo considered a heavyweight and a peer. He perceived Paul as little more than a glorified promotion guy. Grossman was not happy about the fact that Paul and I were starting a new label. He would be losing Fishkin, who had been running his company day to day, and he had a nagging sense that somehow Stevie should be signed to Bearsville, not to our new company, in which he had no financial stake. Grossman and Mo had the same personal attorney, who belittled our prospects to the Warner Bros. chairman.

Even more significant than Albert's opposition to our fledgling business was the growing ire of Mick Fleetwood. I spoke to him the night before we were planning to set up meetings about the label. Suspecting that she hadn't reflected on the consequences of our deal, I had asked Stevie if she had discussed our venture with Mick. I figured that within a few hours of our first calls she would be getting a lot of flack. Stevie turned to me and said in a nervous, quivering voice "No—no. I haven't told Mick"—and then plaintively added, "Can you tell him?"

I had only met Mick in brief encounters going in and out of Stevie's house and explained to him what we were doing. "Well," he said in his deep British-accented voice, "it's interesting that you bring this up, because we actually have a plan for a new deal that includes Stevie that we were just about to show her." I explained that we had already *made* a deal for her solo albums. Mick politely thanked me for letting him know and I reported back to Stevie that I had given him the heads-up.

The next day we and our lawyers met with Mo, fulfilling the promise to Stevie to go to him first. Although short in stat-

141

ure, Mo was a larger-than-life personality, with an unusually loud, deep voice and a commanding presence akin to that of a king of a small but wealthy nation. We would have taken a somewhat lesser deal from Mo than anyone else, but he had no interest at all. He listened to our proposal with gelid eyes and told us, "Maybe I would make a Stevie Nicks solo album, but I am certainly not interested in another joint venture." Which was a way of telling us to go fuck ourselves.

The next day I was called by Fleetwood Mac's lawyer, Mickey Shapiro, who explained that our contract with Stevie was blocking Fleetwood Mac from getting an increased royalty rate. He tried to strong-arm me, saying, "You can't expect Mo Ostin to create a new label around an artsy-crafty album that Stevie is going to make on her own." Fleetwood called Stevie and yelled at her, but she started crying and told him to talk to me. This time the politeness was gone and he was screaming at me at the top of his lungs, "Danny, you didn't tell me she had signed a piece of paper." As calmly as I could I reminded him that I had told him we had made a deal with her. "But you didn't tell me she had *signed*." Apparently he thought that anyone spaced out enough to hang around Stevie's house all the time was too flaky to have a contract drafted.

In retrospect it seems incredible to me that, while they were lovers, both Stevie and Mick had been negotiating business deals that affected each other and never told each other; but at the time it just seemed like par for the course. Stevie was impervious to the pressure from the group. We were helped by the fact that Lindsey Buckingham had also rejected the notion of signing away his solo career to help Fleetwood Mac get a better deal going forward. Stevie was enjoying the empowerment that came with doing her own thing, was protective of her friends, and was offended at the belittling of her solo aspirations. She would show them who was artsy-craftsy. Mo's wife, Evelyn, called Stevie, crying, "Please don't do this to my Mo," but Stevie calmly explained to her that we had gone to him first and he had passed. Paul and I felt a pleasant shock. We seemed to have pulled it off.

But we weren't there yet. The other labels we went to were daunted by the multimillion-dollar package we wanted and were nervous about the negative buzz regarding Stevie's solo project that was emanating from the Warners and Fleetwood camps. Their version of reality was that it was the full group of five that created the commercial sound and that on her own Stevie was too spacey to have commercial success.

We were saved by corporate in-fighting almost as odd as that of the band. Atlantic Records and Warner Bros. were both wholly owned divisions of Warner Communications, but they were fiercely competitive. Atlantic had recently promoted Doug Morris, a former songwriter ("Sweet Talkin' Guy") who was a friend of Fishkin. Doug had built a small record company called Big Tree Records on the strength of his ability to identify hit singles and his shrewd mastery of the motley crew of independent promo people who influenced Top 40 radio. Big Tree had a series of hits with such long-forgotten one-hit wonders as Lobo, Brownsville Station, Hot Chocolate, and England Dan and John Ford Coley and had been distributed by Atlantic. Although Big Tree did not sell many albums, Ahmet was dazzled by Morris's abilities and brought him in to reactivate the Atco label. Anxious to prove his mettle in the rock arena, he acquired in his first deal Pete Townshend's solo album, and he saw Stevie Nicks as a similar opportunity. Although Doug had a gift for self-deprecation, he had a keen grasp of the politics of the record business that led Paul to nickname him "Columbo," a reference to the rumpled TV detective played by Peter Falk who inevitably trapped murderers who underestimated him.

Doug was perceived by the Warners people as a second-tier executive. He resented them and was thus undeterred by their similarly condescending attitude about Stevie's solo project. In future decades Doug would emerge as the preeminent American record executive, but at the time he was still amassing power at **143**

Atlantic and was given permission to make our deal only if we had options for three additional Stevie Nicks albums, making it a five-album deal instead of only two.

Stevie's reaction was mixed on hearing this news, and several days went by with no affirmative response. It took one more episode in the soap opera to get our deal set up. One of Stevie's best girlfriends was a woman named Sara Recor, whose husband, Jim, managed Kenny Loggins. (She inspired Stevie's Fleetwood Mac song "Sara.") One night I visited Stevie, hoping to maneuver her into a talk about the extra albums, and I found her in tears. Sara and Mick Fleetwood were having an affair. Stevie had been betrayed both by her lover and one of her best friends. I tried as hard as possible to empathize, but I had a hard time repressing a selfish hunch that Stevie's romantic disappointment might be good for Paul and me. Sure enough, the next day Stevie called me and solved our problem. "I hadn't gotten back to you because I was worried about upsetting Mick. That's not important to me anymore. You can have the five albums."

The drama surrounding Stevie's solo contract was made even more surreal by the fact that during these negotiations Fleetwood Mac was in the middle of recording the album *Tusk*. Lindsey was obsessed with the edgy music of punk rockers like the Sex Pistols and the Talking Heads and tried vainly to make the album hipper than Fleetwood Mac was destined to be. Stevie contributed three of her best songs, "Sara," "Sisters of the Moon," and "Beautiful Child," any of which I would have been thrilled to have for her solo debut.

I wanted to name the company Goldfish Records, which included both of our names and was also part of one of Stevie's song titles. But that would have put my name first. Paul suggested Modern Records, a kind of ironic reference to the vibe of the halcyon days of the early indie rock labels. That was fine with me too. Stevie hated the name. "I like frilly things, vibey things, *old* things. I am anything *but* modern," she complained, but she had a smile on her face and didn't press the issue and didn't come up with an alternative. So we were Modern Records.

Stevie went into the studio with a young engineer named Tom Moncrieff, who had produced the Walter Egan record. One night Doug Morris came to the studio when they were cutting a new song. After a couple of hours of lying on the floor listening to what was going on, Doug leaned over and whispered to me, "He doesn't even know she is singing out of tune. We're fucked. We need a real producer."

I had been so fixated on getting the deal done and keeping Stevie's spirits up that I had not focused on such a fundamental fact, but I knew immediately that he was right. The problem was that Stevie was devoted to Moncrieff, who had helped her build a home demo studio and who wore one of her golden moons. I immediately thought of Jimmy Iovine, who was the only record producer whom I had a personal friendship with. Fishkin was comfortable with him and most importantly, Jimmy had just produced the album *Damn the Torpedoes* for Tom Petty and the Heartbreakers, and I knew that Stevie was a big Tom Petty fan.

I had first met Iovine shortly after the release of his first hit as a record producer, Patti Smith's album *Easter*. It featured what would be the sole hit single of Patti's career, "Because the Night," which had been cowritten with Bruce Springsteen. Knowing Patti's fierce pride as an auteur I was a little surprised that she would have done the song of one of her contemporaries, and I asked Jimmy if it had been hard. He nodded but explained how they had bonded in the making of the album and when it was almost done he had said, "Patti, it's like this. We need a hit."

Jimmy and I were both clients of attorney David Sonenberg, who was also Meat Loaf's manager and had put us at the same table when *Bat Out of Hell* was performed at the Bottom Line. When I first met him, Jimmy was living with Carol Miller, a **145** much-beloved rock DJ on WPLJ. They soon broke up, however, and Jimmy and I often went to shows together in New York, two single guys in the rock business on the make. Many nights we found ourselves with nothing to do after midnight and would eat a late snack at the all-night Midtown restaurant Brasserie and compare notes on how we each could advance another rung up the ladder.

Iovine was to have an illustrious career, but it was not without its setbacks. Inexplicably, Patti did not use him for her next album but switched to Todd Rundgren (the resulting album, *Wave,* sold less than half of *Easter.*) A similar disappointment had occurred with Bruce Springsteen. Iovine had engineered and mixed the legendary breakthrough album *Born to Run.* For some reason Springsteen and his manager/producer, Jon Landau, had chosen a different engineer for Springsteen's follow-up album. It was a testament to Iovine's self-discipline and perennial view of what he called "the big picture" that he was able to hide his wounded feelings sufficiently to remain friends with both Springsteen and Smith for decades to come. But in 1978, when he had been passed over by both of them, it took great resourcefulness and tenacity to find another genius. After a few forgettable albums he produced to stay in the game and pay the rent, he bonded with Tom Petty and produced the album that would take both of them to the next level, *Damn the Torpedoes.* As had been the case with the Patti Smith album, Jimmy was worried that there was not the right lead single. When the album was almost done he asked to listen to songs that Petty had written but rejected for inclusion on the album and plucked "Don't Do Me Like That" from the reject pile. It became the lead single that broke the album.

I introduced Jimmy to Doug and they hit it off, so the next step was for him to meet Stevie. Jimmy was keenly aware of who had written and sung the biggest hits for Fleetwood Mac, but Stevie's first reaction when I mentioned his name was negative. Her first instinct was to be protective of her friend whom she was already working with and she was dubious about having a "New York vibe" on her album. However, she softened somewhat when I got her an advance copy of the forthcoming Petty record, which she played incessantly.

To get her off the dime I got Petty to come with me to the studio to personally tell Stevie about Iovine's process. I was a little out of my depth. Tom Petty had a look in his bloodshot eyes of a stoner who was pretty sure that even during my hippest moments I was not quite hip enough to be worth his attention. But he did what had been asked out of loyalty to Jimmy. Tom swept Stevie off her feet with his shambling rock and roll intensity and understated Florida charm. He earnestly extolled the virtues of Iovine's indispensable role in the new album. Stevie said the words I'd been longing to hear—she would meet Iovine. Out of Stevie's earshot Petty called Jimmy from the studio and dissipated any lingering anxiety Jimmy had about making the trip to L.A.: "Get your ass right here, Iovine," Tom drawled. "Her voice sounds just like it does on the radio."

By this time Stevie and her piano had moved to a duplex condo on the beach in Marina del Rey. I drove Jimmy out there. At a certain point in the evening she took him for a walk on the beach and when they came back a few hours later it had been decided that he would produce her first solo album. A week later Jimmy had moved in and would be her boyfriend as well as her producer for the next year.

Iovine's streetwise Brooklyn persona added a macho presence to Stevie's entourage. One of Stevie's greatest compliments to a person she considered soulful was to refer to them as "very Rhiannon." Jimmy tended to mock a lot of the mystical affect and told me emphatically, "I am *not* very Rhiannon." He pointedly refused to wear one of the golden moons. But he shared with her a vision of the exquisite balance between Stevie's idiosyncratic rock and roll self-expression and major superstar success. Most of the tracks were recorded with the best L.A. session guys, including Waddy Wachtel on guitar and Russ Kunkel on

147

drums. It was Kunkel who came up with the groove on "Edge of Seventeen." The song title had come about when Jane Petty told Stevie in her southern accent that she had met Tom at the "age of seventeen" and Stevie misheard it as "edge," and then fell in love with the resultant phrase. Henley agreed to re-sing "Leather and Lace." Stevie maintained her sense of a female fairy-tale rock and roll world by adding her friends Lori Perry and Sharon Celani as background singers on most of the album and heavily featuring them on the artwork.

But Iovine fretted that Stevie didn't have "the song." The track record of solo albums by individuals from big groups was decidedly mixed, and in the ensuing months, *Tusk* sold only a fraction of what *Rumours* had, putting Fleetwood Mac on a potential downward slide compared to where they had been even a year or two before. The obvious idea was to see if Stevie could do a song or two with Tom Petty and the Heartbreakers, who were on their way up. The first thing they cut together was a song called "The Insider," which featured a gorgeous blending of Tom and Stevie's voices singing one of Petty's best lyrics, a searing portrait of the rock and roll subculture. But as artistically compelling as "The Insider" was, it did not have the kind of melodic hook that hit songs were made of.

Then they cut "Stop Draggin' My Heart Around," a classic call-and-response duet with a one-listen chorus. Later, when "Stop Draggin' My Heart Around" was the number-one single in America, I posed a question to Jimmy. Tom Petty had written and produced both songs and the tracks were performed by his band the Heartbreakers. Yet "The Insider," which was merely a great album track, wound up on Tom's album while "Stop Draggin' My Heart Around," which was a smash, ended up on our album. How had he convinced Tom to agree to that? Jimmy grinned in appreciation of my recognition of what he had pulled off and replied, "Danny, there is something that you and I both do. When the bad guys do it it's called manipulation. What do we call it when we do it?"

Stevie had originally called the title song "Belladonna," based on having read about the psychedelic drug of the same name. I was nervous that it would attract antidrug attention, which would distract from the mainstream appeal of the album, and in my sole creative contribution to the album other than making the introduction to Iovine, I persuaded her to make it into two words, "Bella Donna," which meant "beautiful lady" in Italian.

Critical opinion was irrelevant to the marketing strategy. The New York reviewers of the time viewed punk rock as the primary purveyor of rock authenticity and had no incentive to chew over the works of massively successful Southern California rock artists. I reprised my Zeppelin strategy, telling writers that she was too big to ignore. Stevie didn't agonize over the press the way Zeppelin or the Eagles did, but she did call David Fricke, weeping in gratitude over the story he had written for a *Rolling Stone* cover. We used her mainstream celebrity to get her onto *Good Morning America*. Meanwhile Stevie had decided that she wanted separate management for her solo career and hired Eagles manager Irving Azoff. The planets were lining up.

Figuring it would be of some use internationally, we made a performance video of Tom and Stevie singing the single, and it was one of the few available by major artists when MTV began broadcasting in 1982, a few months after *Bella Donna* came out. "We used to laugh about how often we played that video," Les Garland, the original head of programming for MTV, recalled. Stevie's cascading golden hair and iconic flowing gowns made her the ideal video artist of the early eighties. For years Stevie, Pat Benatar, Joan Jett, and Ann and Nancy Wilson of Heart were the only female rock singers seen regularly on MTV.

Doug made sure that Atco's promotion and sales teams focused like a laser on *Bella Donna*, and "Stop Draggin' My Heart Around" went to number one on both rock radio and pop radio airplay charts. *Bella Donna* was selling really well but not quite **149** as well as new albums by Foreigner and Journey, two of the most popular of the "corporate rock radio" bands at the peak of their popularity. SoundScan, the system of measuring album sales by toting up over-the-counter sales via bar codes, would not emerge for another decade, and in 1980 the *Billboard* chart was done more or less the same way it had been when I worked there in the late sixties. Hundreds of stores were called for information, but the final creation of the chart was done by one guy named Bill Wardlow. Doug took Stevie to dinner with Wardlow and as a quid pro quo for the personal attention, the next week *Bella Donna* was officially the number-one album in the country according to *Billboard*, despite the fact that anecdotal reports indicated that it was really number three. In response to howls of protest from people involved with the other acts, *Bella Donna* was number one for only a single week—but that still made it a number-one album.

The second single, "Leather and Lace," on which Henley had reprised his vocal, was a huge multiformat hit although Henley was not available for a video. I got it into my head that I should direct a video for "Edge of Seventeen," the third single. I felt that Stevie's own environment, filled with cosmic drawings and knickknacks, and her own private flamboyance would be a great visual accompaniment to the song. Somehow I forgot that the most important thing about a video is how the performer herself looks. The cinematographer we got lit her in a way that was unflattering. The video itself was an amateurish mess and had to be totally scrapped. Luckily she had recently shot an HBO special and we were able to excerpt her performance of "Edge of Seventeen" to maintain her exposure on MTV. I had a significantly enhanced respect for video directors and never tried dabbling in their field again. The experience reminded me that it was the artist's job to be creative and my role was to be their advocate. Although Stevie was irritated for a few weeks, she soon forgave me and never mentioned this embarrassing error in judgment. We then released a fourth single,

150

"After the Glitter Fades," which got the album another couple of months of rock airplay. The album sold three million copies in the year after its release and eventually sold more than eight million.

The vaguely cosmic and romantic nature of Stevie's music produced the kind of fan intensity usually associated with sixties artists. One afternoon while I was out, our receptionist, Larry Flick, was confronted by an agitated young man who was convinced that we had Stevie tied up in the back of the office. He had come to this conclusion because Stevie had not responded to his fan mail. Larry had the presence of mind to say he would go to the back of the office and look for her, whereupon he went into a locked office and called the cops. Another time I got an agitated call from a fan who claimed that her song "How Still My Love" was really written for him. He explained his code name was "Still."

Stevie had a way of translating her life into art. Her song "Beauty and the Beast" drew from her attraction to the Cocteau film as well as from her tempestuous relationship with Fleetwood. One day she bought an Art Nouveau lamp in which the light bulb shone through dark blue glass and soon thereafter turned it into the impressionistic rock song "Blue Lamp," which appeared in the *Heavy Metal* soundtrack. It was a neat trick that reinforced the awe of her entourage. We all saw the same things she saw, but only she knew how to turn them into songs.

The fairy tale of rock drama was abruptly replaced by real life when Robin Snider (her married name was now Robin Anderson) was diagnosed with leukemia. Robin had become pregnant shortly before being diagnosed and gave birth to a baby boy named Matthew shortly before she herself died. Stevie and Robin's widower, Kim Anderson, consoled each other, briefly lived together, and actually got married, although the marriage was annulled several months later.

In 1983, when Stevie was ready to record her second solo **151** album, *The Wild Heart,* her romantic relationship with Jimmy had run its course but he was still her record producer. Whereas *Bella Donna* consisted of songs that Stevie had been culling for a lifetime, the new album had to rely on songs written in the previous year. There was not an obvious hit single like "Leather and Lace," and it had not escaped Tom Petty's notice that Stevie's solo album, buttressed by one of his songs, had sold far more than had the Heartbreakers', so another Petty song was not an option. Jimmy reached out to Prince to play on and produce a track. I arrived at the studio one day to find a giant white-haired bodyguard hulking over the lithe, petite doe-eyed superstar as he added a driving synthesizer beat to the song "Stand Back." "Prince is exactly like Jimmy," Stevie told all of us as Jimmy shrugged his shoulders in bemusement.

In the two years since *Bella Donna* MTV had grown explosively and had become the primary means of exposure for rock music. The first single from *Wild Heart* was originally "If Anyone Falls" and was switched to "Stand Back" at the last minute as the result of feedback from radio people. The video director had written a Civil War scenario for the first song, which he decided to adapt to the more up-tempo "Stand Back." I did a cameo role as an injured Confederate soldier with a bloody rag tied around my head. My gratification from my close-up was short-lived as we all realized that, although the video had lush production values and Stevie looked great, it had no aesthetic relationship to the modern groove of "Stand Back." We had to scrap the expensive video and quickly replace it.

Iovine had struck up a friendship with movie producer Joel Silver, who suggested Jeffrey Hornaday, the choreographer for the recently released hit movie *Flashdance,* and who was anxious to prove he could direct. Stevie and Hornaday concocted a stylized performance video augmented by dancers.

Hornaday was in his mid-twenties, with long blond hair. His boyish appearance masked an intense ambition, which was stoked by his girlfriend at the time, actress Lesley Ann Warren.

She accompanied him at every stage of production, sometimes literally whispering advice in his ear.

During the first rehearsal Stevie asked Jimmy to give her feedback. The two of them had maintained a strong creative connection and Jimmy was able to communicate approval, humor, and concern through body language as he paced back and forth during her run-through. Lesley misguidedly accosted Jimmy and suggested that he was "distracting" Stevie. This almost instantly shattered the video shoot into opposing camps, with Hornaday and Lesley on one side and the people who worked with Stevie on the other.

A couple of days later Hornaday showed Jimmy, Paul, and me an edit, and Jimmy quickly listed half a dozen changes he expected Stevie would want. Hornaday angrily said, "Let's see what Stevie says." A few minutes later Stevie made her entrance into the editing bay, looked at the video, and listed exactly the same problems that Jimmy had predicted. Hornaday began arguing with her about the merits of his "vision." Jimmy jumped up from his chair and, waving his finger at Hornaday, insisted, "There is no argument. This isn't a movie. This is Stevie's record. This is Stevie's video. You do what Stevie wants." Taken aback by Iovine's hostile tone, Hornaday answered, "Fuck you, man," at which point Iovine, still standing, punched him in the face, toppling Hornaday over. Hornaday was a dancer and a natural athlete, but his attempt to retaliate was blocked as we all jumped in to restrain both angry guys and Stevie, weeping, flung her body physically in between them.

Shortly thereafter the editing room cleared out, leaving just me, Lesley Ann Warren, and Joel Silver. "You know," said Lesley, "I think this was really good. Everybody got their feelings out." Silver looked at her with scorn and replied, "Lesley, there is nothing good about this." But in fact, when the changes Stevie wanted were made, it was the right video for "Stand Back." Hornaday's choreography had given Stevie the modern affect the song needed.

When I had started working with Stevie, I was one of very few who believed in her talent outside of the context of Fleetwood Mac. Now she was a proven superstar on her own, supported by some of the most successful executives in the business, and I felt I had little to do other than cram into photos for trade magazines. Modern's contract with Atlantic prevented me from working on outside projects. Moreover, Fishkin and I had personal disagreements, which transformed what had been a joyous partnership into a burden for both of us. So when the opportunity arrived to sell my half of Modern and "cash out," I took it. Fishkin and I made up eventually. I stayed friends with Stevie, who helped me on numerous subsequent occasions, and years later she asked me to write the liner notes to *Enchanted,* an anthology of highlights of her solo career.

Bill Clinton famously used one of Lindsey's songs, "Don't Stop," in his 1992 campaign, so Stevie, as a member Fleetwood Mac, incongruously became a fixture at iconic events of the Clinton administration. Her solo persona also endured. A pivotal scene of Jack Black's film *School of Rock* portrayed the high school principal, played by Joan Cusack, inspired and liberated by listening to "Edge of Seventeen."

In 2000 I spoke to Sheryl Crow just before she produced some songs for Stevie, and she cited her as an inspiration in the same tones in which hard-rock bands talked about Led Zeppelin or punk rockers about Patti Smith. The Dixie Chicks recorded "Landslide," creating yet another generation of weddings at which the song would be played. And in 2007, on a visit to Courtney Love's house in L.A., I noted that in her bedroom there was a single photo, an oversized print of Stevie swirling in full flight.

In her own intuitive and supposedly spaced-out way Stevie helped propel the careers of several executives who would dominate the music business for the next several decades. A quarter of a century after *Bella Donna* was released, Doug Morris was the preeminent executive in the record business, the chairman of the Universal Music Group, by far the dominant record company in the world. Jimmy Iovine was chairman of Interscope, the biggest and most influential label, and Irving Azoff had forged his new company, Azoff Management, into an aggregation of sixty talent managers who collectively represented more musical talent than any other company.

PART III

ROCK'S MIDDLE AGE, 1989–2004

CHAPTER EIGHT

NO NUKES AND
NICK OF TIME

While Stevie was finishing her work on Fleetwood Mac's *Tusk* album, I found a way of reconnecting with my sixties roots. In the years after the Alternative Media Conference, for most of the 1970s, I hadn't seen much connectivity between the work I was doing in the rock and roll business and politics. But while I was making a space for myself in the business, Jerry Brown had been elected governor of California in 1974 with support from the Eagles and Linda Ronstadt, whom he famously dated. In the 1976 presidential campaign, Jimmy Carter had been helped by an unexpectedly enthusiastic piece by Hunter S. Thompson in *Rolling Stone*. The Allman Brothers had performed a series of benefits for Carter, and former *New Yorker* rock critic Rick Hertzberg joined Carter's White House staff as a speechwriter.

My opportunity to join the fledgling political/rock nexus was triggered by John Hall, lead guitarist and songwriter for the band Orleans, a Woodstock-based jam band and two-hit wonder ("Dance With Me" and "Still the One"). John was **159** a first-rate guitarist and had written the song "Half Moon" for Janis Joplin, but he did not have a typical rock personality. He was tightly wound, cerebral, and almost professorial. He hired me to do PR for an ill-fated solo album, which was almost impossible to get ink for. Instead of getting pissed, John took it in stride and shifted my attention to his growing obsession with preventing the building of a nuclear power plant near his home in Saugerties, New York. John had been a physics major, with a keen interest in both science and politics, and gave me a crash course on the issue. Nuclear plants created cancer-causing waste products that were impossible to safely store over the long haul, and were at risk of having accidents that could be catastrophic. He and his fellow activists felt that government investment in less risky forms of energy such as solar and wind power, as well as the promotion of conservation, were much more desirable. Numerous grassroots groups had formed around the country to stop local construction of nuclear plants. *Rolling Stone* writer Howard Kohn had written a series of articles about Karen Silkwood, a technician at an Oklahoma nuclear plant owned by Kerr-McGee. In 1974 Silkwood had confided her concerns about plant safety to a reporter and shortly thereafter mysteriously died in a car crash. Found among her personal effects were tickets to an upcoming concert by Bonnie Raitt and Jackson Browne. When her parents needed money to fund a lawsuit against Kerr-McGee, they contacted Bonnie, who organized a benefit concert for them.

John put together a press conference with Bonnie Raitt, James Taylor, and Carly Simon to announce the formation of a group of artists opposed to the spread of nuclear power. It got a brief flurry of celebrity-driven attention, but the issue really exploded a few months afterward, in late March 1979, when there was an accident at the Three Mile Island nuclear power plant in Pennsylvania. Hall then organized a series of benefit concerts and created a foundation called MUSE (Musicians **160** United for Safe Energy), the board of which consisted of fellow musicians Jackson Browne, Bonnie Raitt, and Graham Nash, as well as several activists including Tom Hayden, Howard Kohn, and Sam Lovejoy, who had become an underground hero for having knocked over a tower in Massachusetts that was to have been part of a nuclear reactor.

Although John had been the sparkplug for MUSE, his relatively low standing in rock and roll's informal hierarchy limited his clout. Jackson Browne, then at the apex of his popularity, was the one bona fide superstar among the group and became first among equals. Hall and David Fenton, a former White Panther who had taken on an organizing role in MUSE, thought that the concerts should be the subject of a documentary film and wanted me to help convince the other artists. My first assignment was Graham Nash, who was considered the easiest guy to deal with. Crosby, Stills and Nash were all graduates of sixties bands and were steeped in protest politics. The hard part was getting them together again after their umpteenth breakup. Graham was mediator of fights between his mercurial bandmates and was a cheerful pragmatist who readily agreed that the impact of the shows would be far greater if a film were made. Bonnie was fine with what everyone else wanted.

But Jackson Browne was said to be against filming, apparently worried that it would be a nerve-wracking distraction. I did not know Jackson and my entire experience in films consisted of the minidocumentary we had made of the Foghat blues concert and of the unsuccessful attempt to develop *Rhiannon*. However, I was intoxicated with the notion of carving out a role for myself and had a zealous certainty that a movie was necessary to elevate the cause.

Jackson's house in Santa Monica was comfortable, albeit modest by rock star standards, and we drank coffee on chairs by the side of his swimming pool. At thirty-one Jackson was a formidable figure. He was good-looking as a model and he spoke with an articulate intensity in a series of eloquent run-on sentences that gave little room for response. His own connec-

161

tion to the issue had come through his admiration for Native American leader John Trudell, who was leading a fight in South Dakota against uranium mining in the Black Hills, sacred ground to several tribes. Somehow I found the nerve to launch into my monologue about the importance of a movie. I have no idea what I said that impressed him, but he agreed at once and never wavered.

The activists had insisted that the celebrated political filmmakers Barbara Kopple and Haskell Wexler shoot some documentary footage but after a few weeks, when Barbara and Haskell figured out that the only way to justify the costs of shooting the concerts was to make a concert movie, they both withdrew. Before she left Barbara had suggested the addition of former Paramount Pictures executive Julian Schlossberg as a coproducer, based on the indisputable fact that I knew nothing about making movies. Julian oversaw most of the shooting, all of the editing, and the rest of the postproduction and arranged a distribution deal with Warner Bros. films. I dealt with the artists, who each had approval over what parts of their performances were included. I had retained David Silver, who had organized the shooting of the Foghat blues concert, to do the same thing at the Garden shows. Schlossberg and I spent several months in an editing room trying to figure out exactly how to weave a political message into a concert film, and as a result we became the codirectors of the resulting film, *No Nukes*.

Jackson was known as a control freak who produced albums at a snail's pace. Landau loved to tell of having accompanied Jackson to the airport at the commencement of the tour to promote *The Pretender* album and Jackson's urgently urging Jon to book studio time to record a rewrite of the lyrics to the first verse of the title song. Landau had to gently remind him that the album was already in the stores. But in the context of the MUSE shows Jackson chose not to be an artiste but an organizer. He was relentless in persuading the Doobie Brothers and Bruce Springsteen to perform and in making sure they were treated with deference. I watched in awe as Jackson literally worked up a sweat vainly trying to persuade Joni Mitchell to perform "Shadows and Light" at one of the Garden shows. Very few artists of his stature would have put themselves in such a vulnerable position.

Jackson was uncharacteristically vigilant in meeting deadlines and budgets, which motivated most of the other artists to follow suit, but there were a few exceptions. James Taylor was famously obsessive about sound quality and spent many extra hours in the mixing room, nursed along by David Silver. Springsteen was my responsibility. *No Nukes* was completed before the advent of MTV, so filmmaking was still exotic in the rock world. It turned out that Bruce had an opinion about every single edit. One of the editors had a passing acquaintance with some members of the E Street Band and had done a cut of "Thunder Road" that had a labored series of close-ups of each musician. Bruce told him kindly but firmly, "I think my fans would like to see more of me."

Getting a rock and roll mix that conformed to the Dolby sound system used by high-end movie theaters took endless tedious hours. While waiting for the technicians to get various pieces of equipment to synch up, Springsteen entertained us with his collection of oldies. He was particularly enraptured by an obscure rockabilly single by one-hit wonder Hank Mizell called "Jungle Rock." Bruce played it over and over, grinning at the primal energy and the silly, infectious lyrics.

Although I loved basking in the Boss's charismatic presence I was simultaneously a nervous wreck, walking on eggs at every moment. When Julian and I had sold *No Nukes* to Warner Bros. it was based on a "presentation" reel, the highlights of which were a Jackson Browne/Bruce Springsteen duet of the Maurice Williams oldie "Stay" and Bruce's bravura theatrical performance of the Gary U.S. Bonds classic "Quarter to Three." The only problem was that we hadn't consulted any of the artists on

163

which songs we were using. Bruce was fine with the film of his own songs "The River" and "Thunder Road" but had serious reservations about the oldies, which he thought, out of the context of a full set, trivialized both his own artistry and the theme of the concerts.

No one else had Bruce's worries. The rest of us considered "Stay" and "Quarter to Three" to be the climax of the movie, a much-needed burst of joy balancing out the earnest but somewhat downbeat balance of the rest of the film. In the emotional context of finishing a movie, the idea of losing those songs seemed like a catastrophe. Julian had gotten his friend and colleague Elaine May to help with the editing, and they asked on a daily basis whether or not we had Bruce's OK yet.

In the meantime we added in a lot of political content, including interviews with Jackson and Graham and a small movie-within-a-movie documentary that fleshed out the rationale for the concerts. We screened our preferred version for Bruce at Goldwyn Studios in Hollywood. A number of Southern California activists, including Governor Jerry Brown, came to the same screening and it was obvious that the film's politics were palpable. I breathed a huge sigh of relief when Springsteen motioned me over at the end, hugged me, and told me we could use the oldies.

A similar problem with a Tom Petty song did not have as favorable an outcome. Iovine had asked me to double-team Landau to get Petty onto the Springsteen shows and when we looked at the film, there was a version Petty did of his song "Breakdown" that was one of the best things we had. But in the intervening months between the concerts and the completion of the film, Petty's career had taken off and he seemed a bit embarrassed to have what was then cutting-edge rock and roll comingled with a hodgepodge of the work of older artists. A hastily organized live recording from the concerts had been released for Christmas 1979 that included songs from such diverse artists as Sweet Honey on the Rock, Peter Tosh, Crosby,

Stills and Nash, James and Carly, et cetera, as well as Petty and Springsteen. "That album makes no sense. The songs have no connection with each other," Petty said to me angrily when I tried to persuade him to let us use "Breakdown" in the film. "Only a geek could like all of it, and it sounds to me like the film will be for geeks as well." Despite my entreaties to Iovine, Landau, Graham, and Jackson to try to change his mind, Petty would not relent. With only days to go until we had to hand in the final edit, Petty was in Japan and I desperately asked Jackson if it made sense for the two of us to fly there and give it one more try.

"Listen," said Jackson to me, playing the role of avuncular grown-up, "the film would be a little more excellent if Petty were in it. A little bit more excellent. But it's not going to be. And years from now when we talk about us, we will give each other a look with a smile that will feel very different from the way you are feeling now." Well, what could I say—Jackson fucking Brown trying to calm *me* down. And of course he was right.

In future years David Fenton would create the largest progressive PR firm, Fenton Communications; Steve Van Zandt of the E Street Band would organize protests against apartheid in South Africa; Jackson, CSN, and Bonnie would do so many benefits that they became known as the "usual suspects" in political circles; and I positioned myself as one of the few rock executives interested in progressive politics. But more importantly, I got to know Bonnie Raitt.

Bonnie came from several traditions—blues, folk, and, less obviously, show biz. Her father, John Raitt, had been a big Broadway star in the 1950s and moved to L.A., where Bonnie grew up in the environs of Hollywood. But she had also been raised as a Quaker and peace activist and was academically sharp enough to have attended Radcliffe. During her college years in Boston she became a prodigy at blues guitar and emerged at a precociously young age as one of the great white blues singers of her generation. She soon became a local favorite at Boston folk clubs, and she would retain the loyalty of many of the rock critics who first saw her in those days. She was signed in the early seventies to Warner Bros. Records and spent several cosseted years there as a critical darling and artist's artist. She befriended blues legends such as Mississippi Fred McDowell and John Lee Hooker and later introduced her baby-boom concert fans to Sippie Wallace. With her flashing red hair and dimples, Bonnie had a natural beauty. She was a died-in-the-wool sixties person who had no interest in fashion, drove a Volvo, never wavered from progressive political views, and was incapable of singing a song she didn't like. She had a warm personality, a gift for friendship, and a cutting, bawdy wit that made her extremely popular among musicians as well as people in the business.

Over the years Warner Bros. had tried a series of name producers to try to convert her cult standing to mass commercial magnitude. The idea was to rival the mass appeal of Linda Ronstadt, but Bonnie was too much the artiste to lend herself to the formulaic pop gems that made Ronstadt a commercial powerhouse. Ronstadt's producer, Peter Asher, carefully selected covers like the Rolling Stones' "Tumblin' Dice" or the Eagles' "Desperado." Bonnie's taste veered more to songs like John Prine's "Angel from Montgomery," which mesmerized critics and cult fans but which were insufficiently facile to appeal to pop radio programmers. She was already in commercial decline by the time of *No Nukes*.

After selling my half of Modern Records I started a management company called Gold Mountain Entertainment (*Gold Mountain* was an anglicized version of Goldberg). Ron Stone, who had comanaged Neil Young and Joni Mitchell with Elliot Roberts, joined me as a partner. One of our first clients was Bonnie Raitt.

This was 1986 and Bonnie's career was at a low ebb. Moreover, the record business was going through a slump, and Warner Bros. decided to drop several artists, including Van Morrison and Bonnie. She had been with the label for fourteen years and they didn't even want to release her ninth album, which at the time was called *Tongue in Groove*. Warner Bros. originally hoped that another label would pick it up, but the culture of the business was such that once a major label rejected an album it was almost impossible to sell it to another company. After some groveling from Ron and myself Mo Ostin reluctantly agreed to release it, even though she was off the label. It was made clear that the release was to help Bonnie do some touring but that little or no promotional support would be forthcoming. Bonnie did some additional recording to update the record, and with a kind of cocky gallows humor she decided to call it *Nine Lives*. The compact disc format had recently been introduced and was only made available to certain artists. It was a particular humiliation to Bonnie that her longtime label would not manufacture a CD of *Nine Lives* but made it available solely on cassette. It sold around sixty thousand copies.

Bonnie was thirty-seven years old and it was to prove very difficult to get another record company excited. Nonetheless, I felt that there had to be a place for Bonnie in the record business. She had breathed life into so many great songs. She had such an extraordinary signature voice. She was the least cynical of artists. She was one of the great live performers. I just felt that if I couldn't find a way to help get Bonnie's career on track, my own career would be meaningless.

Prince offered to produce her next record and recorded song demos in Minneapolis with Bonnie's vocal to demonstrate what he had in mind. The problem was that Prince had simply plugged Bonnie into lyrics that easily could have been written for pop/R&B sex bombs like Vanity or Sheila E. There was no connectivity with her artistic persona. Ron and I tried pitching her based on the idea that she was a great singer who just needed a break. That didn't work either. Every major label had passed on her except our last choice, Capitol Records, whose **167** parent company, EMI, had recently hired Joe Smith as chairman. Smith had started his career as a DJ in Boston, had been a senior executive at Warner Bros. when Bonnie had first been signed, and had a nostalgic affection for her. He agreed to a deal for the then modest recording fund of $125,000. I excitedly called Bonnie to tell her the news and she asked anxiously if I could find out whether or not EMI had investments in armaments. I paused only briefly as I thought about the fourteen labels that had passed on her and answered with uncharacteristic firmness. "No, I won't." It was the first and last time that Bonnie let me have the last word.

Bonnie asked Don Was, of the rock/funk group Was (Not Was), to produce her record. While we had been looking for a deal, Was had worked with her on a version of the song "Baby Mine" from the cartoon *Dumbo* for Hal Willner's compilation of cover songs from Disney films. He had been impressed by her unadorned acoustic club performances, and in contrast to the labored effects of the recent Warners efforts, Was's idea was to let Bonnie be Bonnie.

Bonnie embarked on the rigorous regimen of cleaning up her act, eschewing drugs and alcohol and riding a bicycle and exercising regularly and losing more than twenty pounds, which she would never regain. As had been her approach on previous albums she culled the works of songwriters she admired, such as John Hiatt, but uncharacteristically she also wrote a song of her own called "Nick of Time."

Youth and aging had long been twin obsessions of rock and roll artists. The Who had memorably sung, "Hope I die before I get old." The Beatles' Paul McCartney was still in his twenties when he wrote the musical question "Will you still need me when I'm sixty-four?" By the mid-1980s, various male rockers had written about the rock and roll spirit confronting middle age. Dylan's song "Tangled Up in Blue," released in 1975 when he was all of thirty-four years old, was filled with a wistful nostalgia for lost youth. (Joan Baez's "Diamonds and Rust," about her time in Greenwich Village with Dylan, had come out a few months earlier when she, too, was thirty-four.) Jackson Browne wrote "Running on Empty" in 1977, when he was all of twenty-nine ("In '69 I was twenty-one and I called the road my own"). Bob Seger was only thirty-one when he released the wistful and nostalgic "Night Moves." Dennis DeYoung's "Desert Moon," written when he was thirty-seven, recalled the high school lover who got away. Don Henley was thirty-seven when "Boys of Summer" came out ("I saw a deadhead sticker / on a Cadillac / a little voice inside my head said, Don't / look back, you can never look back"). Springsteen wrote, "So you're scared and you're thinking / that maybe we ain't that young anymore" for "Thunder Road" when he was twenty-seven, and at thirty-five his biggest album, *Born in the USA,* included "Glory Days," a song about the folly of trying to act young. Most notably, John Lennon was forty when he recorded the album *Double Fantasy.*

Bonnie was one of very few rock and roll women to tackle the subject. I teared up as I heard the second verse of the simple demo on my car cassette player of the song "Nick of Time," with its wistful lyrics about watching her parents age. Bonnie was thirty-eight, just eight months older than me.

The press was great from day one. A lot of the people who wrote about music were baby boomers and a lot were Bonnie Raitt fans, especially the women. Both Letterman and Leno booked her promptly and she did a headline tour. Bonnie had a natural rapport with journalists. Although fiercely protective of her privacy regarding personal matters, when it came to her career or politics or the culture in general, she made them feel as if they were in on the joke and they loved her for it.

This was before the days when SoundScan measured over-the-counter sales, but *Nick of Time* shipped around fifty thousand copies and there were reorders of five to ten thousand a week.

The first track released to radio was the Hiatt song "Thing **169**

Called Love." The very grittiness of Bonnie's voice that made her fans connect emotionally made her too "left field" for pop radio. There were a few rock stations that had played Bonnie's previous records and these were the natural conduit to her core fans. But rock radio had always programmed music that was overwhelmingly male. This bias meant that even as hard-edged a rocker as Joan Jett needed pop singles in order to reach a mass audience. "Thing Called Love" peaked at number eleven on the rock radio charts, which was not high enough to make for any kind of breakthrough.

Fortunately, MTV had recently created a second channel called VH1. Although the letters *VH* stood for "video hits," the initial target audience was adult rock fans. As had been the case when MTV first started, there was, at first, a shortage of artists with decent videos to help define the new format. The young, good-looking jazz singer Harry Connick, Jr., would be one beneficiary of VH1's launch. Bonnie Raitt would be another. The video for "Thing Called Love" cost around fifty thousand dollars and featured Bonnie performing the song in a club while flirting with her friend, actor Dennis Quaid. The rock stations only played the song for three or four weeks, but VH1 kept the video in rotation for months and the reorders kept coming. The next track, "Have a Heart," hardly got any radio play at all, but again VH1 was there.

After six months it was finally time to go with "Nick of Time." There was no chance of getting rock play on such a slow song, but with sales now over a quarter of a million I had hopes of getting the Capitol promotion department to work it at the "adult contemporary" format. However, I encountered the classic passive-aggressive resistance from radio promotion people who needed to pay lip service to an "image artist" but who had no appetite for a "work record." It was the same old problem. Radio stations needed vast passive audiences. The "adult" stations revolved their programming around famous-name stars

like Barbra Streisand, whose names were familiar to the 90 percent of their audience who played music in the background. We needed their broadcasts to reach the 10 percent or so of their listeners who were real music fans. We didn't get them.

But then the Grammy Award nominations came out and to our amazement Bonnie received four nominations, including one for Best Album. Historically, the Grammys had not been critical to creating success for rock and roll artists but had flowed to artists after they already had a big record. But this one time, being an "artist's artist" paid off.

I told Bonnie and the people at Capitol not to expect anything other than the "Female Rock" category as an actual victory. Bonnie invited her dad to sit next to her. John Raitt was then in his early seventies but he maintained his broad shoulders and beefcake physique. He had the narcissistic personality that many actors are noted for but also was a warm and witty guy. Like Bonnie he was a nonstop talker. Conversations between the two of them often consisted of a series of interruptions.

On arriving at the Shrine Auditorium where the ceremony was held, I was pleasantly surprised to learn that she had already won the Best Duet for a track she had cut with John Lee Hooker for his album *The Healer* during the pretelecast awards. Bonnie sat next to her dad. My fiancée Rosemary Carroll and I sat next to Ron Stone and his wife, Ellen. Early in the telecast, when Bonnie won the Female Rock Award, we were exultant. She had won a Grammy and mentioned our names on TV. We assumed that the Traveling Wilburys would win Album of the Year, and it was a surrealistic shock when Bonnie won that one as well. It was absurd when she also won the fourth for Best Female. She ran onstage barefoot and said, "Wake me up when this is over."

The telecast was live on the East Coast and delayed three hours for the West Coast, so her mother didn't yet know what had happened. Bonnie's mother always had been a pessimist. Bonnie called her from backstage to tell her the news and I felt by Bonnie's pauses that her mom was searching for the cloud **171** that went with the silver lining. But there was none. Not that night.

The Grammys functioned like a monster version of VH1. It exposed tens of millions of baby boomers to the voice her fans had long loved. The album went gold (five hundred thousand copies) the week before the Grammys, a milestone we were thrilled with. In the next few months it sold an additional three and a half million, becoming certified as quadruple platinum. And she still never had a radio hit on that album.

In the years after the *No Nukes* shows John Hall became more involved with local politics around the Woodstock area. In 2006 he ran for Congress, an underdog in a previously Republican district. Jackson Browne and Pete Seeger did fund-raisers for him upstate. My family hosted an event for him at our house, along with Steve Van Zandt and Bonnie Raitt. "Of all the musicians in the *No Nukes* work," Bonnie told me as she reflected on the path his life had taken, "John was the one who could best talk specifics and the technical side of the nuclear issue. He was the most suited for politics because he could take the heat in an argument, staying as articulate as he was passionate. We always felt he could run for office and do great things." Steve Earle joined Jackson in a concert for John at Town Hall. "We need a guitar player in Congress," Jackson said while exhorting the crowd to elect his old friend. In November John was elected from a previously Republican district, helping the Democrats regain control of the House of Representatives for the first time in more than a decade.

In 2007 as I was writing this chapter I was watching cable news coverage of the Democratic primaries and saw a clip of Bonnie and Jackson singing a duet of "Angel from Montgomery" at a rally for John Edwards in frigid New Hampshire. A few months earlier they had made a video shown on YouTube of the old Buffalo Springfield song "For What It's Worth" with **172** a visual message that warned against the renewed corporate pressure on Congress to build nuclear power plants. When I called Bonnie as I was finishing this book, she had just helped raise money for John Hall's reelection campaign and was deciding which Senate candidates she was going to support in 2008. It was more than twenty-eight years after the *No Nukes* concerts. She wasn't kidding. She never was.

CHAPTER NINE

SMELLS LIKE NIRVANA

My relationship with Kurt Cobain was the most important of my professional career and had many contradictory levels. I was his manager, where I did a decent job, and his friend, where I failed. I saw him as a great songwriter and singer, a visionary about the imagery of rock and roll, as someone who both coveted and reinvented superstardom and who hated many of its by-products. He was an extraordinarily thoughtful and supportive friend, a loving husband and father, as well as a tormented depressive and textbook druggie. Like that of all the great rock icons, his place in history is the result of a combination of his own talents and ambitions and the timing and context in which he did his work.

During the eighties, while I had been building my business and working with relatively mainstream rock artists like Stevie and Bonnie, the punk-rock cultures that had started with the MC5 and Patti Smith and flowered in England with the Sex Pistols and the Clash had created a passionate subculture among punk-rock fans who preferred sparer, **175** more iconoclastic, more political rock and roll. The music was buttressed by the passionate support of rock critics, who, having been marginalized in influence by corporate rock radio, delighted in an alternative rock universe in which their opinions actually mattered.

In 1989 I had married music business attorney Rosemary Carroll, who was a fan of punk and postmodern rock and who focused my attention on the fact that there was an entirely new generation of rock fans for whom the only credible rock and roll was that which came from this alternative culture.

I knew that in order to effectively deal with this new strain of rock artists I needed a colleague steeped in the subculture, and I connected with John Silva, whose clients, House of Freaks and Redd Kross, were struggling on indie labels. John combined a rock nerd's encyclopedic knowledge of punk with a fierce work ethic. In an echo of the underground rock scene of the late sixties, punk rock had spawned new media addressing its audience, including some fledgling alternative rock radio stations (the first of which was KROQ in Los Angeles) and press (ranging from militant mimeographed fanzines such as *Maximumrocknroll* to the slicker *Spin*). There were several hundred small record stores around the country whose consumers primarily consisted of punk-rock fans, clubs that featured the artists live, and agents who booked them. They were all outsiders to the corporate rock world and, in many cases, reveled in their isolation. Having won new major-label deals for John's clients, we set about to sign a bigger act together. After a few false starts we hit the mother lode when Sonic Youth signed with us just prior to their first major label release, *Goo*, on Geffen Records.

Sonic Youth, led by singer Kim Gordon and her husband and lead guitarist Thurston Moore, were among the most respected alternative rock bands. Their impeccable sense of punk style was augmented by a brilliant and innovative musicality. They had made numerous indie records and developed a passionate fan base all over the world, which was reflected and buttressed by the near unanimous adulation of rock critics. Sonic Youth were also great nurturers of the indie scene in general, having given supporting slots to dozens of punk bands.

Sonic Youth's decision to sign with a major label like Geffen had significant reverberations in the indie world, almost like when Dylan went electric. A lot of punk's biggest artists, such as the Dead Kennedys, Fugazi, and Bad Religion, had defiantly started their own companies and championed a DYI ("do it yourself") ethic. Although some of the punk fanzines accused them of selling out, Sonic Youth's integrity was such that the damage was very limited. They told me that they saw their role as that of musicians and that as long as they maintained artistic control of their work, they were happy to get the benefits of financing and marketing from major labels. It was the art that mattered to Sonic Youth, not the business structure that delivered it.

But Kim and Thurston were a bit daunted by the corporate environment of Geffen and wanted managers to help them deal with it. While John handled the day-to-day needs of the band, I handled relations with "the business." The artists I had worked with previously were all approximately my age or older. While I felt wistful that I was now an avuncular figure, less connected to the cultural impulses of the artist, I felt confident that I finally had internalized the various aspects of the business and could actually do a fully competent job both in handling the corporate worlds and knowledgeably advising the band about the mainstream business while John was an aficionado about every aspect of the burgeoning alternative culture.

Sonic Youth was continuing to discover and showcase new bands, which is how John and I met Nirvana. It had become clear to me that Kim and Thurston had their finger on the pulse of postmodern rock and roll, and when I heard their enthusiasm for Nirvana I knew we should try to sign them.

Nirvana had released a couple of singles and an album **177** called *Bleach* (which had been recorded for the princely sum of eight hundred dollars) on Sub Pop Records, a Seattle-based indie label that had begun by releasing singles from local bands at exactly the time when exciting rock and roll was being created by Seattle rockers such as Soundgarden, Mudhoney, and Nirvana. The subculture of college radio and edgy rock critics soon took notice. By the time Nirvana came to Gold Mountain's L.A. office, *Bleach* had sold over thirty thousand copies, which was a significant number for an indie rock band at that time.

Silva had already gotten to know them. "John had a track record in the indie scene," Nirvana bass player Krist Novoselic recalled when I asked him about it as I was writing this book, "and he didn't come off as a shark." And unlike many indie bands who would flirt with the more established rock business, Nirvana had no such ambivalence. They had retained Alan Mintz of the big-time L.A. law firm Ziffren, Brittenham and Branca, and he set up meetings with managers. "We had worked really hard in the underground universe and were ready to take the next step. We liked that John was working with Gold Mountain. We figured out that Mountain meant 'berg,' which meant you. Gold Mountain felt like it was buzzing. There were all these managers working on different kinds of acts. It felt professional. It was compelling." Most of all, we had credibility with Nirvana because we represented Sonic Youth.

John and I met with Nirvana in the Gold Mountain offices on Cahuenga Boulevard West near Universal City. Drummer Dave Grohl was the youngest and best-looking of the three and by far the quietest. He eschewed all talk of business and became animated only when he asked me to tell him Led Zeppelin stories—especially those about John Bonham, whom he idolized. (During the time I managed the band, Dave displayed none of the conceptual brilliance that would later become apparent when he formed the Foo Fighters. He usually opted out of business conversations, insisting, "I'm only the drummer.")

Most of the talking at the initial meeting was done by Krist

Novoselic, an affable giant of six foot six with a keen interest in progressive politics. We spoke briefly about my volun-
teer work as chairman of the local ACLU board, where I had
put the political energy that had been kindled by the *No Nukes*
experience. For most of the meeting the singer, Kurt Cobain,
short and slight, sat quietly, but when he chimed in, always in
a low and understated voice, I quickly recognized his authority
among the three of them. As had been the case when Jimmy
Page spoke during Led Zeppelin meetings, it was clear that Kurt
had the final say.

Sensitive to the fact that many punk-influenced bands preferred indie labels, I asked the band if they wanted to stay with
Sub Pop. I thought it might be an emotional tie, since the press
reports on the Seattle scene made a big deal about the virtue
of indie labels. Kurt emphatically answered, "Absolutely not."
I later was told that although they had affection for some of
the individuals at Sub Pop, they felt they hadn't been paid in
a timely manner and were sick of reading press that gave Sub
Pop credit for the "Seattle sound." Moreover, Krist remembered, "We heard that Sub Pop was talking about doing a deal
with Columbia and we recognized that we were gonna be on a
major label anyway, so we wanted to cut out the middleman."
The band wanted to reach more people. "And you know who
wanted to reach more people the most of the three of us?" Krist
asked rhetorically. "Kurt. He wanted to make it big."

A&R people from Columbia, Charisma (part of Virgin),
Capitol, Geffen, and MCA all wanted the band, which meant
that we would have the leverage to get them an excellent deal.
John went through the motions of meeting with A&R guys at
other labels who had previously refused to return his calls, but
we had a strong preference for Geffen from the beginning because they had shown sensitivity to the alternative culture in
dealing with Sonic Youth. David Geffen had said that "record
companies all do the same thing. What it comes down to for an
artist is—who do they want to talk to?" He had spent top dollar **179**

to get the most sought-after A&R people in the rock business, one of whom, Gary Gersh, had presciently been focusing on alternative rock. Gary had persuaded the marketing department to hire Ray Farrell, a salesman who formerly worked at SST Records and was intimate with the buyers at the indie stores that specialized in punk. Geffen also had a specialist in alternative rock radio, Mark Kates. Former rock critic Robert Smith was head of marketing. Overall the atmosphere at Geffen Records was far more likely to be sensitive to the rebellious artistic attitudes of the members of Nirvana than any other competitor. Gersh didn't take any chances and asked Kim Gordon to call Krist to vouch for Geffen's integrity. "That impressed me," Krist cheerfully acknowledged.

Eddie Rosenblatt, former head of sales at Warner Bros. Records, had been chosen by Geffen to be president of his label. "People come out of Eddie's office feeling like they have had a warm bath," Geffen told me once, adding pungently, "I am not a warm bath." When Rosenblatt assured me that Geffen would give the band creative control and match the highest offer (I think it was a three-hundred-thousand-dollar advance for the first album, fifteen points, plus three points paid to Sub Pop to get out of the way), it was a done deal. (In the wake of Nirvana's success lawyers for the next wave of indie rock buzz bands would often be able to negotiate reversion of the master recording to artists after a term of seven to ten years, but at the time of the Nirvana deal, such terms were not attainable.)

Even though the Geffen deal was excellent for an indie band, it provided only around fifty thousand dollars in cash for each member of the band after a provision was put aside for recording costs, management fees, legal fees, et cetera. Prior to that deal Kurt hadn't even been able to afford his own apartment and had been sleeping on Dave Grohl's floor. Given the A&R buzz about the band there was also competition among music publishing companies to sign them. Susan Collins and Kaz Utsunomiya of Virgin Music had been particularly aggressive in pursuing the band and Kurt took a liking to Kaz, a native of Japan who had previously lived in the UK and who expressed his enthusiasm in heavily Japanese/British-accented aphorisms. (A typical Kaz saying was "Sub Pop is actually subpop," uttered with an intense earnestness that implied he was revealing a secret of the universe.) As I recall it, we got the band a two-hundred-thousand-dollar advance in return for a copublishing deal in which copyrights fully reverted back to the band after seven years.

Although Nirvana wasn't contractually required to consult with him, the band felt comfortable enough with Gersh to discuss production with him. *Bleach* had been recorded by a Seattle engineer named Jack Endino, whom they did not want to use for the forthcoming album. They accepted Gary's suggestion of Butch Vig, who had recently produced the Smashing Pumpkins' debut album, *Gish,* one of the more successful alternative rock albums as of that moment.

In the spring, in Los Angeles, Nirvana recorded the album that became *Nevermind* during which time the guys periodically dropped by the office. On most such occasions Kurt was well aware of the powerful effect of his smile and bright blue eyes. (As British journalist Everett True wrote, Kurt had "something about him like you wanted to find out what the secret was.") But on occasion Kurt seemed depressed and weighed down by the world. One day when Kurt was moping around, Silva asked him why he was in such a bad mood and Kurt snapped back at him, "I'm awake, aren't I?"

The album cover was, like everything else connected to Nirvana, Kurt's idea. He had seen a picture of a baby underwater and made a drawing that showed a baby being lured by a dollar bill on a fishhook. Kurt also sketched detailed designs for Nirvana's T-shirts and posters.

In June, when the band finished *Nevermind,* Gersh felt that the sound was muddier than it needed to be. He convened a meeting at Geffen with the band, John, and me at which he **181** urged that they try a remix and suggested Andy Wallace. (Later, after *Nevermind* had become a huge success, there was some carping about the slick sound of the album. At the time Wallace was not known for commercial records but for having worked with heavy metal bands like Slayer.) Kurt shrugged and agreed to try Wallace as long as there was no implied commitment to use the results. When he heard the remixes he immediately approved them, resulting in the final version of *Nevermind*.

We all wanted "Smells Like Teen Spirit" to be the first track released to radio, because it seemed to sum up the essence of the band. We assumed that the song would have a life span of six to eight weeks, after which the label would release the more midtempo song to try to cross over to a wider audience.

I finally saw Nirvana in concert when they were booked as the opening act for Dinosaur Jr. at the Palace. Standing in the back by myself on the periphery of the audience I was completely overwhelmed. Although most of the songs the band played were from an album that had not come out yet, Kurt had a mystical and powerful connection with the audience that took my breath away. After years of increasing cynicism about what rock and roll had turned into, I felt the naive excitement of a teenager. Somehow Kurt Cobain was able to be both on the stage and in the audience, rocking the crowd out and yet also among them. It was only then that I realized that Kurt Cobain was not just a smart, quirky rock artist but also a true genius. I shivered at the thought of how casually I had taken the signing of them. What a lucky break!

To make sure that Nirvana was not seen within the offices of the record company as the sole province of the indie-rock partisans, we booked them into the old-school rock club the Roxy, which was down the street from Geffen Records on Sunset Boulevard. Dozens of Geffen executives joined several hundred of Nirvana's L.A. cult fans for a fully realized preview of what Nirvana was about to become. Kurt was worried that the show had been impaired because of a couple of broken guitar strings. I was not bullshitting him when I reassured him that the band had nonetheless been spectacular. Afterward I walked across Sunset with several of the Geffen people. Robin Sloan, who was in charge of videos, gushed, "This must have been how people felt when they saw the Who in clubs in the mid-sixties." But the excitement was still in the context of a subculture. Krist recalled feeling that although "Faith No More and Jane's Addiction had broken ground for us, it was really generous of Geffen to print up fifty thousand copies. That was a lot for an indie band."

A couple of days later the band shot the video. As has been widely chronicled, Kurt had a concept for the "Teen Spirit" video that he called "pep rally gone bad." In fact, he wrote out every single shot. When Rosemary and I and our one-year-old daughter Katie visited the set at CMT Video in Culver City, the members of the band themselves were serene, waiting in between takes. The director, Sam Bayer, was worried that the crowd of extras had overreacted to the band's lip-synched performance and that some of the "punks" looked pretty stoned. But the video benefited from the authenticity of the fans' glassy stares.

An early edit of the video had a shot of Kurt looking right into the camera while he walked toward it, making a direct connection with the audience. In one version Bayer took it out because he thought it was too "commercial." He told Silva he thought it was the worst shot in the video. Tellingly, Kurt disagreed and insisted that the shot be put back in, delaying completion by a day. He wanted his fans to be able to look him directly in the eyes.

Prior to the album's release Nirvana had joined a Sonic Youth tour of Europe. Like a lot of American punk bands, Sonic Youth was bigger overseas than in the U.S., and they headlined a minifestival tour, playing in front of thousands of people per night in Holland, Germany, and the UK. Thurston had the foresight to ask filmmaker Dave Markey to document the tour, **183** which was later released under the title *The Year Punk Broke*. Perhaps Thurston saw what Nirvana was about to become or just had a general sense of the coming tectonic changes in the mass rock audience. He prophetically told Markey, "Nineteen ninety-one is the year that punk finally breaks through to the mass consciousness of global society." The film documented what would be among the last innocent weeks of prestardom life for the members of Nirvana. More than any time in my career before or since, the rush of events to come seemed to take over. I always felt like I was on a bicycle chasing a car I could only catch up with at traffic lights.

"Smells Like Teen Spirit" got an incredible reaction right away. At a Guns N' Roses concert in New York the crowd, a mainstream rock audience with little if any awareness of the punk subculture, roared in approval when the first few chords of "Smells Like Teen Spirit" were played over the public address system. WFNX in Boston played the entire album from beginning to end, the kind of thing that was done for established bands like the Rolling Stones, not indie bands on their first major label album. I remember sitting next to Mark Kates at a marketing meeting in which he read a series of dozens of comments from alternative radio and retail. There were stores that had a waiting list of people who had advance-ordered the record. "Nothing like this has ever happened before," the usually unflappable Kates said, unable to mask his astonishment.

Peg Yorkin, who led a group called the Feminist Majority, told me that the female alternative group L7 was doing a Rock for Choice concert with the rock band Sister Double Happiness, and that they wanted Nirvana to headline. Silva already knew about it. Dave Grohl was friends with a member of L7 and had promised that Nirvana would do the benefit. Although Nirvana was not as overtly political as Fugazi or the Dead Kennedys, they were committed to certain ideals, especially those related to personal freedom.

A few days later I was told that a fourth group, Hole, had

been added to the show. Hole, whose lead singer was Courtney Love, was a client of Rosemary's. Courtney had persuaded Kim Gordon to produce the band's first album, *Pretty on the Inside,* which had been released a couple of months earlier to an encouraging reception by punk-rock fanzines. Rosemary said that Courtney was not happy with the length of Hole's set. Echoing Silva's attitude, I told her that she should be grateful that Hole was in the show at all. Rosemary said prophetically, "You don't know Courtney."

Within days of the September 24 release of *Nevermind* it was clear that Nirvana was not just another cult band. The casual and earnest guys who had cheerfully worked on the album in relative obscurity were about to become rock stars with a velocity that the music business had not experienced since the days of *The Ed Sullivan Show.*

The week after the album's release Nirvana headlined at the Palace in Los Angeles. Afterward, as hundreds of people milled around, basking in the glow of his performance, Kurt was invisible to most of them, so new to rock stardom that his face and body language weren't yet recognizable signatures. I was quietly standing next to him, savoring the moment. Kurt leaned over to me and in his voice that on the surface sounded like a slacker's but with a precision that no slacker ever had, alluded to the first round of press interviews that Nirvana had done in anticipation of the release of *Nevermind.* "We've been getting a lot of questions about politics." He paused to choose his words carefully. "I don't mind talking about politics a little, but I don't want it to be the main thing people write about us. I want them to know we have a sense of humor."

I knew he was right. It was important that the band not come off as pretentious, but I didn't know what he wanted me to do about it. It seemed like one of those pointless conversations about the press for which there could be no answer but empathy. But Kurt patiently continued, "I was trying to figure out why we were getting these questions and so I read the bio **185** the record company hands out, and in the second paragraph there's a reference to punk politics."

I was supposedly the middle-aged old-school rock pro, but in thirty seconds I had gone from feeling avuncular to feeling like a novice. Kurt had made a connection that had eluded me. He understood that Nirvana, within the first few days of the release of *Nevermind,* was no longer limited in appeal to the punk-rock press. Until the day he died, he would always make himself available to the fanzines who had supported Nirvana as an indie band, but he also focused on the larger rock and roll audience. He understood that mainstream writers, who were not intimate with Nirvana's roots, would be heavily influenced by the press kit. The changes Kurt suggested were made and the tone of the feature articles about the band immediately reflected them.

Eddie Rosenblatt had come to the Palace with Axl Rose, who wanted to meet Kurt. Eddie was in an impossible position. Guns N' Roses was Geffen's biggest artist of the previous year and Nirvana was the hot band of the moment. As Eddie feared, Kurt had absolutely no interest in meeting Rose, who had the kind of macho rock persona that Kurt detested. In order to prevent Eddie from looking impotent, I walked Kurt out of the dressing room, and then gave Eddie two passes that could get him and Axl into the dressing room, where Eddie could pretend to be surprised that Kurt wasn't there.

Up until this point Krist had been doing most of the interviews. Kurt created the materials behind the scenes but had chosen to stay out of the spotlight. He couldn't even figure out what he wanted to call himself, experimenting with spelling his name Kurdt and Curt, before deciding on the original. Shortly after the record came out Kurt decided that he would be the primary spokesman for the band.

There was a period of around two weeks in which I still felt my job was to make sure that all of Geffen focused on the album, not just the indie rock lovers. Having been disappointed by the limited exposure MTV had given to Sonic Youth's "Kool Thing," I huffed and puffed to get MTV to increase the video rotation from medium to heavy. It took MTV only a week to increase it. I had asked, in one meeting, if the pop promotion people could try to get Top 40 airplay in at least one market, say Seattle. I was lectured by the head of pop that Seattle's Top 40 station was not particularly daring and focused on artists like Paula Abdul. I ran into Daniel Glass, president of SBK Records, on a plane. SBK had gotten pop airplay on the British rock band Jesus Jones, who, while not as hip and cutting-edge as Nirvana, were more alternative than not. Daniel told me that KRBE in Houston had been the first pop station to play it and I called the Geffen promo guy back with this info.

Other than making me feel good these efforts were a complete waste of time. The record was magic and needed no human help. "Smells Like Teen Spirit" was no mere setup track. It went to number one on three radio formats, alternative rock, mainstream rock, and even Top 40, and became the most played video on MTV. *Nevermind* had come out in October. By Christmas it was number one, having overtaken Michael Jackson's *Bad*. The year before *Nevermind* commercial rock had been reduced to one of its most uninspiring iterations, melodic, predictable ballads that were poor copies of Bon Jovi and Def Leppard, bands like Poison, Winger, and White Lion, whose videos revolved so much around their coifs that they were known as "hair bands." The closest thing to authenticity had been Guns N' Roses, which featured undeniable musical brilliance but which perpetuated a macho stereotype for rock stars. Suddenly, that era was over.

Shortly after the sales for *Nevermind* exploded, *The New York Times* business section asked Geffen president Eddie Rosenblatt what the label's marketing plan had been for *Nevermind* after the album had made its quick and improbable journey to number one. Rosenblatt said that the "plan" was "Get **187** out of the way and duck." We all loved that line. Real men did not take credit for the accomplishments of others' genius.

The band, Silva, Gersh, and I met at Jerry's Deli in Studio City to decide on the second single. After an interlude in which Kurt unsuccessfully tried to convince Gary to sign Mudhoney (the band, close friends of Nirvana from Seattle, would end up signing to Warner Bros.), we went over the possibilities and agreed it should be "Come as You Are," both because it was a great song and on the theory that a ballad might reach an even wider radio audience. At the last minute Kurt cautioned that the song sounded a lot like a Killing Joke song. We all told him not to worry and he shrugged and went along with the decision, but as usual he had a point. Killing Joke later sued for copyright infringement, although they didn't prevail.

Nirvana's tours were booked by the William Morris Agency's Don Muller, who was one of the creators of the Lollapalooza festival and was highly attuned to the alternative rock world. I was convinced that Nirvana should headline their own shows and eschew the traditional step of opening for bigger acts. I did not think they belonged on Lollapalooza, comingled with other "alternative" acts. It seemed to me that Nirvana could put their own shows or festivals together if and when they wanted to. Kurt wanted to emulate Sonic Youth and offer exposure opportunities to obscure artists that were his favorites. Two that were on the tip of his tongue were Captain America, a melodic Scottish alternative band, and Björn Again, an ABBA cover band. However, just prior to the release of the album the band was offered eight dates at ten thousand dollars a night to open for the Red Hot Chili Peppers. This fee assured that, with their spare production and road crew, plenty of money would be left over for Nirvana at a time when we weren't sure what their income would be for the year, so we accepted. By the time the Chili Peppers dates actually occurred, I kicked myself that we had underpriced them.

Not long thereafter, Cliff Burnstein, one of the managers of Metallica, called to propose a three-act stadium tour with Guns

N' Roses, Metallica, and Nirvana. There was a lot of money on the table. I knew that Kurt really liked and respected Metallica but that he detested Guns N' Roses, and I told Cliff that I was sure the band would pass. Kurt indeed had no interest, even after Metallica's lead guitarist, Kirk Hammett, called to try to cajole him into doing it. For the rest of their brief career Nirvana was a headliner.

Nirvana played one more time in the indie-rock venues that had nurtured them before they went on to conventional arenas, and I went to see them play the four-hundred-seat Chicago club the Metro on October 12. In the dressing room before the show, a tall blonde introduced herself to me as Courtney Love of the aforementioned band Hole. She said she had come to keep her friend Lori Barbero, of the band Babes in Toyland, company. Lori apparently was the latest alt-rock woman who had a crush on Dave Grohl. I was charmed by Courtney's self-effacing affect, although I would soon learn that she had numerous personas that she could call up at will and this would be the last time I would ever see Courtney as quite such as underdog. After the show in the dressing room I saw her sitting on Kurt's lap, a somewhat comical image given how much bigger she was than him. But there was nothing comical about their connection. From that night on they were inseparable.

Until Courtney came along, Kurt had never spoken to me about anything personal. I had been positioned as the old-school music-biz guy with liberal politics and Silva was the one closer to the band's age and culture. But in part because Rosemary was Courtney's longtime lawyer I connected with her easily and recognized quickly that this was no one-night stand. Since Silva had a strained relationship with Courtney, I became the prime management contact for Kurt. Kurt was moody, prone to depression, and capable of quietly scathing bitterness. Similar to Jimmy Page, Kurt could create a distancing aura that made me feel that I needed to walk on eggs when I approached him about even the most routine issues. But most of the time Kurt had a **189** sweetness and gentility about him. He rarely took out his bad moods on the people around him. And when the clouds of despair parted, his scintillating smile and wry humor could light up any room. Kurt and Courtney often visited our L.A. house on weekends and Kurt, who had been a teacher's assistant in a kindergarten when he was younger, loved to play with Katie.

MTV requested (it was more like a demand) that the band record a few songs "live" in their New York studio before Nirvana embarked on a European tour. Their research told them that there would be an immediate hunger for more Nirvana, and MTV was going through one of their periodic aggressive moves against possible competition (moves that assured that competition was never able to develop). Given the hegemony over the rock business that MTV had during those years, I was a firm believer in kissing its ass.

I joined the band for the first week of the European tour. As we walked through Heathrow Airport, Dave Grohl noticed that cassettes of *Nevermind* were on sale at one of the newsstands and he exclaimed in shock, "I never wanted to be in a band whose records were sold at airports." But he was. *Nevermind* had exploded in the rest of the world with the same velocity as it had in America.

Silva had hired a wild-eyed fanzine writer named Anton Brooks as Nirvana's indie UK publicist. Anton, terrified that Geffen's UK distributor, MCA, would somehow pollute Nirvana's integrity, asked me to go to the label with him to "explain the philosophy of the band." Although I felt wholly inadequate to the task, I explained, to Anton's relief, that Nirvana would not want to talk to the British dailies (the ultimate pop media) and would restrict themselves to music writers and TV appearances. Anton needn't have worried. Like record company executives the world over, the MCA people were perfectly happy to cooperate with the wishes of an artist who was selling lots of records and in any event, Kurt had very clear ideas about whom he did and didn't want to talk to.

On the *Top of the Pops* TV telecast Kurt deconstructed the already ubiquitous "Smells Like Teen Spirit" by crooning the vocal like a combination of Jim Morrison and Mel Tormé. The producers of the venerable BBC show grumbled with distaste that the band had not delivered a note-for-note replica of their hit single.

The next day they taped *Friday Night with Jonathan Ross.* Ross was known as the David Letterman of the UK because of a TV manner that, in the context of British chat shows, was considered edgy and eccentric. However, Ross's producers were not sufficiently tuned in to musical culture to have the slightest idea how Nirvana was different from a typical pop group. The guest prior to the band was a novelty performer from France who worked under the name Monsieur Mangetout. His "act" consisted of literally eating metal, in this case a small laptop computer. As if to comment on the surreal nature of appearing on such a broadcast, Nirvana, without alerting the TV producers, substituted "Territorial Pissings" for "Smells Like Teen Spirit" and ended the performance with Kurt breaking his guitar and Dave kicking over the drum stand. Ross lamely quipped that Nirvana was "available for birthday parties and Bar Mitzvahs." John struggled to keep a straight face as the irate production crew of the TV show berated him for Nirvana's supposed lack of professionalism.

Kurt was already obsessing about how to reinvent Nirvana in light of the unexpected speed of the band's commercial ascent. He would keep its integrity and commitment to the punk subculture while simultaneously maintaining a relationship with the bizarrely large worldwide audience his music was creating. Above all, he wanted to avoid repetition now that the international rock media covered everything the band did. In Europe, keenly aware that he was being photographed, he wore a different shirt for almost every show. Back home in the U.S. he wore a dress for the band's first appearance on MTV's metal show *Headbangers Ball,* a frontal assault on the macho metal stereotype. Not all stereotypes were rejected. Nirvana exulted in breaking guitars and drum sets onstage with regularity.

Courtney's very presence was a metaphor for the end of one era in the band's life and the beginning of another. She influenced Kurt to leave Alan Mintz and have Rosemary represent his interests. She introduced Kurt to Kevin Kerslake, who then did four Nirvana videos. Often Courtney was just a mouthpiece for what Kurt himself wanted and didn't want to ask for.

Like many bands Nirvana had agreed to divide equally all of the band's income, including songwriting royalties, despite that fact that Kurt wrote all of the songs by himself. This practice was based on the reality that for many bands, the cost of recording ate up most or all of the royalties generated by record sales, the cost of traveling consumed most of the touring income, and songwriting royalties ended up being the one source of disposable income. "I thought we would be as big as the Pixies," Kurt explained to me on the day he announced that he wanted the full reward of being the actual songwriter now that it was clear that the other members of the band would make plenty of money from other sources in light of their huge success. Kurt floated the notion of being paid as the sole writer.

A confrontation about songwriting income is one of a manager's worst nightmares, but the other members of the band didn't fight about it. "Look," Krist told me after having discussed the matter with Dave, "Kurt does write the songs and I have no problem with him getting paid for it." (In 2006, when Courtney sold half of Kurt's publishing for nineteen million dollars, it became clear what a big issue this was.)

Although I knew Courtney could sometimes be difficult, it was also obvious to me that Kurt's attachment to her was no passing fancy. It also was clear to me that she was genuinely talented. Shortly after *Pretty on the Inside* came out, Rosemary and Courtney had started looking for a manager for Hole. Gary Kurfirst, who had made his reputation as manager of the Talking Heads, was a leading candidate and the matter was going to get resolved soon. I asked Kurt one night if he would like it if I managed Hole. "That would be awesome," he said with a palpable sense of relief, as if I were validating the relationship.

Silva insisted that I be the one to deal with Courtney, to which I readily assented. To me it was a no-brainer. Rosemary was irritated at me for swooping in and using my relationship with Kurt to circumvent the orderly process she had set in motion of choosing a manager for Hole. I explained to her that this was simply something I felt I had to do to protect my own business. "Why do you think," she asked angrily, "that if Gary Kurfirst managed Hole he would try to manage Nirvana?" I answered with true conviction, "Because I would." I hired Courtney's friend Janet Billig to help.

As had occurred with Nirvana, my appreciation for Courtney's talent increased even more after I had signed her as a client. I sat in a BBC radio studio while she recorded three new songs with an acoustic guitar. One of them was "Doll Parts," which, while rooted in the anger of her earlier work, had a level of subtle songwriting sophistication beyond anything she had previously written. I just loved it. (In 2007 "Doll Parts" was performed by the main character in the Oscar-winning film *Juno,* a reflection of the brilliance of the song.)

Courtney's involvement with Kurt, her flair for self-promotion, and the general music-biz excitement about grunge created immediate major-label desire for Hole. Armed with "Doll Parts" it was easy to get Gersh and Rosenblatt to offer a state-of-the-art deal from Geffen. With some misguided encouragement from Courtney the rock press reported the deal as having been for a million dollars, but it wasn't. It was around three hundred thousand for the first album and a good royalty similar to the Nirvana deal.

The weekend in January that Nirvana did *Saturday Night Live* for the first time was a turning point that put into sharp relief the heroin problem that was to haunt Kurt for the rest of his life. (Kurt dyed his hair pink for *SNL,* which somehow added a sense of dissolution.) Courtney called me at home on a Saturday morning and asked me to please get Kurt five thousand dollars in cash so they could do some "shopping." Ron Delsener, who promoted the New York concert Nirvana was doing that week, was unfazed by my request even though it was the weekend, but I felt pretty weird and uncomfortable as I shlepped up to his office and then delivered the package of hundred-dollar bills to Courtney at the hotel. Abruptly, the dark cloud of drug excess had entered the band's life. I was confronted by the baroque façade of lies and the awful glassy-eyed deadness that regular heroin use creates. I resolved to confront them about it, but first we needed to get through the next few days in New York.

Backstage at *Saturday Night Live* I was told that Kurt had nodded out several times earlier the same day during the photo session the show did for all of its guests. But the sweet intoxicating perfume of Zeitgeist trumped everything, at least for the moment. Victoria Jackson, one of the cast members, told me that her friend Weird Al Yankovic had asked her if he could set up a phone call with Kurt to discuss a parody of "Smells Like Teen Spirit." This seemed like a good idea to me. The success of the band had come so intensely and rapidly that it was important for the band to show it wasn't drinking its own Kool-Aid. Jackson called Weird Al from her dressing room, and after listening to a five-minute pitch, Kurt gave a groggy assent.

Nirvana performed capably on *Saturday Night Live,* but Kurt and Courtney both seemed stoned before and after. Kurt's mother, Wendy, who had flown to New York to see the show, hovered in the dressing room. In her mid-forties, Wendy was blond and had the same flashing blue eyes that Kurt did. Courtney explained, "She was the prettiest girl in Aberdeen" as a teenager. Kurt was glassy-eyed and exhausted and wanted to go back to the hotel. "Don't you want to go to the party?" Wendy asked with childlike longing. Kurt looked as if he had the weight of the world on his shoulders and mumbled quietly, "You go, Mom," and quickly departed with Courtney to return to their hotel room.

Right after *SNL*, *Nevermind* went back to number one on the album charts, around the same time it went double platinum. Johnny Rotten was quoted as saying, "Nirvana has done what the Pistols and the Clash could never do. They've taken punk to the top of the charts."

Nirvana did some more taping for MTV. Kurt seemed completely out of it, almost nodding out, but he insisted on seeing how MTV was editing the performances. He would slump almost unconscious with eyes closed until they played him an edit. Then he would utter crisp, decisive directions about which camera angle to use and exactly when to cut to the next one. He glanced up at me with a defiant look that seemed to say to me, "Get off my back. I've got this under control." Invariably his choices were right. Then he would slump again until it was time to look at the next song. (MTV aired the versions exactly as Kurt directed.) I was torn between awe at the clarity of his judgment about Nirvana's music and image and a deep anxiety and sadness that he was willing to act stoned even in such a semipublic situation.

Nevermind was named the best album in the annual "Pazz and Jop" poll of rock critics published in *The Village Voice*. It was the first time since the seventies that an artist had so utterly ruled both the sales charts and the hearts of rock critics. I got great satisfaction out of working for an artist that my former rock critic colleagues so respected, but such moments of triumph were marred by the behind-the-scenes drama.

One minute Nirvana was a punk band who barely could afford cheap apartments, the next they were number one. One minute the heaviest drug backstage was beer, and now suddenly there was heroin. I was shocked and disappointed. I had hoped to have seen the last of cocaine and heroin, forgetting that merely because baby-boom rockers were now flocking to AA, that didn't mean that the next generation had the same body of experiences or was in the same frame of mind. It was even weirder for Silva, who had lived in a state of grace with mature alt-rockers like Sonic Youth.

To underscore the urgency of the situation the San Francisco–based rock magazine *BAM* published a piece that noted the rumors and signs of Kurt's heroin use. When the band got back to L.A., John and I decided not to let William Morris book any more dates and I asked around for suggestions on whom we could get to help us do some sort of intervention on both Kurt and Courtney. David Geffen put me in touch with Tim Collins, the manager of Aerosmith, a band that had successfully dealt with heroin addiction through therapy. Collins recommended a counselor in Los Angeles who had been an addict himself. The counselor affected the look of a rock star, sporting long hair and tattoos. I was a little nervous when he quickly dropped the names of several other bands he had worked with, but he clearly had experience that very few people had: helping famous rock musicians deal with drug and alcohol dependency.

Silva, Gersh, Rosemary, Janet Billig, and Hole guitarist Eric Erlandson and I met the counselor at Cedars-Sinai Hospital. The idea was that we would do the intervention and then consult with Dr. Michael Horowitz, who was head of chemical dependency at the hospital and ran some programs that could be helpful.

I forget the pretext under which we got Kurt and Courtney to come, but the plan for the intervention collapsed almost immediately when Courtney revealed that she was pregnant. The tattooed counselor pulled Gary, John, and me aside and said, "I have never dealt with something like this before—a couple, a pregnant woman . . ." He stammered, unable to finish his thought, and then said anxiously, "I've got to go." The three of us looked on in amazement as he stepped into the elevator and the doors closed. We never heard from him again.

We tried to reason with Kurt and Courtney, telling them

we loved them but that we were very worried that they were killing themselves or ruining their lives. Dr. Horowitz tried to give clinical advice, suggesting to Courtney that it was not a great idea to have a baby while dealing with addiction. "You're not *telling* me to have an abortion, are you?" asked Courtney, her voice rising with her trademark hostile whine, "I mean, I'm pro-choice but that doesn't mean that anyone has the right to tell me to have a fucking abortion." Horowitz suggested that it might not be safe for the baby, and Courtney, who was only six weeks pregnant, went into a confrontational mode. "Is that a medical fact or is that just your opinion? I want to see it in a medical book." She was interested in medical facts, not a sermon. Horowitz sheepishly acknowledged that at this early stage of pregnancy a woman could discontinue heroin with no physical or psychological damage to the fetus. Courtney looked triumphant as she towered over the doctor seated at his desk. The next day Kurt went into the first of many visits to rehab. I felt somewhat lame and somewhat helpless, but at least we had done something.

Courtney did stop using heroin and was healthy for the duration of the pregnancy, a fact that was to prove very significant later on. She became a patient of Dr. Paul Crane, who was Rosemary's longtime OB/GYN and who saw Rosemary through the births of our own children. Crane assured us that if she followed the recommended protocol the baby would be born healthy.

Kurt and Courtney got married on February 24, 1992, in Waikiki, Hawaii, where they had stopped on the way back from Australia and Japan. It was a very small wedding, attended by the other band members and some of the crew. In the early months of his marriage Kurt spoke about Courtney in terms that were almost courtly, a fantasy of the way he imagined a loving husband would talk about his wife. (Kurt's own parents had divorced when he was nine, which he always regarded as one of the central traumas of his life.) Kurt was deeply offended by anyone who registered disapproval of Courtney. "I can't imagine that people would think it wouldn't bother me," he said in a plaintive tone of voice, as one married guy to another. "I feel as any man would if his wife were insulted."

Kurt's sentiment about his marriage was reflected in a cover story on the couple in the teen girl magazine *Sassy*. "In the last couple months I've gotten engaged and my attitude has changed drastically," Kurt explained. "I can't believe how much happier I am. At times I even forget that I'm in a band, I'm so blinded by love. I know that sounds embarrassing, but it's true."

Kurt, alas, was not willing to go to AA meetings. Rosemary and I had become friends with Buddy Arnold, who had created the Musicians' Assistance Program (MAP) to help advise and facilitate musicians with drug problems on treatment and therapy. Buddy had been a jazz saxophonist and had played with the Buddy Rich and Stan Kenton bands in the 1950s, and as a younger man he had been a junkie whose addiction landed him in jail on more than one occasion. At sixty-five years old Buddy was bald, wizened, and spoke with a thick New York Jewish accent, but he always had a twinkle in his eye. He had been sober for more than thirty years and was devoted to helping other musicians get sober. (According to Steve Earle, John Coltrane had twice kicked heroin on Buddy's couch.) Buddy had the kind of compassion for druggy rockers than only could have come via his own experiences, and he never dropped names. Both Kurt and Courtney immediately felt comfortable with him. One day Kurt solemnly told me that I was "really haimishe" and then giggled, admitting that Buddy had taught him the Yiddish word for "down to earth" and suggested he surprise me by saying it in his northwestern drawl.

Kurt, like most junkies, would often insist that he did not have a problem and that other people were wildly exaggerating his use of drugs. When those of us around him rolled our eyes at that tactic, he insisted that he had frequent, terrible, and debilitating stomach pains. It was possible that his stomach really did hurt, but a series of L.A.'s best stomach doctors were unable to figure out what the problem was. Buddy recommended that Kurt see a Dr. Robert Fremont, another sixty-something Jewish character who had an expertise in dealing with drug addicts. Kurt didn't feel guilt-tripped by Fremont, who periodically gave him injections that relieved the pain in his stomach. "He's a compassionate man," Kurt told me earnestly. I asked Fremont what he gave Kurt and the doctor sighed. "Don't tell him," said Fremont, "but it's a placebo." In other words the psychological effect of getting any kind of shot was making him feel better. I never could figure out if Fremont was being candid with me or if he was giving Kurt a less benign drug, but there is no question that Kurt always felt and acted better after he saw him. Courtney soon became a patient of Fremont as well. One day when I asked how she was doing, he said gruffly to me, "Well, let me put it this way—thank God neither one of them is Jewish."

Courtney called me one day from the Australian tour, alarmed because Alex MacLeod, their road manager, had gone bungee jumping, gotten drunk, and was pounding on their hotel room door yelling at Kurt to stop acting like a spoiled child. Kurt grabbed the phone from her and reiterated that he felt it was ridiculous for him to be treated like this by his own crew. Of course, I immediately offered to have Alex fired, but even in his exasperation Kurt wouldn't hear of it. By the next day they had made up and Alex stayed with the band for the rest of their career. In his own way Kurt both gave and inspired deep loyalty.

Rolling Stone belatedly decided they wanted to do a cover story. Kurt had long complained that *Rolling Stone* had ignored the punk rock culture he cherished, writing little if anything about bands such as Mudhoney, Jesus Lizard, Vaseline, and the Melvins that he considered the most creative and authentic of the previous several years. Kurt preferred the sensibility of *Spin*, which had put Nirvana on the cover the week that *Nevermind* **199** came out. But always somewhat in thrall to rock iconography, he consented to do the interview. When it came time to take the cover photo, Kurt had second thoughts and I got a hysterical call from the Geffen Records publicist. There is nothing more aggravating for a publicist than the possible loss of a cover story and since the problem occurred at the last minute, she would be blamed by the magazine for having screwed up their newsstand plans.

When I got him on the phone, Kurt grumpily reiterated his deep distaste for the passé version of rock culture that *Rolling Stone* was then associated with. I told him that I supported him no matter what he did but that he had to understand that if he didn't pose for a picture, the band would not be on the cover. From the tone of his response I assumed that he would not take the photo, but the next day he did. He posed for the photo wearing a T-shirt that said, CORPORATE ROCK MAGAZINES STILL SUCK. At the time I thought it was pretty silly. How could he credibly be putting down a magazine that he was posing for? But with the passage of time the photo has become one of the defining images of Kurt Cobain's concept of rock and roll. It was a way of telling his fans he was playing the game but on his own terms.

The *Rolling Stone* piece had an unfortunate put-down of Pearl Jam from Kurt ("jumping on the alternative bandwagon"). Kurt was clearly irritated that Pearl Jam was selling as well as Nirvana had. On one occasion he called me to complain because he thought Pearl Jam's videos were played more frequently than Nirvana's. On another occasion he did the same kind of tabulation of letters to the editors of *Rolling Stone* regarding the respective bands. But when they saw each other face to face, Kurt and Eddie Vedder always got along, and at one point there was a party at which they slow-danced across the floor with each other to publicly dissipate any residual tension.

In January the Democratic governor of Washington State, Booth Gardner, made a "state of the state" speech in which he proudly boasted that Washington was the "home of Nirvana." A couple of months later both houses of the Washington State Legislature passed a bill that would have made it illegal for kids under eighteen to attend concerts that included profanity. Given the nature of the rock culture in the nineties this effectively would have kept younger teenagers away from all of the music that had made Seattle famous. Like the rest of the Seattle rock community the members of Nirvana were livid about the legislation, believing it would suffocate much of the state's rock culture. One day, after getting off the phone with an outraged Krist, I called the governor's office, identifying myself as Nirvana's manager. After thanking him for his generous reference to the band in his speech, I asked Gardner to veto the bill, pointing out that it would demoralize and damage the very culture that had produced the music for which the state had become internationally famous. The governor countered, "I'm planning to sign it but don't worry, it will never become law. It's not constitutional." Why then, I asked, was he signing it? "To send a message." What message, I queried, did he think he was sending? It seemed to me that the message that musicians would receive was that their work was not respected by politicians. "It's going to send a message that I think should be sent," the governor answered. But what *was* the message? "A message that needs to be sent," he repeated, evidently bereft of any further talking points. (The law was indeed rejected by the Washington state courts.)

A news report from Colorado revealed that two teenage boys had raped a girl while singing the Nirvana song "Polly," which Kurt had written as an indictment of violence against women. A distraught Kurt asked if there was anything he could do for the victim. Somehow he and Courtney were able to send her some flowers, and Kurt issued a statement pleading with his fans not to misinterpret his lyrics.

The spring was a relatively calm time. Kurt and Courtney were renting a place in Hollywood where Kurt and Kevin Ker- **201** slake began the project of assembling footage for the long-form video that would eventually be called *Live! Tonight! Sold Out!* He had an inexhaustible appetite for international TV coverage of the band's unlikely ascent to superstardom. Working doggedly and enthusiastically on the video, he carefully culled quotes from dozens of hours of footage to create his own definitive narrative for his fans about Nirvana. His other creative juices were expressed in a pile of ornate, dark, and trippy drawings and poetry fragments that were strewn everywhere around the living room.

A right wing group in Oregon had gotten sufficient signatures for an antigay ballot initiative called Proposition 9 that would, among other things, prohibit gays and lesbians from being schoolteachers. The director Gus Van Zant, who lived in Oregon, was one of the leaders in the Oregon gay community opposing the measure and contacted me through mutual friends about Nirvana doing something to raise money for the "No on 9" Committee. Rosemary and I had a dinner for Gus to meet Kurt and Courtney, and Kurt promptly committed Nirvana to headline a benefit concert in Portland.

The success of Nirvana affected many of us around the band. Sub Pop suddenly was worth millions of dollars. Gary Gersh, after years of credible near misses, finally had his first big signing. Silva, after years of dealing with club owners, now added promoters of arena shows to his Rolodex and would soon sign the Beastie Boys to Gold Mountain. (In subsequent years he would build a great management company of his own, representing the Beasties and the Foo Fighters, among others.) I accepted a job as senior vice president of Atlantic Records. My deal with them included the sale of half of Gold Mountain to the company and an understanding that while at Atlantic I would continue to be available to comanage Nirvana, Hole, Bonnie Raitt, and Sonic Youth for the next year.

As a way of paying homage to Kurt I signed two of his favorite bands, the Scottish band Captain America (who changed their name to Eugenius) and the seminal Seattle grunge band the Melvins, whose first Atlantic album Kurt agreed to produce.

Because of the huge commercial success of *Nevermind* Thurston wanted to include five Nirvana songs in the final version of *The Year Punk Broke,* even though every other artist except Sonic Youth was limited to one.

Not long after, Kurt was working on video for the song "Lithium." The video primarily consisted of footage taken at the Halloween show, but Kurt, always looking for a way to make his videos more interesting, told me he wanted to add some live shots from other sources to add some exciting images to the "live" video. One of these was a ten-second shot of Kurt being carried around on Krist's shoulders from the European footage shot for *The Year Punk Broke.* That clip was actually from the song "Negative Creep" and had been shot a year before the Halloween show, but Kurt figured out a way to edit it into a montage that flowed beautifully and added a sense of playfulness and anarchy to the "Lithium" clip.

Before I had started managing Hole, Courtney had decided to cooperate with journalist Lynn Hirschberg for a profile in *Vanity Fair.* Over several months I kept hearing about their conversations and finally went to a photo session Courtney did for the article, which Lynn also attended. Courtney was riffing in her brilliant free-associative way about a movement in the Northwest rock community called the riot grrls. As I watched the New York killer journalist pretend to be Courtney's fawning girlfriend, I had a sinking feeling.

Hirschberg's article hit the newsstands the same day that Frances Bean Cobain was born. Frances was born in perfect health, as Courtney and Dr. Crane had predicted. However, the *Vanity Fair* piece proved to exceed all of my worst nightmares.

What set the article apart from a PR mistake and made it a full-fledged crisis was the following section:

> *Twenty different sources throughout the record indus-*
> *try maintain that the Cobains have been heavily into*
> *heroin. . . . "It was horrible," recalls a business associ-*
> *ate who was traveling with them at the time. "Courtney*
> *was pregnant and she was shooting up. Kurt was throw-*
> *ing up on people in the cab. They were both out of it."*

There was a huge moral difference between doing heroin before she knew she was pregnant and after. I was appalled that *Vanity Fair* would print the latter charge based on an unnamed source without giving the subject any opportunity to comment. There weren't "twenty people" in the record business who even *knew* Kurt and Courtney. And based on what Dr. Crane had told us, I was convinced that the pregnancy had been handled responsibly once Courtney became aware of her condition.

I asked Eddie Rosenblatt if he would visit the hospital with me, figuring that the appearance of her record company president would make Courtney feel like less of a pariah, and he immediately agreed. "Of course, I love babies. Let's go right now," he said brightly. Courtney appreciated the visit but wept copiously as she talked about the piece. "Don't give me any of your optimistic shit," she moaned. "I will never recover from this." Although the future would show that she could recover from quite a bit more, her sense of foreboding was on the mark.

Within days the social services agency of Los Angeles County put a legal hold on Kurt and Courtney's custody of their daughter on the theory that they had already endangered her. A Xerox of the *Vanity Fair* article was stapled to the complaint. To me, the notion that any possible good could be served by taking Frances away from her parents and enmeshing her in the legal system was grotesque and immoral. This was the downside of the celebrity culture at its worst.

Courtney was convinced that Dr. Horowitz was out to get her, a fear that seemed justified when the *Los Angeles Times*

somehow got hold of files from the hospital describing her behavior there. In December, Courtney would sue Horowitz and Cedars-Sinai Hospital for this breach of confidentiality, a case that was quickly settled. But the urgent priority was to get Kurt and Courtney custody of Frances.

Rosemary found an attorney specializing in L.A. family law who explained to us that the agency would release temporary custody of Frances to a family member while they went through the legal process to determine if Kurt and Courtney were fit parents. Typically in cases like this a grandparent did the trick, but neither Kurt nor Courtney trusted either of their parents. Kurt's mother, Wendy, was the most sympathetic, but she seemed too fragile to deal with the public pressure. His father, Don Cobain, having abandoned him when Kurt was nine, was persona non grata, as was Courtney's father, Hank Harrison, who had left Courtney's mother, Linda Carroll (no relation to my wife), when Courtney was three. Linda Carroll had married several subsequent times and had an extremely contentious relationship with her daughter. She flew down to Los Angeles supposedly to "help," but when I met with her she spent the first half hour giving me a defensive monologue about how difficult and rebellious Courtney had been as a child to justify having sent Courtney to reform school when Courtney was caught shoplifting at the age of twelve. She then pitched me the idea that she herself should have permanent custody of Frances. I was appalled. I concluded that Linda was not to be trusted.

Courtney decided on her half-sister Jaime Manelli, a student at the University of Oregon. They were not particularly close, but Courtney shrewdly assessed that Jaime would be controllable because she needed money. I offered her five thousand dollars to come to L.A. for a month and be the official guardian of Frances, on the condition that she would live in an apartment we rented for her a few doors down from Kurt and Courtney's house in Hollywood and would defer to the real parents while cooperating with the legal process.

Jaime turned out to be a friendly, if slightly ditsy, girl who **205** gave us no problems at the outset and satisfied the legal requirement. Courtney had to report in weekly to Children and Family Services, where she irritated the social worker the first time she was asked if she was seeking employment and answered grandly, "I'm a rock star." After a few weeks Jaime came to see me. "You know, Courtney has always belittled me and she has been doing it more and more the longer I stay here," she complained. Supposedly, Courtney in a nasty fit of temper had told Jaime that her "real" father was someone other than the man who had raised her (apparently an invention but nevertheless hurtful). I made as many sympathetic noises as I could, although it occurred to me that she had known what Courtney was like when she agreed in the first place. Jaime doggedly continued, "As this thing drags out it's delaying my ability to graduate; I'm not sure how long I want to keep doing this." A light bulb dimly flickered in my mind. "Would it be easier for you to deal with that stress if we paid you another three thousand dollars?" I asked. Jaime beamed. "That would be great," and the subject of Courtney's "abuse" did not come up again.

The supermarket tabloid *The Globe* ran a front-page story headlined "Rock Star Baby Born a Junkie," with a picture of a deformed baby that they said "might look like" Frances. A week later Axl Rose, perhaps feeling diminished by Nirvana's commercial and critical eclipse of Guns N' Roses, said onstage that Kurt and Courtney should go to jail.

Kurt insisted that Nirvana keep its scheduled appearance at the Reading Festival in England. He had himself rolled out onstage in a wheelchair to mock the reports of his supposed druggedness and proceeded to perform an energetic and powerful show. At the end of the performance he persuaded the crowd of forty thousand to chant, "We love you, Courtney."

While Rosemary dealt with the lawyers, I worked the press. It seemed to us that if the authorities had been adversely influenced by the *Vanity Fair* piece, they might be equally influenced by something positive. I turned to Robert Hillburn of the *Los*

Angeles Times, who considered Kurt a member of the highest
level of artists in the rock pantheon. The custody challenge was
still a secret when I called Hillburn and offered him a scoop: the
first postchildbirth interview with Kurt and Courtney. A few
days later his piece appeared, portraying the couple as lucid,
normal, loving parents.

A week or so later Hillburn, having figured out my agenda,
called and said in a tone that was as close as he got to anger, "I
feel like I was used." I was temporarily speechless. Hillburn had
busted me. I started to formulate a response, but Hillburn filled
the silence with a gentler tone of voice. "Well—if I'm going to
be used, it might as well be to help a genius."

As part of the strategy to deal with the custody challenge,
Kurt and Courtney both went into therapy, supervised by Dr.
Fremont. Kurt went into rehab. He had a few more days to
go when I got an urgent phone call from MTV president Judy
McGrath insisting that Nirvana perform on the MTV Awards,
which were to be broadcast live from L.A. I told her that it was
not a good time for Kurt, which I assumed came as no shock
to her, since she was well aware of the adverse consequences
that had occurred in the wake of the *Vanity Fair* piece. But over
the next couple of days Judy called several more times, with
increasing pressure in her voice.

Calling Kurt in rehab was not my proudest moment, but my
role in his life certainly included the obligation to advise him
about major issues in his career, and I had been dealing with
MTV long enough to recognize the implied threat that came
with the pressure. Kurt agreed right away, but the melancholy
in his voice was unmistakable. The punk rock persona he had
originally created dreaded the idea of being on an award show,
any award show. But, of course, he was also the guy who spent
hours thinking up and writing ideas for music videos and who
kept careful track of how many times Nirvana videos were
played on MTV.

Judy called me again the day of the rehearsals for the MTV **207**

Awards and said worriedly, "My staff tells me he is singing some song about rape." I assured her that Kurt was passionately against violence toward women. I got him on the phone backstage and he explained that he had indeed written a new song called "Rape Me," which wasn't about rape but one of Kurt's signature vague poetic musings. He thought it would be much cooler, for both the band and MTV, that Nirvana debut a brand new song on the award show instead of doing one from an album that had already had so much exposure. Judy would later say that her reaction was a mistake. She had been spooked by the word *rape* and hadn't wanted to answer for it. Kurt grudgingly agreed to do "Lithium" instead. I felt like I'd let him down.

There was a backstage area at the award show in which performers and presenters could sit and eat before the show. Rosemary, I, Kurt, and Courtney, with the month-old Frances in tow, found a table that turned out to be next to one at which Axl Rose and his girlfriend, the model Stephanie Seymour, were sitting. Courtney leaned over and asked in a voice drenched in sarcasm, "Do you want to be godfather to our daughter?" Perhaps to break the tension, or perhaps sarcastically, Seymour asked Courtney sweetly, "Are you a model?" Courtney instantly replied with a question of her own. "Are you a brain surgeon?" At this point a glowering Axl Rose, who was accompanied by two huge bodyguards, shouted at Kurt, "Shut your bitch up or I'll knock her to the pavement." For the next fifteen minutes or so the people at the two tables studiously ignored each other, and then we went our separate ways. As the night wore on, Kurt got increasingly upset as he reflected on Rose's boorish threat.

Just after Kurt and Courtney left the table to go to one of the dressing rooms, Jaime, who technically still had custody of Frances, ran up to me beaming with a big smile on her face. "I've got to say, for all of the problems I was having, this is really great seeing all of these stars up close. I can't believe I was just now sitting rapping with Whitney Houston." I couldn't wait to share this one with Courtney.

Nirvana won two awards. To make his own statement about the banality of the occasion Kurt had a Michael Jackson impersonator accept the first one. The second time Nirvana's name was called, the band accepted it and Kurt solemnly told the television audience, "Don't believe everything you read."

The next day, based in part on an affidavit from Dr. Fremont, L.A. County finally granted Kurt and Courtney permanent custody of their own daughter, providing they took regular drug tests.

The day after that was the "No on 9" benefit in Portland, Oregon. At one point Kurt talked to the audience about the purpose of the event, describing the incident at the MTV Awards at which Axl had threatened Courtney and decrying the evils of violence and prejudice against women and gays. Suddenly a fan rushed up onstage, yelling something at Kurt. Security guards rushed over to remove him, but Kurt motioned for them to let him go and gave the fan the microphone. "Kurt, man," the teenage boy said, "I love you and I love Axl. Why do I have to choose? I just want to rock." I thought the kid had a point, and there were a few scattered cheers. Kurt reclaimed the microphone and spoke gently but firmly. "You can't say it's okay to take a woman to the pavement, or be prejudiced against gays, and still really appreciate what we do." The audience roared its approval. The kid nodded in stoner understanding, shook Kurt's hand, and walked off the stage unaided. Again, I was dazzled by Kurt's ability to be at one with his audience.

The next night Nirvana did a benefit in Seattle for the Washington Music Industry Coalition, the group that had been formed to fight censorship in response to the dopey legislation with the nebulous message from Washington State politicians.

My assistant Lisa Derrick was a member of a small feminist group called the Bohemian Women. They had booked a night at the small Hollywood club the Café Largo, and Lisa asked **209** me if Courtney would be interested in playing acoustically. I thought it would be really good for Courtney to do something small on her own, and she played a riveting acoustic set that included "Pennyroyal Tea," a new song written by Kurt, all the more remarkable coming from a man because it was convincingly written in the voice of a woman who had an unwanted pregnancy. The Nirvana version of the song would appear on *In Utero*.

One day in late September I got a copy of the finished Weird Al parody that he called "Smells Like Nirvana." I messengered it to Kurt, and when I didn't hear back from him I was wracked with anxiety that he might have hated it and might have blamed me for talking him into allowing it. (Any artist can record a cover version of a popular song but approval is required to rewrite the lyrics for a song parody, permission that Kurt gave after I had put him on the phone with Weird Al backstage at *Saturday Night Live*.) After another twenty-four hours I called him and chatted about various trivialities until finally I casually asked what he thought of the video. "I laughed my ass off," Kurt answered, and my blood pressure returned to normal.

Then we got word from Buddy that Dr. Fremont was dead. Kurt wept when he heard the news. Officially the word was that he had had a heart attack. A journalist later told me that Fremont himself was an addict who actually died of a drug overdose and implied that the shots he gave Kurt had had narcotics in them. All I know is that while he was seeing Fremont, Kurt didn't seem stoned or nod out in front of people and seemed to be capable of enjoying his life. After Fremont's death Kurt was never able to find a doctor he was really comfortable with.

Melodrama was soon to return. Two British journalists, Victoria Clarke and Britt Collins, were peddling an unauthorized biography of Nirvana called *Flower Sniffin', Kitty Pettin', Baby Kissin', Corporate Rock Whores*. The title came from one of the Nirvana T-shirts Kurt had designed. Collins had edited a Nirvana fanzine called *Lime Lizard* but in some interviews the two conducted in the Northwest, they were given credence to Lynn Hirschberg's description of Courtney and had even interviewed Hirschberg herself. To Courtney this meant that they were out to demonize her. Kurt, who was hypersensitive to attacks on his wife after what the couple had recently been through, developed an animus toward the writers as well and asked Rosemary if there was anything she could do to stop the book from being published.

Steve Hochman of the *Los Angeles Times* informed me that Britt and Victoria had played him tapes from their message machine of Kurt and Courtney physically threatening them. I found Kurt and Courtney on the road and asked them what the fuck they were doing. Courtney started ranting about how evil the writers were. I screamed at them that it was impossible for me to help them if they did idiotic things like this. I was going to deny that it was their voices on the tape and if anyone asked them they were to deny it as well. The couple contritely agreed. I called Hochman and said that Kurt and Courtney denied having left the phone messages. "Danny, I've interviewed both of them and I know their voices," Hochman said quietly, in a tone that seemed to beg me not to bullshit him. Like his mentor Hillburn, Hochman was a real rock fan. I felt guilty but I had to protect my clients. "Steve, you asked me for a comment and this is my comment. I am denying it is them. You have to print that they denied it if that's what I say." Steve sighed, knowing I was lying but sympathetic to my dilemma, and he dutifully ran the denial.

The New York Times reporter let me get away with a little more spin, printing my quote that the messages on Clarke's machine were "either a prank that someone has played on these women or this is something they are fabricating to publicize an unauthorized biography."

Notwithstanding my plea to them not to speak to reporters, Courtney couldn't resist granting a telephone interview to *Entertainment Weekly,* which reported that during their chat they could hear Kurt in the background yelling at her not to talk to journalists.

Regarding Britt and Victoria's book Courtney said that at first they had seemed like supportive fans but then "all of a sudden their whole agenda changed. All of a sudden they're calling people who claimed to have slept with Kurt. Britt got ahold of one of my ex-boyfriends. They went to Kurt's aunt Judy [Milne]—all they do is talk about me. What do you think of Courtney? What do you think of what she wears? What do you think her influence on Kurt is? They're obsessed with the fact that me and Kurt got married and had a child. It's very sexist and stupid. They're discussing me as if I'd never had a band or made any sort of contribution to my culture, which is, you know, punk rock. Their whole point is that I'm not an artist, all I am is this crazy, dysfunctional, manipulative person."

Under a barrage of threatening letters from Rosemary and an apparent lack of enthusiasm about the quality or marketability of the book, Hyperion eventually canceled publication of the biography.

For the next couple of years it seemed like Courtney always was in the midst of a feud with some woman. At various times she was livid with Nymphs singer Inger Lorre; Kurt's ex-girlfriend, singer-songwriter Mary Lou Lord; and her old friend, Babes in Toyland lead singer Kat Bjelland (Courtney claimed that Kat stole the "kinderwhore look" from her), among others.

Kurt was always worried about money. He had no interest in luxuries, but he was afraid of being broke as he had been only a few years earlier. Every time a tour was planned he asked me to prepare a breakdown for him of what he would personally net "after taxes and after commissions." One day he called me, annoyed that Courtney had just ordered a Lexus similar to one I had bought a few months earlier. "Do I need to have a car that expensive?" he asked. I figured that maybe Courtney had told him that in order to be taken seriously as a star he needed

a certain kind of car. I carefully answered, "Kurt, if you are asking me whether or not what kind of car you have has any relevance to your career—it doesn't. This is totally a personal decision. Get whatever car you want or don't have a car at all. Your career is based on your music." Kurt replied, "That's what I thought," and he canceled the order. Notwithstanding the periodic problems between them and within each of them, my take on Kurt and Courtney was and remains that they were deeply in love with and protective of each other.

In August, Kurt began producing the Melvins album up in Seattle. He would do it in pieces, in part because the Melvins took their time writing the songs. Kurt liked the idea of producing the Melvins, but the reality of being a producer was weird for him. Although he had idolized the Melvins' live intensity and uncompromising punk energy, he never went into the studio without complete songs on his own records. At one point Buzz Osborne asked Kurt to write some songs with them. Kurt was back on drugs at the time, but he had not lost his critical faculty when it came to music. "I'm not going to do that," he said to me. "I'd just end up writing the songs myself." He wanted to save his best songs for his own recordings.

Given the occasional complaining about how the magnitude of *Nevermind* had distorted Nirvana's life and aesthetic, I was surprised when Kurt told me he wanted to do a fourth video for the album, to the song "In Bloom." As with the other videos he had a vivid and specific idea, which was to spoof the contrived rock performers in the era of *The Ed Sullivan Show*. He obsessed about how to get the precise amount of visual distortion into the picture to simulate black-and-white TV images of the mid-sixties. It became one of MTV's most popular videos.

In December the Scottish band Eugenius, whom I had signed at Kurt's suggestion, came to L.A. as part of an American tour with Mudhoney to play a concert at the Palace. Kurt was in an ebullient mood the night of the show and suggested that he and I pose for a photo. He earnestly said, "We're throwing our first party. We're inviting the guys from Mudhoney and Eugenius **213** over to our new place and want you guys to come." Always terrified about getting lost driving around L.A., I carefully wrote the directions down. It turned out that the house was on a little known side street in the Hollywood Hills with a poorly marked door. After being buzzed in we had to step into some sort of a lift that took us up to the house. When we got there we discovered that we were the only people who had come to the "party." We figured he had just given the address to the bands without directions. Rosemary and I had planned just to stay for a few minutes but we couldn't leave our hosts without any guests. So the four of us spent an hour or two fussing over the baby and gossiping; it turned out to be one of the few drama-free nights we would all spend together.

Earlier in the year, when Nirvana had gone to number one, Gersh got a call from Jonathan Ponemon of Sub Pop, reminding them that the Seattle indie had in its possession a number of unreleased early Nirvana recordings. They cynically called the potential compilation of the early material *Cash Cow*. In a successful effort to have their cake and eat it, too, they avoided the animosity of their most famous alumnus by selling the tracks to Geffen, who paid them a six-figure amount and an override on the condition that the band would create and approve the release of an "early years" album for Christmas.

The album, now christened by Kurt *Incesticide,* was released in time for Christmas. In lengthy liner notes Kurt commented on the previous few months of his life, sending "a big fuck-you to those of you who have the audacity to suggest that I'm so naive and stupid that I would allow myself to be taken advantage of and manipulated." Referring to Courtney, he wrote that nothing in his life had been "half as rewarding as having a baby with a person who is the supreme example of dignity, ethics, and honesty." He exhorted people who were prejudiced against women and gays not to buy his records.

Early in 1993 Nirvana began recording the album that would become known as *In Utero.* Kurt had been writing songs for months. He was very focused on balancing songs with punk energy against those that could work on the radio. When he finished "Heart Shaped Box," he called and ebulliently announced to me, "I've got the first single." While he was writing "All Apologies," he played the Beatles song "Norwegian Wood" over and over again, hour after hour.

As an effort to reconnect with his roots he decided to hire Steve Albini as his producer. Albini, a legendary figure in punk-rock circles, had worked with many of the most respected indie rock artists, including the Pixies, Fugazi, and the Jesus Lizard. Albini's dedication to indie rock and his prodigious output were indisputable. He saw himself as a champion of artists and his role in the studio to record them, not to interfere with their creativity. He had a theory about the placement of microphones that resulted in a more "real" sound. Most of the albums he had worked on had very low budgets, hence he liked to record very fast. Since Kurt finished songs before going into the studio and because Nirvana's ability to create arrangements of his songs was second nature to them, there was no need for more than the few weeks Albini had scheduled. (Albini made much of the fact that he would get no royalties on the record, but he received a hundred-thousand-dollar fee, which was not bad for a few weeks of work.)

When I heard the result I had two reactions. The songs were great. Again Kurt had crafted a series of hard rock songs, which also had distinctive melodies and choruses. But Kurt's voice was buried too deeply in the mix. Courtney was also very worried. "You've got to tell Kurt what you think," she pressed me. It turned out that Kurt was not that thrilled with the mixes himself but dreaded the idea of confronting Steve Albini, who had declared the process complete.

David Geffen, who had never met Kurt, asked if he might be introduced to the man who had become his label's biggest star. I drove Kurt out to Geffen's house in Malibu. In later years it would be expanded to become one of the most prominent **215** mansions on Carbon Beach, but at this point it was a relatively modest house, albeit with a stunning beachfront view of the Pacific Ocean.

Clad in T-shirt and jeans, Geffen told Kurt a little about his own life, including the process of coming out of the closet as a gay man. He spoke of his love of the songs of his first management client, Laura Nyro. Geffen actually half-sang a few of Nyro's best-known songs, such as "Wedding Bell Blues," but he got no look of recognition from Kurt, whose rock and roll canon did not include Nyro.

As we were leaving Kurt asked Geffen if he had heard the mixes of *In Utero*. Geffen had not. Kurt explained that he was torn between his desire to be faithful to the original version and his concern about getting songs on the radio. "Don't think about the radio," Geffen said dismissively, "and don't pay any attention to what anyone else says or thinks. Give us the record that you like. Our job is to sell it."

In the car on the way back to Hollywood Kurt looked relieved. "He was really different than I expected." Kurt was favorably impressed with the simplicity of Geffen's furnishings, with the lack of an entourage, and with the relaxed agendaless nature of the conversation. Although I had taken Kurt out there as an accommodation to Geffen, it turned out that the visit really helped to calm Kurt down.

Notwithstanding Geffen's supportive posture, Kurt was still uncomfortable with the sound of the record. However, he had been stung by some of the punk fanzine attacks on *Nevermind* as having sounded "slick," a verdict that, in my opinion, had had more to do with the huge success of the album than its sound. Nonetheless, Kurt did not want to go back to Andy Wallace. The obvious choice was Scott Litt, who had coproduced and mixed the last several albums by R.E.M., a group whom Kurt held in high esteem. After Kurt met Litt to discuss remixes he called in the best mood he had been in for weeks. "He's so nice," Kurt gushed, "no wonder he's really successful."

Albini was furious about the remix. It was impossible to tell where Albini's sense of violation stopped and his gift for self-promotion started, but he was clever enough to avoid criticizing the band when he falsely told Greg Kot in the *Chicago Tribune* that the "band's management and label hate the record." Kurt asked me to release a statement on behalf of the band that said simply, "We asked Scott to remix tracks on a few tracks because we felt the vocal wasn't loud enough."

The truth was that while nobody at Geffen "hated" the record, I did bridle at the condescending tone of one promotion exec who damned it with faint praise. Once the record was in Geffen's system, the influence of the gossip faded and they did an excellent job. Although *In Utero* did not do as well as the phenomenal *Nevermind* or Pearl Jam's second album, *Vs.,* it did sell more than four million records in the United States and millions more worldwide, and in retrospect I still believe it stands up as every bit as great a collection of songs as *Nevermind* was.

When *In Utero* was about to come out, Geffen Records heard from the head buyer at Wal-Mart that the massive chain would not carry the album unless a different album cover was created for their stores, because the original cover included pictures of fetuses. Kurt had personally designed the controversial artwork and I assumed he would resist any pressure to change it, especially in light of the recent public drama about the final mixes. I was delighted to have an opportunity to show Kurt that I would stand up for him.

I reassured Kurt that the band was coming off of a number-one album and that he could hold firm. There was no need for him to feel intimidated. Geffen would quickly back off, and in any case the band's contract gave them final say about the cover art. Nirvana fans, I assured him, would find the album elsewhere. After all, N.W.A. had just sold two million albums without any presence in Wal-Mart. Kurt calmly but firmly interrupted me and said in his earnest slacker monotone, "Of course

I want our records in Wal-Mart. When I was a kid, the only place near where we lived to buy records was a Wal-Mart. One of the reasons I make records is for kids like me." He had no problem creating an alternate cover in order to reach Wal-Mart shoppers.

Kurt had an elaborate idea for the "Heart Shaped Box" video. He found images in photo books and magazines and then combined them with scene ideas that he thought would go with the song and at the same time create a work of art that could stand on its own. Kurt conceived of a part in the video he thought Katie could play, a girl around her age (then three), with long blond hair, dressed in a Ku Klux Klan outfit. Rosemary and I felt that our daughter was too young to deal with the kind of visibility that a heavy-rotation MTV video would create, so we declined. A blond child actress who looked a lot like Katie was cast. Kevin Kerslake, who had directed the last three Nirvana videos, budgeted the concept of "Heart Shaped Box" at well over half a million dollars. Since Nirvana's royalty account was, and would remain, fully recouped, half of the cost of the videos would come directly from the band, and Kurt was offended by the proposed cost. Anton Corbijn did an excellent job for around two-thirds of the price. I took Katie to the video shoot in Hollywood, but it turned out to be a depressing experience. Kurt was obviously stoned out of his mind, and he barely seemed to recognize us through opaque heroin eyes.

After the video was aired, Kerslake sued Kurt, claiming, absurdly in my opinion, that he was responsible for the idea of "Heart Shaped Box." Kurt was deeply offended. After he died the remaining members of the band settled with Kerslake.

In September there was another MTV awards show, on which the band performed "Heart Shaped Box." Kurt reluctantly agreed to the performance. "I'm doing a lot of things I never thought I would do. I guess someday maybe I'll even wear a tuxedo," he said with an edge of self-loathing that my demurrers were unable to wash away. But at the show itself Kurt was excited to meet Peter Gabriel.

One of the most poignant things about Kurt's self-destructiveness was that it was focused almost entirely on himself. To me he was incredibly gracious and generous. Shortly before the Melvins album was delivered, Courtney read some disparaging comment in a fanzine that the band's lead singer, Buzz, had made about her and she told me she was going to insist that Kurt take his name off the album as producer. When I called Kurt and told him that if he did so it would be embarrassing to me, Kurt gently replied, "I know. I would never do anything like that." One night my boss at Atlantic, Doug Morris, joined Rosemary, Kurt, and Courtney for dinner, during which we made routine small talk. As he was leaving, Kurt shook Doug's hand and said, "I don't know what it is that you do, but you are a very nice person and it's really been a pleasure to meet you." Of course, Kurt knew exactly who he was.

I had continued my work for the ACLU and one night I was debating conservative talk host Dennis Prager at a Hillel in West L.A. about whether or not separation of church and state was a good idea. I was amazed to look into the mostly Jewish audience and see Kurt and Courtney there. Prager had asked rhetorically if one were to see a group of people coming down a dark street would one be more or less comfortable if informed that they were deeply religious. I did not have much of an answer, but later, during the period reserved for comments or questions from the audience, Courtney said, "Well, if you were a doctor who performed abortions you would probably prefer that the people walking down the street weren't the kind of religious Christians who shoot abortion doctors." Afterward we ate at the Jewish deli Canter's while Kurt assured me that watching me grapple (rather poorly, I thought) with a right-winger was "total entertainment."

Rosemary was a few weeks away from giving birth to our son Max and we were still living in Los Angeles, so I missed the **219**

November taping of *Unplugged,* about which Kurt enthused with pride, "This is really going to make people appreciate our band"—as if the appreciation they had received still wasn't quite enough, not as deep as his talent justified.

Whenever he was with Frances he was a doting father who took delight in her every grunt and movement. But such moments of satisfaction were brief and he was frequently restless and troubled by his career. There were days when he grew frustrated at what he perceived as the musical limitations of Nirvana. He asked me if I thought he could have a solo career without a formal breakup of Nirvana. Obviously, he could do both. He was feeling pressured to let Nirvana headline the Lollapalooza tour and asked what I thought about it. Knowing of Kurt's propensity to cancel shows from time to time, it seemed to me that he would resent the liability he would have as part of a tour he didn't control. Moreover, I always had felt that Nirvana should stay on a level all their own and avoid being lumped in as part of a general alternative trend. So I was against it. I don't know who was pushing the idea, but he sounded surprised and relieved by my answer and the band declined the offer to headline the tour.

A lot of the time he sank into depression and drug abuse. His chronic excruciating stomach pains were impervious to conventional medical care, making the lure of opiates, legal and illegal, all the more potent. On March 4 Courtney called in a state of hysteria. Kurt was in the hospital in Rome, where Nirvana was in the middle of a European tour. He had overdosed on Rohypnol, which he had taken after he and Courtney had had a fight. It was unclear whether or not he would survive. Courtney always had a spiritual side. She was seriously into doing Buddhist chants. I was a big believer in the power of prayer and affirmation and we prayed a little together on the phone.

There was not a phone in the intensive care unit where Kurt was recovering, so Courtney was checking in with Janet Billig every hour or two. The last report indicated that things were looking pretty good but that they wouldn't really know Kurt's condition until the next morning. Over the next hour or two the news of his OD broke on the wire service. And my phone began to ring incessantly with queries from the concerned and the curious.

My secretary told me David Geffen was on the phone and when I picked up he said in a somber voice, "Well, when people are determined to kill themselves there is nothing that you can do." I started to give him the same spiel I had been repeating to people who called, that we wouldn't know for sure until the morning, when Geffen interrupted me and said in a tone of voice one would use to calm down a demented person, "Danny, he's dead. Courtney just called me and told me he died." I was speechless as my mind raced. If Kurt had died, why wouldn't Courtney have called Janet or Rosemary or me? One didn't lightly contradict David Geffen, but I was pretty sure he was wrong about this. I carefully explained that it was possible that the call may have been a hoax.

Janet tried to track down Courtney. Although unlikely, we couldn't rule out the possibility that Courtney might have called the most powerful person she could get on the phone to tell him the news. Fifteen minutes later Janet called with the news that Kurt was not dead. An imposter, pretending to be Courtney, had called Geffen's office with the false report. We never figured out who placed the call.

Ever since Dr. Fremont had died, it seemed like Kurt had been fighting a losing battle against drugs. "I don't know another Bob Fremont," Buddy Arnold said dejectedly. There was a British doctor who sent pills derived from opiates that weren't legal in the U.S., stomach doctors, and a series of rehabs and unsuccessful efforts to get him to AA or NA meetings. Not surprisingly, Kurt developed a coterie of hangers-on who did drugs with him. According to British journalist Everett True, some friends of Kurt viewed the music business itself as the source of **221**

Kurt's bouts of anguish and depression and drugs as a positive element. True wrote that one of them grew angry at Courtney for encouraging Kurt's relationship with me and viewed my visits as "the devil coming over for tea."

I was commuting weekly from New York to Los Angeles. We would not move full-time back to New York until the summer, by which time our newborn son, Max, would be seven months old. During the third week of March Courtney called me at my New York office to ask if I would fly to Seattle instead of Los Angeles to participate in another intervention to get Kurt to go back into rehab. She was desperately worried about the way Kurt had been acting. She said that Kurt was the worst he had ever been in terms of his use of heroin and that she feared for his life.

I had no way of knowing then that the intervention would be the last time I would ever see him. I was burned out from the twice-weekly transcontinental trips I was making and resented the idea of carving out an additional day away from my family. Given the fact that Rosemary was persuaded that I should go and my sense of obligation to Kurt, I knew I had to do it. But I didn't go with a great attitude, which I have regretted ever since.

Janet Billig had arranged for David Burr, yet another drug counselor steeped in interventions, to fly with us from New York to help organize the confrontation we were to have with Kurt. Silva was flying up from Los Angeles. Burr appeared to be in his late thirties, was bearded, barrel chested, and had a warm, teddy-bear quality. He appeared oblivious to rock and roll or showbiz glitz. He spoke the twelve-step language with a quiet zeal. His advice to us was to be firm in confronting Kurt and to focus on the effect his drug addiction would have on Frances.

Courtney greeted us at the house in a state of high anxiety. Kurt was sitting outside with his friend Dylan Carlson, the singer in a drone metal group called Earth. I walked over to them and awkwardly started talking about the need for him to go into rehab. Kurt didn't seem particularly stoned, just subdued and depressed. He said that his problem wasn't drugs, it was anxiety brought on by the weirdness of always being recognized. I knew that this was just an avoidance of talking about drugs but answered literally, reminding him that I had been with him many times when no one recognized him. In my experience Kurt, in part because of his small physical stature, was naturally inconspicuous unless he went out of his way to dress garishly.

Then he got more argumentative, recalling that William Burroughs had told him it was possible to live a normal life and take heroin. That might be theoretically possible, I said, but it certainly wasn't working for Kurt. His life seemed out of control.

"You're being influenced by Courtney," Kurt said emotionally. It seemed like they were fighting all the time now. He insisted that she had a far bigger drug problem than he did. I agreed with him that Courtney needed to go into rehab, too, but that any problems he and Courtney were having could be much better worked out one way or the other after they were both clean.

We batted it back and forth for a while as we walked into the house. Burr approached him and did the AA rap about the fact that he had been where Kurt was and knew what he was going through and added, "Think of your daughter." Kurt got really angry for the first time, looking at him and saying, "You don't know me and you don't know anything about me," and then Kurt snapped at me, "I'm not going to talk to this dick." He went upstairs to go to the bathroom and a minute or two later he called me urgently to come upstairs. In the tone of voice one would expect from a kid tattling on a sibling he indignantly told me that Janet had taken his pharmaceuticals from his bathroom and was flushing them down the toilet. Janet looked mortified. I knew she was just trying to "do something" to help.

I tried to control my impatience and took a deep breath. I said I could understand why he was upset, but he had to understand that we were all there because we were worried about him. Kurt plopped himself down on a couch and started frantically rifling through a copy of the Seattle phone book's Yellow Pages. He said he wanted to find a psychiatrist. I suggested that there were better ways to find one and he shouted in a paranoid tone that the only way he would trust anyone is if he found someone himself, not through anyone with an agenda. My heart ached. The poor guy was so freaked out and, though surrounded by well-meaning people, totally and terribly alone.

But I was also very antsy to get out of there. If I left soon I could get a plane to L.A. that would get me home that night. Kurt grudgingly said that he would go into rehab if Courtney would.

I got home in the early evening, weary and depressed. I called him and said quietly, "Kurt, I just want you to know that no matter what, I love you." In a subdued, defeated voice he answered, "I know." Katie heard me say his name and asked to say hi. When I took back the phone he still sounded utterly drained. "I'm gonna go now," he said, which were the last words he ever spoke to me.

As Kurt had promised, he checked into the rehab facility Exodus a few days later—but two days after that, Kurt jumped over its fence and disappeared. There must have been some coverage of his latest rehab in the rock press, because I got a call from a woman whose name I did not write down, who said she had been a former girlfriend whom Kurt had stayed in touch with over the last few years. She spoke knowledgeably about his obsessive-compulsive disorder and went on about how worried she was about him. Callers like this usually had some weird agenda, but she said she was calling because she'd had an intuition about a single fact. Kurt was on antidepressants (something I didn't know), and she was worried that withdrawal from the antidepressants at the same time as the heroin withdrawal would send him over the edge. I didn't know what to say except to thank her for the call and promise that I would look into it when I heard from him. As I hung up I had another in a series of sinking feelings.

On April 8, I was back at Atlantic's New York office. I was in a meeting with Stevie Nicks to discuss her next solo album when Rosemary called. She was driving to Exodus to tell Courtney that Kurt had been found dead in a room above the garage at the house in Seattle, having shot himself in the head.

A few days later I was back in Seattle with Rosemary, the night before the funeral. We went to that same house, where the intervention had been, where he had later shot himself, where friends and family were now gathered. Among those present was Kurt's mother, Wendy, his sister, Kim, who looked uncannily like Kurt, as well as Krist, Peter Buck of R.E.M., and Kat Bjelland, her feud with Courtney set aside. Courtney planned out the program for the private memorial the next day and asked me to speak last. "You know," Courtney said to me in a choked voice, "Kurt and I wanted to be Danny and Rosemary, but the trouble was we both wanted to be Rosemary." She cried as she wiped her eyes.

Courtney asked if anyone wanted to come with her to see Kurt's body in the morgue before he was buried. Rosemary, Wendy, Kat, and I all urged her not to do so. "Don't you want to see his little monkey foot one more time?" she sobbed plaintively. After she calmed down, she showed us a long suicide note that Kurt had written. It began

To Boddah
Speaking from the tongue of an experienced simpleton
who obviously would rather be an emasculated,
infantile complain-ee. This note should be pretty
easy to understand.

225

Courtney said, "I can't believe he was so fucking stoned he didn't even know how to spell Buddha right," pointing to the word *Boddah*. Now it was Wendy's turn to howl in anguish, "That's not a misspelling," she sobbed. "Boddah was the name of an imaginary friend Kurt had when he was seven years old."

Other than a passage from Ecclesiastes ("To everything, there is a season," et cetera) I don't remember exactly what I said at the memorial service the next day, but I recall deciding to focus on things that would mean something to the people whom I was close to who were alive. I remember seeing Silva sitting there and saying something about Kurt's ambivalence about success: He was loyal to his punk origins but focused on things like MTV. I remember saying how much he loved Courtney and I ended with something spiritual about the eternal nature of the soul. I believed that geniuses like him really are sent to earth by God. Years later, when I read Everett True's book, I learned that this sentiment was offensive to some of his older friends. Not everyone wanted a cosmic context. Many people felt that there was a lot to be angry about. And not everyone felt that it was appropriate that someone associated with the commercial aspect of the rock business should be framing his life and death.

Afterward, as I mingled, I saw Eddie Rosenblatt and suddenly started crying uncontrollably while he hugged me. A little later a short middle-aged man with a beard came over to me and thanked me for what I had said. He introduced himself to me as Kurt's father, Don Cobain, who had divorced Wendy when Kurt was nine years old—an event that Kurt had frequently referred to as a traumatic moment in his childhood.

Later I mentioned to Krist how surprised I had been to meet Kurt's dad. Krist sighed and said, "Yeah, Kurt and I both had problems with our dads. I'm a forgiver but Kurt had a hard time forgiving his dad." After the service Courtney went to a vigil where thousands of Nirvana fans had gathered and read Kurt's note to them.

Rosemary and I went back to our hotel and gathered up the kids to get back to L.A. The limo that took us to the airport was driven by a woman who figured out by our conversation that we had come from the funeral. She told us that she had driven Kurt on several occasions, including his last trip to Seattle. When she told him how much her son loved him, Kurt had suggested she drop by her own house before taking him home. He told her son, "You know, your mom is a really great driver."

The aftermath of Kurt's death was pretty intense and surreal. MTV had covered the vigil with the somber intensity of a cable news channel. Wendy was widely quoted as saying that she had begged him not to join the "stupid club" of rock geniuses such as Jimi Hendrix, Jim Morrison, and Janis Joplin who had all died, as Kurt did, at age twenty-seven.

The day after the funeral a fax was circulated in various parts of the rock community, a hoax that purported to be a letter from Silva to me celebrating the money we would supposedly make from Kurt's death. By this time I was making no money whatsoever from Gold Mountain, and in any event Gold Mountain would have made far more from Nirvana tours later that year than from the increased record sales. More to the point we were consumed with grief and devastated at any inference to the contrary.

I figured that it had come from somewhere in the Northwest. I certainly understood that people who had known and loved Kurt from his early indie days in Seattle might have a resentment toward people he later met in the mainstream music business.

A week or so after the funeral Rosemary told me about Tom Grant. Grant was a private detective whom Courtney had retained to look for Kurt after Kurt left rehab. In keeping with the dubious theory of "independence" that Kurt had articulated during the latter stages of the last intervention, Courtney had gotten Grant's name from the Yellow Pages. She retained him to try to find Kurt and told Rosemary to cooperate with him in every way possible. The day before Kurt's body was found, Grant and Dylan had searched the Seattle house but had neglected to look in the greenhouse, where Kurt had shot himself. Now, Rosemary told me, Grant had come up with a theory that Kurt had not committed suicide but had been murdered.

I met Grant in his modest one-room Hollywood office. He was husky, a bit paunchy, and sporting what looked to me like a bad dark-brown hairpiece. Grant had been with the Los Angeles Police Department for a few years in the early seventies before embarking on a career as a private eye.

I felt that Grant was intoxicated by his unexpected proximity to the media limelight and seemed to be savoring every moment as he told me his theory that Kurt was murdered. He claimed that Kurt's body had had enough heroin in it to have rendered him unconscious and thus unable to have shot himself. I suggested that Kurt may well have developed a very high tolerance for heroin. He suggested that part of Kurt's note had been forged to change a note to his fans about leaving the music business to a suicide note. I just didn't see it that way. It seemed like a suicide note to me.

Why, I asked, would people want to kill him anyway? It was clear that he thought Courtney was in on whatever "it" was. Grant said the reason was money. I explained that Kurt was worth a lot more money alive than dead but Grant, who knew nothing about the music business, smiled cynically as if I was either naive or duplicitous. "Are these just theories," I asked, "or do you have proof?" Grant looked at me cagily and said, "I'm not going to show it to you. I don't know what your relationship is to this." I asked why, if there was compelling evidence of a murder, the Seattle Police Department wasn't investigating. Grant snorted and said that as a former police officer he knew about police departments. At this moment the last, most tenuous thread of Grant's credibility vanished as far as I was concerned. The idea that Courtney could have masterminded a **228** conspiracy that included the Seattle police was absurd. In any event, Grant's whole shtick violated every instinct I had about both Kurt and Courtney. I rose, shook his hand, and told him I had to go.

We later found out that Grant had surreptitiously taped some of his conversations with Rosemary, including one in which she had mentioned that Kurt and Courtney were contemplating a divorce. This was what Grant considered "evidence" of some dark plot. Of course, it was common knowledge among all of their friends and colleagues that Kurt and Courtney had a tempestuous relationship, and Courtney herself had told Rosemary to be completely open with Grant. In years to come Grant would achieve a sort of minicelebrity as the result of his conspiracy theory. He was the primary source for two books, and a dozen years later his Web site, with tapes of Rosemary's voice, was still up. In 1997 Grant had another tenuous brush with headlines when he was briefly hired by Paula Jones in connection with her lawsuit against Bill Clinton.

The following year Courtney was cast as Althea Flynt in the film *The People vs. Larry Flynt*. She gave a great performance and was nominated for a Golden Globe Award and made her peace with *Vanity Fair* when they put her on the cover. The film's director, Milos Forman, was honored by the Southern California ACLU, and at my request Courtney agreed to present Forman with the award at the dinner, the program of which I emceed. As the event drew to a close, a slight man with a British accent climbed up the steps to the hotel ballroom stage and took the microphone. He starting talking about the supposed hypocrisy of the ACLU for having Courtney participate in an evening devoted to free speech when she herself had supposedly not been forthcoming about her husband's death. I ran onstage, grabbed the microphone, shouting, "You are not part of the program, you don't belong here, now get off the fucking stage," and escorted him off. I later learned that the man's name was Nick Broomfield and that he had a friend filming his ejection with a portable camera. The footage is included in his vapid

229

documentary *Kurt and Courtney,* which regurgitated some of Tom Grant's theories.

Though these contrived conspiracy theorists possessed no merit, the same could not be said of some of those who questioned whether or not more could have been done to get Kurt off of drugs. Those around Kurt did everything we could think of, but in the awful and permanent aftermath of his death I have never stopped wondering whether more vigorous research would have revealed some alternative therapy that might have reached out to him in a way that twelve-step programs did not. I have always wished that in my last conversation with him I had invited Kurt to come without Courtney and stay in our guest room for a few days. I don't know if he would have done so or what would have happened to him if he had. But it would have been worth a try.

CHAPTER TEN

PROS AND CONS OF BECOMING A RECORD COMPANY GROWN-UP

As I previously mentioned, I had gone to work for Atlantic Records in 1992 and gradually phased myself out of Gold Mountain. I had loved managing artists, but as a first-time father at the age of forty I felt that the particular way that Gold Mountain was structured made it much more financially insecure than the Atlantic deal was for me.

In prior years I periodically wondered why no major label had offered me a job. In my heart of hearts I knew the answer. I wasn't a finance person or a lawyer or a heavy radio promotion guy. People like me were only valuable to record companies to the extent that we could identify and sign commercial talent. And the way that the business world judged your talent for picking and signing and working with artists was not how smart you were, how much you loved music, how hard you worked, what skills you had, or what critics thought of your taste. To be taken seriously by the grown-ups you had to be associated with big hits. That was the coin of the realm.

In the years immediately following the success **231**

of *Bella Donna* in 1981, I hadn't been associated with such hits. Then, in 1989, came *Nick of Time*. Shortly thereafter another one of my clients, Allannah Myles, had *Black Velvet*, a worldwide number-one record on Atlantic for which she won several Juno Awards, the Canadian equivalent of the Grammys. Her eponymous album sold four million copies worldwide. Then Nirvana's career exploded and suddenly I was treated by the big shots in the business as if I'd gained a hundred IQ points. Doug Morris offered me a job as senior VP for Atlantic, in which capacity I would be in charge of the West Coast A&R staff with a mandate to "bring in things that sell."

In the years after *Bella Donna* Doug had put together a string of hits, mastered corporate finance and politics, and he now shared the title of cochairman, co-CEO with Ahmet, who had long since relinquished day-to-day operations. All of the senior executives reported to Doug, but Ahmet remained a significant corporate influence, and he was an invaluable asset from time to time when we tried to sign artists. At one point the Warner Music company in Germany was trying to sign the Scorpions away from Polydor. Although only a midlevel rock band in the United States, the Scorpions sold millions of albums in Germany, so poaching them would be a big deal for the company. Ahmet and I had a short meeting at which I briefed him on the band's history. "Klaus is the singer and Rudolf is the guitar player," he repeated, and then added with a wolfish grin, "That ought to be enough. The bass player and drummer usually don't have anything to say." I joined him in a cynical giggle. We met with the Scorpions for about an hour, during which Ahmet regaled them with stories of old R&B artists and uttered platitudes about what it took to be a real international superstar. The band committed to Atlantic the next day.

One of Ahmet's oft-repeated stories involved a conversation with a jazz musician after Ahmet had given David Geffen his first label deal. The musician asked Ahmet dubiously if David Geffen really had a good ear for music. "I'm not sure,"

Ahmet replied, "but he definitely has a nose for music." Having a "nose" meant that you could find artists or records that had an audience and sign them before the competition did. Thus, in the argot of Atlantic, there were successful A&R guys with ears who made judgments based on their own musical taste and those with noses who tried to figure out what was hot. With few exceptions I was a nose guy.

My initial mission was to focus on alternative rock. Phil Collins, Atlantic's biggest commercial superstar, was starting to cool off. Atlantic's head of A&R, Jason Flom, proficient with both his ears and his nose, would continue to be one of the great developers of talent in the business and would later become president of Virgin Records; but Atlantic's initial foray into alternative rock had not been successful, so I was supposed to help fill the gap.

The week before I moved into Atlantic's offices, Flom asked to meet with a band he was desperate to sign. One of his young protégés, Tom Carolan, had brought him a tape of Mighty Joe Young, an L.A.-based rock group who Jason believed was going to be huge. Other record companies knew about the band, and it looked like they were going to sign elsewhere because Atlantic didn't have an "alternative" image. Jason hoped I could turn it around.

Mighty Joe Young visited me at the Gold Mountain offices. I don't recall being particularly eloquent that day, but the Nirvana posters on the wall must have done the trick, because the band signed with Atlantic. Shortly thereafter they had legal problems with their name and they rechristened themselves Stone Temple Pilots (STP). Over the next few months I had a few nice talks with the lead singer, Scott Weiland, who had classic good looks, almost like a movie star playing a rock star. He wanted his piece of rock and roll history and he had the overwhelming self-confidence that many successful performers develop or learn to fake. Notwithstanding Scott's affection for rock and roll clichés (he had an affinity for eyeliner and rarely had the same hair color two weeks in a row), he had a sincere brooding intensity and poetic soul that touched me. In contrast to Scott's flamboyant persona, bass player Robert DeLeo looked more like an executive than a rock musician. But behind his shy personality and buttoned-down look, Robert wrote brilliant musical tracks, which blended perfectly with Scott's lyrics. Robert's brother Dean added an authoritative lead guitar to the mix.

STP's album, *Core,* and its lead tracks, "Sex Type Thing" and "Plush," fit into the Zeitgeist of alterative rock radio and MTV and the Nirvana/Pearl Jam/Soundgarden audience so precisely that the album sold eight million copies. Weiland told several journalists they had signed to Atlantic in order to work with me. It wasn't particularly fair to Jason or to Tom, but Scott's very public acknowledgment of me burnished my image as an executive immensely. (Tom always maintained a self-effacing humor about the role of an A&R person. He repeated a saying from his native Iowa that "even a blind chicken finds a piece of corn every once in a while.")

Then Kim Gordon and Thurston Moore focused my attention on Matador Records, which had, among others, the indie-rock favorites Pavement and Superchunk, and I negotiated the acquisition of half of Matador for Atlantic. Matador's gifted and tenacious founders, Gerard Cosloy and Chris Lombardi, were great at finding important music at a very early stage and had enormous credibility with the indie magazines, college radio stations, and indie stores, many of whom would support any album that had the Matador label. But Chris and Gerard were very loose about asking for long-term contracts. Liz Phair, whose low-budget album *Exile in Guyville* sold several hundred thousand copies and was the critics' album of the year, had been signed as a "one-off" and thus we had to compete for a contract for her next albums with several other labels.

Matador's mystique engendered great loyalty among many of their artists, but Liz was not an indie purist. "Let me make it clear, I like limos and nice dressing rooms," she said at one of our first meetings about a new contract. When she played a Los Angeles show, Mo's son Michael Ostin, a senior A&R executive at Warner Bros., showed up with an impressive entourage including actress Rosanna Arquette. But the Matador team, with a little help from me, was able to win the battle and re-sign Liz. This was the first time in many years that Atlantic had beaten Warner Bros. Records in this kind of a beauty contest, and I think it solidified Doug's faith in me as a valuable piece of manpower. Not long thereafter he named me president of Atlantic, which made me officially the number-two executive at the company.

Doug spent a lot of time explaining to me how to be a record company president. He had the kind of self-confidence that allowed others to shine. Identifying and mentoring executives was one of Doug's many talents. By 2008 all of the label heads at three of the four U.S. majors had worked for and been trained by Doug at one time or another.

Having spent the better part of my career trying to cajole radio promotion departments to work records I was invested in, I loved having Atlantic's vaunted promotion department report to me. However, I soon learned that my main job was to support them and keep their morale up. Their job was to identify which records were causing positive reaction at radio stations and causing local sales, and then to spread the airplay on those hot records so that the entire country heard them. This was called "bringing a record home." As president my opinion set the tone in the prerelease period, but after that public reaction to the records dictated priorities. Contrary to the mythology that record companies "made" hits, Doug showed me that the best we could do was to recognize them. I suspect that this was part of what Jerry Wexler had meant years earlier when he told me there were "no secrets."

There existed A&R people who had a hands-on relationship with the making of records, who found songwriters and cowriters and producers, and who were hands-on with the mixing. But my own orientation was to look for artists who were auteurs, who, even if they needed occasional advice, had a self-contained vision of their own music, essentially my own version of Ahmet's bump-into-a-genius theory. This hands-off approach didn't always work commercially, but it fit my idealized notion of rock and roll artists, and in the mid-nineties at Atlantic it gave me a timely hot streak.

Over the next couple of years I signed, among others, Collective Soul, Hootie and the Blowfish, and Jewel, who collectively sold more than twenty-five million records. Actually, it's a bit of an exaggeration to say "I" signed them. In every case there was an A&R person who did most of the work. Both Collective Soul and Hootie were originally identified by a guy who called record stores for Doug to find out if indie releases were selling locally. I sent Tim Sommer, a young friend of Rosemary's I had hired as an A&R guy, to see Hootie live, and Tim signed them to an inexpensive deal. He then got John Mellencamp's longtime producer, Don Gehman, to produce the record and championed them in the corridors of Atlantic, at first against great odds. When asked to do so by Tim, I did call David Crosby and get him to sing harmony vocals on the record, and I met the band once or twice and saw their New York show. The album eventually sold more than fourteen million records, generating around seventy-five million dollars in profits for Warner Music. I was a little more involved with Jewel's first album, helping her sift through her dozens of songs, but most of the work was done by Jenny Price, another A&R person in the Los Angeles office.

A lot of my time was spent looking at numbers. Doug had mastered the ability to "manage the bottom line," which, for the most part, meant cutting costs quickly enough when sales were down.

Recording costs and overhead came out of a budget that was set annually. Marketing costs were the biggest variable in the business and could be continually tweaked and adjusted. To make a profit margin the corporation wanted, it was necessary to try to keep the marketing spending in the neighborhood of 20 percent of the total amount of billing. On big hits that percentage was less and on flops it was more. Every week Atlantic's senior executives sat with the finance people, looked at the previous week's sales, studied the marketing spending, and decided whether the "present view" conformed to expectations. We then adjusted go-forward marketing authorizations based on the new information.

I soon came to realize that in a public company, everything revolved around meeting or exceeding projections for quarterly profits. Projections were presented at annual meetings of division heads with the Warner Communications finance people. The first time I went, Doug did most of the talking, explaining carefully what the sales projections were and how they related to expenses. Then Ahmet spoke up and said, "You know, this is the record business, and the truth is if we have hits we'll do well and if we don't we won't. The rest of this stuff is bullshit." The corporate CFO laughed and said, "Ahmet, you've been saying the same thing for twenty years," to which Ahmet replied with a shrug, "But it's still true," and everyone laughed. Alas, the corporate culture that understood and put up with such vagaries was soon to expire.

My entry into the ranks of executives at the Warner Music Group coincided with a time of transition and turmoil. A year earlier Steve Ross had delegated oversight of the music companies to Robert Morgado. Morgado's predecessor, David Horowitz, had seen his role as being nurturer to Mo Ostin, Bob Krasnow, Ahmet, and Geffen during a time when the record business was booming and when the cash flow from the Warner Music Group was helping fund the acquisition of cable companies. Morgado was a more traditional corporate numbers guy, whose style grated on the record company heads. Ostin insisted that he report directly to Steve Ross instead of to Morgado.

Elektra chairman Bob Krasnow was a protégé of Ostin's and shared Mo's contemptuous attitude toward corporate orthodoxy. Doug was the only label head whom Morgado could relate to.

Morgado approved investment to expand Atlantic. He green-lighted the funding of an Atlantic Nashville office, a home video company, the acquisition of Rhino Records, bringing me into the company, and, most significantly, the funding of Interscope Records, which was originally set up as a joint venture between Atlantic and Interscope's owners, Ted Field and Jimmy Iovine. Between the expansion and a series of hit records, the Atlantic Group overtook Warner Bros. Records as the number-one record division within the Warner Music Group, both in terms of volume and profits.

Morgado brooded over the fact that Mo did not report to him as if it had been an insult to his manhood. In December 1992 Steve Ross unexpectedly died of cancer at the relatively young age of sixty-five. He was replaced by Jerry Levin, who had no emotional attachment to any of the record company chairmen and whose primary focus for the corporation was on the growth of cable TV. Morgado was given the power he had coveted, and in short order he fired Krasnow and Ostin on the basis that their profit margins were far smaller than Atlantic's. A new job was created for Doug, in which he would be in charge of all three U.S. Warner Music Group labels. I ran Atlantic day-to-day. Doug's protégée Sylvia Rhone became the new chairman of Elektra. Lenny Waronker, who had been Mo Ostin's longtime protégé and number-two guy, was named the new chairman of Warner Bros. Records.

A few months later, as Waronker was about to take over as chairman of Warner Bros., he abruptly decided he did not want to replace his longtime mentor. (Lenny would go on to join Mo at DreamWorks Records.) Without discussing it with Doug, Morgado decided that Rob Dickens, who ran the Warner company in the UK, should become the new chairman of Warner Bros. Doug felt that he, and not Morgado, should pick the new Warner Bros. chairman. After a bitter fight Doug prevailed and named me to the job. I hated leaving Atlantic, but I wasn't really given a choice. Nevertheless, there was a giddy exhilaration at the fact that after only a few years as a record-company executive I was going to run the most prestigious record company in the world.

Mo Ostin's departure attracted enormous media coverage. He was a giant of the business and was widely beloved by Warner Bros. artists and executives. When I had been at Atlantic I was walking on a path that had been carefully prepared by Doug. At Warners I felt as if I was on my own. I was again commuting every week between New York, where my family had moved when I became president of Atlantic, and Los Angeles, where Warner Bros. was headquartered.

The wounds from the fight between Doug and Morgado did not heal. I think that Doug felt the authority of his new position was being undermined almost as if he had been kicked upstairs. I felt obligated to loyally support Doug any way I could. Moreover, I was now working every day at Warner Bros. Records trying to get the trust of people who detested Morgado for having fired Ostin, so I liked the idea of being adversarial to Morgado. At times I had a perverse enjoyment of combat in the rarified corporate air. My rapid ascent had made me an object of curiosity within the world of Time Warner and I was meeting the people who ran the film, book, and publishing divisions. Between the jet lag, the scrutiny, the intoxication of the attention I was getting, and a desire to be a loyal aide to the man who had twice promoted me, I frequently lost perspective. I have long wished I could take back several dozen sentences I uttered during this period under the stress of various pressures, or while I had delusions of grandeur, or both.

The few months I spent at Warner Bros. Records provided me with a memorable overview of one of the great record companies. The senior and middle executives were among the most accomplished in the business and it was fascinating to meet Prince, Paul Simon, Quincy Jones, Madonna, and others. However, a lot of my focus was in trying to re-sign two superstars whose contracts were about to expire, R.E.M. and Neil Young.

R.E.M. wasn't ready to make a new record, so there was not a time crunch. They eventually did re-sign with Warners, although the deal was closed after I left. My own ability to communicate with them was enhanced by the fact that I knew Patti Smith. The time period during which I was courting R.E.M. coincided with a tragic time in Patti's life following the death of her husband, MC5 guitarist Fred Smith. For the previous fifteen years Patti and Fred had lived in Michigan and she had been inaccessible to most people in the business. After Fred's death, Patti and their children, Jackson and Jesse, moved back to New York and stayed at our house until Patti got her own place. Rosemary, who had idolized Patti since she was a teenager, became Patti's lawyer. One day the three of us were walking down the street in our Greenwich Village neighborhood when a couple of Japanese tourists stopped and begged us to take a picture of them with Patti. The man looked like he was going to faint from excitement as he repeatedly said in broken English, "I so lucky." R.E.M.'s lead singer, Michael Stipe, was that kind of Patti Smith fan.

Stipe had originally conceived the R.E.M. song "Everybody Hurts" as a duet with Patti but had been unable to get her on the phone. He carried around a pin that had been issued by a fan club created when her *Radio Ethiopia* album came out while Stipe was still in high school. A few days after I met with the band I noticed Jackson Smith, then fourteen years old, wearing an R.E.M. T-shirt, and I told him that Michael Stipe had been a big fan of his mother. Jackson looked at me as if I were bullshitting him, but less than a year later Patti and Stipe had become good friends.

240 The Neil Young situation was more urgent. Neil Young, rightfully, was considered one of the great geniuses and iconic artists in the music business, valuable out of proportion to his recent record sales. A *Newsweek* article speculated he might leave Warner Bros. because of Mo's departure. Doug and Jerry Levin recognized that the Warner Bros. brand would be damaged if we lost him. Neil's longtime manager, Elliot Roberts, astutely milked the moment to the point that a five million dollar advance was required to close the deal. This was several times what Neil's previous record sales warranted, but at least two other companies were willing to pay it, so I got corporate permission to make the offer.

I met Neil with some trepidation. His long hair and well-lined face would fit on any rock and roll Mount Rushmore. Unique among artists who had emerged from the 1960s, Neil Young had maintained an artistic edge and relevance. He was as much of a hero to punk rockers as he was to hippies. When he asked me what music I had listened to as a kid I mentioned Dylan, the Beatles, and Phil Ochs. Young's face came to life and he repeated, "Phil Ochs," and the ice was broken as he launched into an animated talk about the late, great political singer-songwriter.

Young had been working with the members of Pearl Jam as a backup band on an album called *Mirror Ball,* and shortly after the contract was signed he told me that he had decided that he wanted the artist credit on the front of the album to read Neil Young and Pearl Jam. I could understand his desire to have the commercial association with Pearl Jam at a time when they were America's most successful rock band, but the fact was the Pearl Jam lead singer Eddie Vedder did not sing any of the leads on the album. More to the point, Pearl Jam was signed to Sony Music (who had been one of the companies trying to sign Neil). In cases like this it was almost never a problem to list superstars on other labels in small print on the back as sidemen, but the use of their name on the front as a marketing tool was a totally different matter. I knew that there was no way Sony would allow the Pearl Jam name to be used so prominently on a record released by one of their competitors.

As calmly as I could I explained this to Neil, who implacably responded, "Yes, but things have to be called what they are. And this record is me and Pearl Jam." I knew better than to try to argue with the famously stubborn genius about the existential nature of one of his recordings, but I called Elliot Roberts in a panic. Part of the rationale I had given my corporate bosses for the deal we had given Young was the impending release of *Mirror Ball*. It would be a disaster if it were shelved and even worse if it came out on Sony. Elliot understood immediately and said he would take care of it.

I was in a state of high anxiety for the next few days until Neil called and told me he had recorded organ solos that would go in between the rock songs on the album. "Now that I've added those pieces that I did myself, it's a Neil Young album." I thanked Elliot for having worked his magic.

Neil's practice was to personally "deliver" his new records and play them for the chairman. He and his wife, Peggy, sat on the floor and smoked a joint as Warner staffers crowded into my office and listened wide-eyed to the album *Mirror Ball*. I still think it is a great album and I wish I had been able to oversee the marketing of it, but I was gone from Warner Bros. by the time it was released two months later.

The fighting between Doug and Morgado got so bad that Time-Warner chairman Jerry Levin got rid of Morgado. But instead of giving Doug the top music job he made him report to HBO chairman Michael Fuchs. It soon became clear that one of Fuchs's missions was to get rid of the temperamental record executives. Doug Morris, CFO Mel Lewinter, and I were all fired and soon thereafter Fuchs sold the company's share of Interscope to Universal. (By 2008 Interscope had long been the most successful American record company and Jimmy Iovine the most accomplished record executive of my generation.) My tenure as chairman of Warner Bros. Records had been seven months. The Warner Music Group's U.S. market share, which was close to 30 percent when we all left, would plunge to half of that a few years later.

Doug was given a well-funded joint venture with Universal Music. It was called Rising Tide and he offered me a senior role in it, but around the same time I was offered twice as much money to become president of Mercury Records in the United States, which was a division of PolyGram. (A few months later Doug was made the chairman of all of Universal Music.)

PolyGram was run by Alain Levy, a native of France who had spent a lot of time in the United States. The company's major shareholder was the Dutch electronics company Philips and they had funded Levy's vision of an expanded PolyGram, which had been largely accomplished by the acquisition of three of the most powerful remaining independent labels, Motown, Island, and A&M Records.

Mercury had been a competitor of Atlantic in the 1950s, had been acquired by PolyGram in the 1970s, and had been most recently run by Ed Eckstine, a great R&B developer of talent who had signed and overseen the careers of Vanessa Williams, Brian McKnight, and Tony! Toni! Toné! However, the rock roster revolved around Bon Jovi and John Mellencamp, both of whom were cold at the moment (they would both have great comebacks long after I left). Ed had left me with the big Joan Osborne hit "One of Us," which was exploding just as I arrived. Levy and British executive Roger Ames, to whom I would eventually report day-to-day, wanted me to modernize the roster and make the division profitable.

My first acquisition was the second incarnation of Phil Walden's Capricorn Records. Walden's first version of Capricorn was known for southern rock and included the Allman Brothers. He had eventually sold the catalog but kept the name and had created a new roster. Walden was a flamboyant and brilliant native of Macon, Georgia, whose first career had been as Otis Redding's manager. In 1976, while managing

243

the Allmans, he had arranged for the group to do a series of fund-raising concerts for Jimmy Carter that financed the early primaries. Phil was a great storyteller who always liked to get in the last word. One night over dinner Peter Wolf and Phil were trying to one-up each other. Peter told of having had an affair with Hank Williams's second wife and Phil said he had had one with Williams's first wife. Peter told a story about being on the set of *Chinatown* with Faye Dunaway, whom he had been married to at the time. Walden looked momentarily flustered and then exclaimed, "Well, I took Andy Warhol to the Grand Ole Opry." No one could top that.

The first two releases from the Capricorn/Mercury deal were by the rock groups 311 and Cake and they each had their first platinum records, fueled by modern rock airplay and MTV. As had been the case with Stone Temple Pilots at Atlantic, this quick early success solidified my corporate standing.

The biggest hit brought in under my Mercury regime was Hanson, whose teen-pop hit "MMMBop" and the album it was on were overseen by Steve Greenberg, who had worked for me at Atlantic and whom I had brought in as head of A&R. Greenberg was a brilliant hands-on music guy who got involved with every detail of the making of the record, and the result was the sale of ten million units worldwide.

By my second year at Mercury we had increased the gross U.S. billing to two hundred million dollars, up from eighty million the year before, with hardly any increase in costs. As a result of this success I was promoted to chairman of what was now called the Mercury Records Group, charged with overseeing the hip-hop label Def Jam, the classical labels Deutsche Grammophon, Philips, and London, the jazz label Verve, and legendary R&B company Motown. As had occurred at Warner Music, my promotion paid me well and gave me corporate prestige but removed me even further from day-to-day work with artists.

To satisfy my inner hippie I had Mercury fund a poetry label called Mouth Almighty, which released recordings by William Burroughs, Sekou Sundiata, and Allen Ginsberg, and albums by the Fugs, Spalding Gray, Jim Carroll, and Ringo Starr. We also funded a New Age label called Triloka, which released records by Krishna Das and Baba Ram Dass. None of these sold very well, but they were all very inexpensive to record. Consequently, Mercury was able to break even while enhancing its cultural appeal to it employees, the media, and other artists.

One of the last deals I made was to acquire Lucinda Williams's album *Car Wheels on a Gravel Road*. It had been recorded for Rick Rubin's American label, but at the time Rick was not in a position to compel either of his distributors, Warner Bros. or Sony Music, to release it and they had both passed. Rosemary had represented Lucinda for many years and she had played the album for me several times. I really loved the final version, which had been produced by Steve Earle and Ray Kennedy. When I closed the deal to release it, I called to congratulate Earle on his work. This was the beginning of what would turn out to be one of the most important relationships I ever had with an artist. In the waning months of my time at Mercury I drove the promotion department crazy, and they were able to get *Car Wheels on a Gravel Road* a substantial amount of Triple A play. The music press, which had always supported Lucinda, made it one of the best reviewed albums of the year. Lucinda had never sold more than seventy-five thousand units, but *Car Wheels on a Gravel Road* sold over half a million, her first gold album.

For the calendar year 1999 the Mercury Records Group had the largest market share of any American label group, beating out Columbia Records for number one. Although that fact validated some of the work my team had done in the previous year, it was irrelevant to the macroeconomics of PolyGram, which had started an expensive, money-losing movie division. Against Alain Levy's wishes Philips decided to sell PolyGram to Universal Music, and Levy was out. Doug Morris would run the consolidated company. For the merger to make economic sense six labels would be compressed into four.

For several years rap music had been eating away at rock's dominance of the teenage market. By the end of my years at Mercury rap was the number-one record-selling genre. Rock did not disappear as a voice of teen culture the way jazz and swing music had when I was a kid, but it became a much smaller percentage of the Zeitgeist and thus of the business. I had great respect for hip-hop culture but I never developed more than a superficial expertise in the hip-hop business. Thus Lyor Cohen of Def Jam had a lot more corporate value to Doug in 1999 than I did. So I was out again.

The reorganization of Universal resulted in a company that would dominate the music business for at least the next decade, although of course that decade would be fraught with challenges from the Internet that were still not apparent (at least not to me) in 1999. We PolyGram people remained on for several months after the merger was announced, pending the various government approvals that were necessary, and during that time Universal had corporate consultants interview the senior people to get a handle on the record business. One of the consultants asked PolyGram executive Roger Ames about the company's customers and Roger asked him who he thought a record company's customers were. "The people who buy the records?" the guy guessed, but Roger shook his head. "The retailers?" Again there was a negative response. Roger gave him the point of view of a record person: The customers of a record company are the artists. Get the right artists for the right price and the rest takes care of itself.

I was in the mood to do something where I could work more closely with fewer artists, and an investor named Michael Chambers wanted to fund an independent record company. We called it Artemis Records. The first two artists I signed were Steve Earle and Warren Zevon.

CHAPTER ELEVEN

WARREN ZEVON: LIFE WILL KILL YOU

Warren Zevon was the most literary of rockers. He counted among his friends Carl Hiaasen, Paul Muldoon, Hunter S. Thompson, and Mitch Albom. He was fluent in both classical and modern poetry and he loved the hard-boiled mysteries of Raymond Chandler and Ross Macdonald (to whom he dedicated his album *Bad Luck Streak in Dancing School*). He even agreed, on occasion, to play with the Rock Bottom Remainders, the vanity "band" that consisted of writers Amy Tan, Dave Barry, and Stephen King, who sometimes sang Warren's biggest hit, "Werewolves of London."

But the writer Warren most reminded me of was the literary hero of his teenage years, Norman Mailer. Like Mailer the writer, Zevon the rock artist was a man's man as well as a woman's man who combined sensitivity, intellectual acuity, macho sarcasm, wit, crudeness, and aggression. He was the tough guy who wore his heart on his sleeve.

Like Mailer, Zevon also knew how to get attention. Even if he lacked the internalized laserlike **247** connection with mass success that Bono or Springsteen possessed, he had a sense of show business that propelled him far beyond mere cult status. Truly unique and utterly uncompromising as a songwriter and performer, he was, as his son Jordan pointed out, an artist who developed "an intuitive savvy of marketing." When told of his fatal illness Zevon said to his son, "I'm not going out with a record that sells ten thousand copies."

Jackson Browne introduced me to Warren in early 2000, a few weeks after the formation of Artemis Records, asking me to listen to new demos that Zevon had made. Artemis was, by design, a small indie label. There were lots of great things about running big record companies—the money, the perks, the way almost anyone in the world would take your call, the demystification of decision making at the top, and the occasional joy of team building—but for me they were not jobs in which one worked closely with individual artists, nor were they platforms on which it made sense to spend much energy on midlevel sellers. Although I missed the status of the big jobs, I was relieved that I now had a professional agenda where meeting with someone like Warren Zevon made sense.

Part of what I wanted to do with Artemis was to provide a home for artists who were still creative and who had impassioned fans, but whose sales base had dropped beneath the level that meant something to the majors. Warren's last album, *Mutineer*, which had come out five years earlier, had sold fewer than forty thousand albums. Dropped by the label Giant Records, he had been without a record deal ever since.

As a young man, Warren had stood out among the dozens of artists and songwriters who entered the bloodstream of the rock business from Los Angeles in the seventies. Many would be more commercially successful, such as Fleetwood Mac, Linda Ronstadt, Jackson Browne, and the Eagles, but all of them, and many others who labored to write poetic, relevant, and musically accessible songs, would point to Warren as the most talented. "He was the best of us," Jackson said to me not long after Warren died, "the best songwriter"—the latter words uttered in a choked voice that combined admiration, sorrow, and envy.

Jackson had discovered Zevon at a low point in his career in the mid-seventies. Zevon had played piano with the Everly Brothers and made a forgettable debut album and was without a deal just as he had found his writer's voice. Browne began performing Warren's songs in concert, got him signed to Elektra, and in 1976 produced the album *Warren Zevon,* which put him on the map. (Several members of the Eagles played on it, and Linda Ronstadt had a hit covering the song "Poor Poor Pitiful Me.") Jackson also produced Warren's commercial breakthrough album, *Excitable Boy,* which included two of the songs he would become most famous for: "Werewolves of London" and "Lawyers, Guns and Money."

Zevon also became famous for being a drunken and drugged-out wild man and for his recovery, which was memorably documented in a 1981 *Rolling Stone* cover story by Paul Nelson. Precisely because of his intellectual and musical integrity and his rebellious, unwavering commitment to a certain vision of himself as an artist, Zevon's subsequent sobriety had a lot of credibility in the rock world. (He would stay straight for more than twenty years, deviating only at the end of his life under doctor's care and orders.)

Nelson, the rare rock journalist who became a character in an artist's life, wrote of the intervention that finally worked in the form of a visit from Ken Millar, who, under the name Ross Macdonald, had written hard-boiled detective novels that both Nelson and Zevon adored. As Nelson described it:

> *Zevon was in bad bad shape. People had been trying to get him to go back to the drug center, and the only way I could see his actually doing it was if Ken Millar came and told him: somebody he really respected, a major fa-*

ther figure. So I said to Millar, "I know this guy just reveres you, he looks up to you like a god; would you be willing to go and talk to him?"

Zevon later told Tom Nolan (in *Ross Macdonald: A Biography*),

This was a time when the attitude towards drug and alcohol renunciation had a lot more to do with medallion-wearing therapists than it did with twelve-step programs. So I was sitting in my palatial shithouse in Montecito, in terrible Valium withdrawal, with instructions not to miss therapy the next day. I was in really bad shape. And I remember him coming to the door. Ken was wearing some kind of plaid fedora, like a private eye. He was a very comforting presence; you know, Valium withdrawal involves considerable fear and trembling. Everything he said was informed by a tremendous amount of compassion. There was a big book about Stravinsky on my coffee table; I'd known Stravinsky. I said, "Here's a guy that lived to be eighty-eight. Worked up to his last day, never had problems with alcohol or drugs." Millar said one word: "Lucky." Of course, that word stayed with me all my life—coming from someone who really didn't have anything to do with the world of rehabilitation or Recovery Nation, but could just say a word: "Lucky."

Zevon told Nelson,

As I was storming around the house, I came to the realization that all that stuff in the media that made me into F. Scott Fitzgerald, the two-fisted drinker, the adventurer—all that stuff was just bullshit. I said [to

*myself], "You're not a fucking boy and you're not
a fucking werewolf, you're a fucking man, and it's
about time you acted like it." I'd say, "There's nothing romantic, nothing grand, nothing heroic, nothing
brave—nothing like that about drinking. It's a real
coward's death."*

Zevon recovered a lot quicker than his career did. He spent
many sober years making records for labels who dropped him
and played for diminishing live audiences. But he always retained a core group of fans who included the most celebrated of
his peers, hence Jackson's call to me.

I was genuinely excited by the new demos. Zevon had lost none
of his mastery of the language and retained a unique balance of
dark and light. As Springsteen had put it, he was "a moralist in
cynic's clothing." One of Zevon's distinguishing characteristics
was his impulse to write about subjects not typically accessible
to rock and roll. Bonnie Raitt's *Nick of Time* had dealt with the
advent of middle age from a rock and roll perspective. Zevon's
new songs dealt with the advent of death. I had never heard
anything like them. The song that jumped out at me first was
"Life'll Kill Ya," which started with a solo semiclassical intro
and then launched into a verse and chorus that only he could
have written:

> *You've got an invalid haircut*
> *It hurts when you smile*
> *You'd better get out of town*
> *Before your nickname expires*
> *It's the kingdom of the spiders*
> *It's the empire of the ants*
> *You need a permit to walk around downtown*
> *You need a license to dance*

> *Life'll kill ya*
> *That's what I said*
> *Life'll kill ya*
> *Then you'll be dead*
> *Life'll find ya*
> *Wherever you go*
> *Requiescat in pace*
> *That's all she wrote*

My only questions were whether Warren had a realistic idea of what the limited economics were of a comeback and what he would be like to deal with day to day.

I wanted to meet him face to face. Artists who do not have big radio hits are particularly dependent on their ability to schmooze.

Any anxiety I had faded quickly over lunch with Warren and Artemis marketing head Michael Krumper at Cafe Un Deux Trois on West Forty-fourth Street across from our office. In place of the wild-eyed anarchic figure of my fears, the real Warren was the very model of the rational middle-aged battle-scarred rocker. Any sense of grandiosity had been knocked out of him, but he was no burnout. His weather-beaten face was offset by his impeccably groomed blond hair. He was trim with broad shoulders, the result, I was later to learn, of compulsive hours spent in the gym. He wore a gray Armani suit over a gray turtleneck. In a deep and resonant, world-weary voice he alternated wiseguy witticisms about the cast of characters in the business with all of the right phrases about moderate ex-pectations. I was, and would always be, somewhat in awe of Warren's piercing intelligence, and I felt a little guilty that he felt impelled to be on such good behavior.

I committed to sign him the very next day. Warren didn't have a manager at the time, so I asked him who his lawyer was so we could get him a contract. "Why do I need a law-yer?" he asked. "Jackson Browne told me to sign with you.

I'll sign whatever you give me." When I insisted that he retain a lawyer, he said that his business manager, Bill Harper, had recommended Ken Anderson, who then negotiated the deal on Warren's behalf. For the next year or so I often told this story as an example of Warren's innocence when it came to business, but it was essentially bullshit. In fact, Anderson had been his lawyer for years. Warren's pose was attributable to a desire to flatter me or to try to avoid paying a legal fee or both. Anderson represented Warren for the rest of his life.

The budget for the album, which was called *Life'll Kill Ya*, was seventy-five thousand dollars. The demos were excellent, particularly the vocals. Many of the songs were written with his longtime collaborator Jorge Calderón, who also played bass and who had helped make the demos so strong. But I thought some additional production might help give Warren a better commercial chance. I suggested Paul Kolderie and Sean Slade, with whom I'd successfully worked on the Lemonheads and the Mighty Mighty Bosstones albums. Warren quickly hit it off with them. The production paid off on "Porcelain Monkey," the hardest rock song on the album, which was a sardonic retelling of the story of Elvis Presley's death, and "I Was in the House When the House Burned Down," an apocalyptic, Dylanesque combination of poetry and prophecy. Other songs that stood out were "Hostage-O," perhaps the most explicit S&M song recorded by a major artist from the masochist's point of view, and "Don't Let Us Get Sick," which returned to the album's central theme of the anticipation of death.

Warren's one reliable ally in the media was David Letterman, who always booked Warren to sing whatever song was being promoted at radio and also used him as a substitute band leader whenever Paul Shaffer was on vacation. The Artemis staff did whatever they could to promote the record, setting up in-stores and interviews on the Triple A radio stations. (Triple A originally stood for "acoustic, adult, alternative," and they were often the only radio stations that would play artists such as

Lucinda Williams, Bonnie Raitt, Jackson Browne, Steve Earle, et cetera. Unfortunately, only a few of them had audiences big enough to impact record sales.)

We also got him a new booking agent, Marsha Vlasic, whose other clients included Neil Young and Elvis Costello. At first Warren fell into the outmoded rock-star adversary relationship with the Artemis promo people. "Your staff is treating me like Sting," he griped to me one day but then, characteristically, admitted, "Of course, most of the time I kind of like being treated like Sting." On another occasion Artemis president Daniel Glass asked him why he berated the promotion people for minor sins such as the absence of Diet Mountain Dew in club dressing rooms. "I always figured that they would take me more seriously if I was an asshole," Warren explained candidly. Daniel disabused him of this notion, and thereafter Warren was considerably nicer to the promo staff.

He did not completely abandon all traces of irrational rock grandiosity. As a favor to Artemis, Steve Earle, whom I had also signed to the label, offered Warren a special guest-star slot at the South by Southwest conference in Austin. Steve had grown up in Texas and drew thousands of people in Austin, but Warren demurred. It was obvious to me that if it had been the Eagles he would have opened, but he just could not live with the idea of playing second fiddle to Steve, even in Austin. We selected "I Was in the House When the House Burned Down" as the track to be promoted at radio but needed an edit without the word *shit*. Warren went through the motions of agonizing over it and told me he needed to discuss it with Carl Hiaasen and other "real" writers to determine if he would be sacrificing his writerly integrity by sanctioning a clean radio version before he gave his permission.

Warren toured with no accompaniment, playing piano and guitar and masterfully controlling the stage. One night at the Bowery Ballroom in New York a fistfight broke out in the au-

dience and Warren stopped playing, walked to the edge of the stage, and asked sternly, "What's going on?" The two drunken brawlers looked sheepishly up at Zevon and stopped fighting, and Warren gracefully completed his song.

The press was not quite what I had hoped for. I never found the lead sheep. *Life'll Kill Ya* got excellent reviews, but they didn't run with the size and impact required for an adult artist to break through. Beyond Letterman we didn't get much more TV.

VH1 had long since abandoned the playing of "adult" rock videos and had become a Hot AC (Adult Contemporary) format playing the likes of Sheryl Crow. The one vehicle VH1 had to promote an older artist was *Behind the Music,* a series of hour-long documentaries that tended to revolve around melodramatic scenarios in the lives of musicians. I called, cajoled, and begged every executive at MTV networks who would take my call. I figured he was perfect for the show, with his history of drug abuse and the number of famous rock stars such as Radiohead and R.E.M. who professed admiration for him. I hit a brick wall. The big shots took my calls, made encouraging noises, but referred me to the middle executives in charge. George Moll, the producer of the show, went to bat for me, but the executive who was the ultimate arbiter of programming at VH1 felt that Zevon had no relevance to the twenty-five-to-thirty-four-year-old audience they wanted. This was a moment when VH1 was turning over more and more control to TV producers without any sense of the music culture. "You know why I know that our audience doesn't care about him?" the executive asked me rhetorically. "Because I don't care about him."

Bill Flanagan, the VP at VH1 whose portfolio included liaising with critically acclaimed singer-songwriters and aging hippies, apologetically offered as a consolation prize a five-minute piece on Warren on the VH1 show *Where Are They Now?* I knew that Flanagan respected Warren, but the show was mostly about one-hit wonders and, I thought, beneath Warren's dignity. In addition, unlike *Behind the Music,* it had no history of helping to sell records—so I passed.

We made one final effort at widening the album's audience. As was his wont, Warren had recorded one "cover song," a poignant version of Steve Winwood's "Back in the High Life." In Winwood's version the chorus was defiant; in Warren's it was agonizingly wistful. The way Warren sang the lyric just killed me, as if he was singing for all of the aging rock artists (and executives) who wanted one more chance.

Peter Asher, who had produced all of the big Linda Ronstadt hits, had been one of Warren's managers in the past and now was working for Sony Music, which did the international distribution for Artemis. As a favor Asher did a radio remix of "Back in the High Life" at literally no cost. (Asher typically would have charged at least twenty-five thousand dollars for such a task, but he was another one of Warren's loyal friends.) We struck out when we tried to get commercial radio to play it. It was one of those ideas that sounded good in theory but had no practical result.

Ultimately, I failed to get *Life'll Kill Ya* the audience it deserved. But the record did get Warren back into the market, increased his live audiences, and reconnected him to his core audience. The effort on the ground of fighting for every inch, and Warren's touring, resulted in doubling the sales of *Mutineer,* which reached around seventy-five thousand. It drove me crazy that I hadn't been able to figure out how to attain the heights of Bonnie Raitt's latter-day success for Warren.

Zevon had a diverse and interesting group of friends. In addition to the usual suspects of the L.A. rock scene and his array of literary pals, he hung out with Tennessee state senator Steve Cohen, jazz pianist Michael Wolff and his wife, the actress Polly Draper, Billy Bob Thornton, and seemingly every one of the dozens of women he'd had affairs with in the past, all of whom, as far as I could tell, still adored him.

Another close friend of Warren's was his dentist, Dr. Stan Golden, who, by coincidence, also looked after me and Rosemary. Stan was one of the authentic characters that only Los Angeles can produce. His white hair, beard, and motorcycle gave him the affect of a painter, but he was extremely serious about his vocation. His office was arrayed with photos and testimonials of movie stars whose teeth he had worked on, but his true love was rock and roll.

Stan was Bob Dylan's cousin and had grown up with him in Minnesota. In addition to signed photos of George Harrison and Mick Jagger, Stan proudly displayed the sheet music to "Blowin' in the Wind" with an inscription from his cousin affirming that Stan was "the best dentist in the world." Tapes of classic rock played perpetually in Stan's office. Stan was thrilled that I had signed Warren and asked how we had met. When I told him I had been introduced by Jackson he said earnestly, "Boy, I'd love to be Jackson Browne's dentist." I told Stan that in all of my conversations with Jackson the subject of his teeth had never come up, but that I'd keep it in mind.

Warren loved Stan. Part of the appeal was undoubtedly the Dylan connection. Part of it was that Stan gave him a good price for veneers on his teeth. As he had gotten older, Warren had become more and more obsessed with his appearance ("the job of looking good," he explained to his nonshowbiz friends) and Stan was a key ally. But at another level Stan played a paternal role that Warren coveted and appreciated.

A few months after the end of the *Life'll Kill Ya* tour, Warren told me with trepidation (or feigned trepidation) that his next oeuvre was going to be a "spiritual album." He didn't mean religious but more generally upbeat. "Hunter Thompson thought the last one was too morbid," Warren growled. "If *he* said that . . ." Warren and I both laughed at the notion of being too dark for Thompson. (Not that I ever met Hunter Thompson, but it was seductive to feel that Warren thought I knew him or pretended that he thought so.)

Instead of writing with Jorge Calderón or working with a producer again, Warren wanted to set up a home studio and **257** do everything himself. I figured that since we weren't paying very much for his albums, and since Warren was essentially an auteur, it would be inappropriate to argue. In retrospect I probably should have questioned him more seriously about this approach.

Warren had internalized the idea that adult albums needed PR "hooks," and he had decided to use the literary "angle" for all it was worth. He cowrote with a number of writers, including Thompson, Mitch Albom, Paul Muldoon, and Dave Barry. (Hiaasen used the lyrics of the song in his latest novel and the recording on his Web site.) Warren and Albom wrote a song about a hockey player called "Hit Somebody," which included a guest voice-over by David Letterman. Artemis had had unexpected success with the Baha Men novelty song "Who Let The Dogs Out," in part by getting it played in sports arenas, and we hoped that hockey teams would embrace Warren's song. They didn't. The title song, "My Ride's Here," was another poetic reference to death. Although I liked several of the songs, the album seemed less focused to me than *Life'll Kill Ya*. The one fully realized recording on it, the song "Genius," was a classic Zevon masterpiece, but it was particularly ill suited for radio play, even Triple A, because of the length of time it took to get to the chorus.

On the previous album Warren had been able to make money on the road by touring acoustically, without a band, accompanying himself on piano and guitar. He insisted that the songs on *My Ride's Here* couldn't be performed in concert without a full band. This would have meant that instead of making money on the road, he would have lost something like five thousand dollars a week, and he asked Artemis to pay for it. We couldn't afford it and Warren called my bluff and refused to tour—which also meant forgoing the interviews and in-stores that were scheduled in tandem with tour dates.

Shortly before *My Ride's Here* was finished, Warren was **258** asked to do the theme song to the TV show *Action,* an edgy parody of Hollywood that had a burst of publicity. Artemis VP Michael Krumper handled the liaison between the show and Warren, and for some reason the next thing I heard was that Warren was livid with Michael. I never could quite figure out what Warren was upset about, but I was pretty sure it involved an economic request that Michael turned down. Artemis was, of necessity, pinching pennies and Michael would have simply been trying to carry out my wishes. In any event, Warren told me that Krumper had gravely insulted him. I told Warren that he did not need to talk to Michael in the future but that I hoped that Warren was not asking me to fire him. Warren's tone immediately changed and he said, "Danny, if you fired him because of me I'd hang myself."

My Ride's Here only sold half as well as *Life'll Kill Ya*, and feelings were frayed on both sides. Warren, with the careful politeness he always used with me when there was any kind of stress, explained, "I'm very sensitive and when I hear a tone of voice that is less than enthusiastic, I get very discouraged." I knew this and I also knew that on any given day the people who worked at Artemis, or at any record company, might be under any number of pressures that could affect their tonality. He needed a manager or some kind of buffer to deal with the label. I also wanted some help. We had done everything we could, and Warren was still a brilliant artist, but without some sort of a gimmick such as a TV ad or a soundtrack I couldn't figure out how we could get him the audience he deserved.

Warren didn't mind the idea of a manager, but he said he couldn't afford to pay management commissions on his current level of touring income, which was the primary way he made a living. After racking my brains I could only come up with one person who would appreciate Warren, had enough clout to help, and made enough money that he could afford to waive commissions except on income growth: Irving Azoff. It wasn't a hard sell. Irving knew that Warren was a genius and he knew that both the artists he already worked with and the wealthy

259

baby boomers he did business with admired Zevon. He took him on with the proviso that the day-to-day work would be done by Brigette Barr, who had previously worked with Warren when she worked for Peter Asher.

The disputes in connection with the last album had left a little chill between us, and at Rosemary's urging, in August 2002 I met Warren for lunch at Ivy at the Shore in Santa Monica. I quickly told him that we would like to make another album with him, and the relief on his face was palpable. He had, after all, been dropped by four previous labels. As a peace offering he sheepishly said that "the new songs I'm writing I can perform acoustically," which was his way of acknowledging that it had been a mistake to refuse to tour on the last record even though there wasn't a record company subsidy for a band.

As always, Warren found a way of complaining about a couple of rock writers, this time quoting verbatim not only nasty phrases that Bay Area critics Joel Selvin and Greil Marcus had used in describing his work in years past but also things they had written about Jackson Browne and J. D. Souther. I was a little surprised that Warren considered an insult to Souther an unpardonable sin, but Warren looked at me like I was crazy. These guys were his brothers. He gleefully told me that he had recently been able to veto the inclusion of Selvin from jamming with the Rock Bottom Remainders.

I told him he had fans in unexpected places. Rosemary and I had hosted an event for the Creative Coalition that, to our dismay, the flamboyant right-wing writer Ann Coulter attended. When introduced to me Coulter gushed that she was a huge fan of Warren's and thought that she had heard that he had recently dedicated a performance of "Excitable Boy" to Bill Clinton, which she took for Zevon's endorsement of impeachment. Warren and I had never discussed politics but he blanched on hearing this anecdote. "Oh, my God, that's depressing," he growled, shaking his head with the same horror Kurt Cobain had when

contemplating his more Neanderthal fans. As we parted, Warren said he felt a little tired. Always impressed by Warren's bulg-
ing biceps I told him in words that would come back to haunt
me, "You look the picture of radiant health."

A few days later Warren called me at the house we were
renting in Malibu. I have imbedded in my memory a vivid image
of stopping in my tracks as I walked up the stairs holding a portable phone as I heard his halting voice. He wanted to discuss
something personal. My stomach clenched up, anticipating that
he would want to borrow money, which is usually what people
mean when they say that. I listened with growing shock as he
explained that he had seen a series of doctors at Stan's suggestion because he was having trouble breathing. Within a couple
of days Warren found out information that had not dawned on
him as a possibility earlier in the week: He had a terminal form
of cancer called mesothelioma in his lungs and liver and had,
perhaps, as few as three months left to live. I asked him if he
needed any money or other kind of help and he said he did not.
Stunned, I uttered some platitudes about prayers and got off of
the phone.

The form of cancer he had was not the result of smok-
ing but of exposure to asbestos, and Warren seemed slightly
relieved that his vices hadn't brought this on him and added,
with false levity, that he was perversely flattered to discover that
Steve McQueen had died of the same disease. Warren reiterated
that he didn't need money but I still felt, somewhat desperately,
that I should "do" something. My partner, Michael Chambers,
arranged to have Deepak Chopra meet him privately. Although
Warren liked Chopra, he decided not to use any of the time he
had left attending one of his retreats.

Warren wanted to record. His son Jordan recalls, "He
started to do the record because that was the only thing really
that dad ever did—he was a surfer and he was a musician."
Warren told me that since his children were grown up, his legacy was his music. His wiseguy intellect had previously resisted **261**

formal or sentimental words like *legacy*, but there was no reason for that now. Sentiment was no longer unhip.

For most of his career songwriting had been an agonizingly slow process for Warren but now, he said, the songs were coming almost spontaneously. "I told Brigette we really have to use this. I want her to be the most manipulative, exploitative manager she can be. I want to milk this for all it's worth." He insisted on a press release announcing his disease and did several interviews, telling *Entertainment Weekly*, "I'm okay with it, but it'll be a drag if I don't make it till the next James Bond movie comes out." He added prophetically, "If you're lucky, people like something you do early and something you do just before you drop dead. That's as many pats on the back as you should expect."

Brigette didn't know if it was one song or two or three. We certainly didn't anticipate he would live long enough to do an entire album. I figured that even if he just did one song, we could release it as a bonus track on a "best of" or something. I didn't know what we would do with the recordings, but I just opened up a budget. I initially sent $25,000. We ended up spending around $160,000 on the album, not much by normal standards but around double what the previous albums had cost. I justified this both in consideration of the celebrity duets that Warren was getting and because I just couldn't say no to him at this point. The whole thing was so devastating.

Jackson Browne reminded me that Warren's relationship with Jorge Calderón was creatively "very significant. . . . Warren with Jorge is different from Warren alone." Jorge was a Chilean native who had played bass on many of Warren's albums, produced a few, and written a dozen songs with him, more than any other cowriter. He was, as Jackson had predicted, Warren's choice as a collaborator and producer of the music that would become Warren's last album.

Jorge was sad-eyed, melancholy, self-effacing, and focused

on Warren's record. Everyone involved in the recording found it a bittersweet experience, dominated by the sense of the impending loss of Warren but filled with an artistic and spiritual energy that only could have occurred in the context of the awful and inspiring drama.

Jackson was floating an idea for a tribute album, with other artists doing Warren's songs. "Warren's songs are so great, and it would be great to hear them with different voices." Flashing back to his frustrations as a producer recording Warren's vocals, Jackson recalled, "He always insisted on being recorded like a manly man, like Ian Tyson." (Tyson was the deep-voiced lead singer of the Canadian folk duo Ian and Sylvia.) Warren's singing voice was indeed deep and unique, the kind of voice heard more often singing sea chanteys than popular rock and roll. Jackson was convinced that many of Warren's songs could take on a different life sung by different singers. I mentioned the idea to Warren, who snarled, "Tell Jackson to make the fucking tribute album after I'm dead. Right now I want to concentrate on my own new album."

Grimly focused on commerciality, Warren told me conspiratorially that in addition to his new songs he was covering "Knockin' on Heaven's Door," the Dylan song about death written originally for the movie *Pat Garrett and Billy the Kid*. It was a haunting, powerful idea coming from a guy who was actually dying. "Radio will have to play that, right?" he asked with a dark and poignant chuckle.

Most of the recording was done at Sunset Sound in Hollywood, which had been around since the late 1960s. Sunset had neither velvet couches nor video games, but all of the recording equipment was kept up to date and it had a great staff. Having recorded his last two albums mostly at home, Warren was pleased to be back in what still felt like the big time to him. With a proud grin Warren pointed out the gold albums on the studio walls representing recording done at Sunset: the first several Doors albums; the Rolling Stones' *Exile on Main Street*; Led Zeppelin's second and fourth albums; the Beach Boys' *Pet*

Sounds, Prince's *Purple Rain,* James Taylor's *Sweet Baby James,* Neil Diamond and Barbra Streisand's single "You Don't Bring Me Flowers," and Jackson's Brown's *The Pretender* as well as albums by Elton John, the Who, the Doobie Brothers, Van Halen, and, more recently, Rage Against the Machine, Sheryl Crow, and Sugar Ray.

Cutting off any chance of inquiries about his health, Warren greeted me with a hug and a grin and asked gruffly, "How did you like your press?" He had mentioned me very generously in recently published articles in *Rolling Stone* and the *L.A. Times.* I thanked him and acknowledged that I enjoyed seeing my name in print. "All of us in show business do," he said wistfully.

The song they were working on was "Dirty Life and Times," the lyrics of which showed Zevon at his most sardonic, a farewell from the lovable rogue, an elegy for Warren's defiant side:

> One day I came to a fork in the road
> Folks, I just couldn't go where I was told
> Now they'll hunt me down and hang me for my crimes
> If I tell about my dirty life and times

He felt good about the lyric because it wasn't maudlin. I suggested that it might not make a bad album title, which Warren politely appeared to consider, although he wisely jettisoned the idea later on and went with *The Wind.*

Jorge was bursting with excitement that Ry Cooder had played on the track. "Warren had wanted Ry to play on his other albums and Ry always blew him off. Until the minute he got here I was worried, but he showed up on time and he played great." Jorge gushed.

Brigette had nervously asked me if Artemis would pay for the famed fashion photographer Matthew Ralston to take an album cover photo. Even at a discount this was an extravagance, but I caved because I knew how much something like this symbolized status to Warren. But I stressed to him that the real key to making an impact was not the cover photo but the proposed VH1 special that required giving them access to the recording studio. This time around George Moll had been able to sell it internally, based on the death "angle" and the anticipated superstar guests. He had selected a British filmmaker named Nick Read, whom Warren was to meet the following day.

On October 30 Warren flew to New York to make his last appearance on the *Late Show with David Letterman*. It was a huge ordeal for him just to get the strength to get onto the plane. "I wasn't going to do it," he told me in the dressing room beforehand, "but then I remembered how Sammy Davis in *Yes I Can* wrote about dancing when he had cancer, so I figured I should make the effort." Warren, dressed in a gray Armani suit he bought for the occasion, was accompanied by Kristin Stefl, a tall, very pretty young woman who had been a flight attendant on a plane ride Warren had taken shortly before having been diagnosed. Kristin was at Warren's side most of the times I saw him the last few months, glamorous and sexy but also sweet and oozing compassion and regret. According to Brigette's cynical view Warren was actually closer to a number of other girlfriends even during this time. Warren was a classic ladies' man. He had dozens of girlfriends over the years and stayed in touch with most of them. But he had decided that Kristin gave him the right rock star image for his final days, especially for the VH1 special. As was typical with Warren, he found a way of merging cynicism and sentiment. The warmth and emotion between Warren and Kristin was very real, but so was his focus on his image.

Rosemary and I watched in the green room with Michael Wolff and Polly Draper. Warren was the sole guest for the entire hour, an honor shared, in the history of the Letterman show, only with Al Gore. There was reason to worry about whether Warren would really have the energy to do the whole thing but he sailed through it, performing "Roland the Headless Thompson Gunner" at Letterman's request, joking about having "the flu," acknowledging that having gone more than a decade without a physical checkup hadn't been such a great idea. In response to Letterman's question about whether or not he had anything to share with the audience—now that he was confronting his mortality—Warren shrugged and answered, "Just to enjoy every sandwich." Letterman tearfully repeated Warren's phrase when he did the sign-off at the end of the broadcast.

Backstage we were all choked up. I assured Warren he had been great and sounded great. Having beamed self-assurance and gruff charisma during the show, he suddenly seemed to shrink and hugged me, saying, "You know, I wish I did really just have the flu." I barely could get out the words "So do I." It was a terrible reminder that for all of Warren's showbiz bravado and Zen equilibrium, he really was living with the dream and finality of a fatal illness. It was, when all was said and done, no fucking joke.

A couple of weeks later I visited Sunset Sound again. Nick Read and the VH1 crew were documenting the proceedings as Warren cut live tracks on two new songs, "Prison Grove" and "Numb as a Statue." The band consisted of Jorge, who, in addition to producing, was playing bass, Cooder (again!) playing lead, David Lindley on multiple instruments, and drummer Jim Keltner, a legendary L.A. player whose credits include *Layla* as well as numerous Dylan and Neil Young albums.

Warren was again almost gleeful at being able to preside over such an august musical assemblage. Jorge gushed that "there is a guardian angel over this project. We're getting everybody we want when we need them."

Handing me some lyric sheets, Jorge singled out the line in "Prison Grove" that read "Take one last look at the prison yard." Jorge earnestly explained, "It's prison as a metaphor for death. And you know a prison yard—if we were to look at it, it would look ugly and spare. But to a person condemned to death, looking through the bars, you see the beauty even in a piece of gravel." Some part of Jorge was living in Warren's head. This is one of the things that great artists can do—bring out and enhance the soulfulness of the people around them.

For an hour or two there was the typical studio anxiety—getting sounds, connections, and headphones right and so forth. While waiting around I told Warren how much I loved one of the lines in "Dirty Life and Times," where he sang "I'm looking for a woman with low self-esteem." He grinned conspiratorially and told me, "Billy Bob called me and asked me if he could please sing it." The idea of Angelina Jolie's ex-husband insisting on singing that line delighted the Hollywood voyeur in Warren. Warren added, "Billy Bob is coming over later today too. I really like the way he sings with me." I mentioned that he was using a lot of the same people on a lot of songs and he nodded. "Exactly—it's an album and it's really gonna sound like an album." This is one of the prosaic studio clichés—to say that a group of songs is going to "sound like an album." But in the heightened atmosphere of this project it seemed like a revelation.

Ry Cooder was larger than life in the studio. His guitars were treated like rare antiques. His opinion about takes was always first among equals. He wore striking tortoiseshell glasses and said that they had been custom-made by a Moroccan designer he knew from Paris. When I mentioned Cooder's glasses to Warren he said, his respect tinged with envy, "These guys always have good shit. They have the shit and they have the shit." As he was about to go back to work in the control room, I told Jorge that I was nervous that Jackson Browne might be feeling left out. My concern wasn't commercial—the celeb guests were coming in thick and fast: In addition to Thornton and Dwight Yoakam, Warren's album had already attracted Tom Petty and Don Henley. But spiritually and emotionally it would be terribly wrong for Jackson not to be part of it.

Jorge had the solution in hand. "Jackson is in town—I called him. Warren finally said to me that it would be a good idea to get Reggie [one of Warren's many nicknames for Jackson] in here. I thought he could sound great on the chorus on 'Knockin' on Heaven's Door.'" Jorge shrugged apologetically and explained, "You know, Warren needed to start the album—to get the ball rolling—and then invite Jackson in." After all these years, even at this moment, was Warren still paranoid about Jackson having some sort of "control"? But Jorge delivered. Jackson came in a few days later, did several vocal parts, and had a great time with Warren.

During a break Warren said how pleased he was with a long piece that David Fricke had written about the recording of the album in the new *Rolling Stone*. "Pretty good, huh?" he growled in a satisfied tone. "If I was in midcareer it would be unethical to thank him, but given the circumstances I'd like him to know how I feel."

When I told Fricke of Warren's reaction, he was gratified. "Everyone at the magazine gave it a lot of care." Although *Rolling Stone*, like all music media, needed to attract younger readers, they had kept the connection between their older readers and older artists. Fricke laughed at the "unethical" line— only someone who put writers on a pedestal would have that concern.

I had asked Stan if Dylan was going to appear on the album. He responded that "Bob wants to do something but thinks that singing on the album would be too shallow." Warren and I figured that this meant Dylan didn't want to be part of a crowd. Soon thereafter Dylan started singing "Mutineer" and a couple of other Zevon songs in concert. Warren told me that he had gone with Stan to Dylan's L.A. show the night before last. "You know—it's almost worth it"—meaning almost worth dying to have that kind of acknowledgment. "I love Bob Dylan so much," Warren said with a rueful sigh.

Not withstanding his respect for the session guys, Warren **268** was very much in charge. After several takes of "Numb as a

Statue" he told Keltner, "Let's not get too Caribbean here—we don't want to go with James Bond down to Jamaica." A few minutes later, still unsatisfied, Warren told Jorge, "It's a little calypso for me—we need more slash, bash, and bad taste." Eventually the band got the idea and did the rockier version that appeared on the finished album.

During a break for lunch the now sober former party animals Zevon, Cooder, Keltner, and Lindley argued the merits of various caffeinated drinks. "Jolt and Bull shredded me," Lindley complained. They concluded that Warren's favorite, Mountain Dew, was the gold standard.

Later, Warren took me aside and confided that he had started taking painkillers and other drugs. "I told my doctors that my program required me to avoid these drugs, and they said that is not an option," he solemnly told me. He could now have his cake and eat it too: drink or take drugs with no opprobrium from himself or others—not much of a trade-off for a fatal illness, but there it was.

Just as I was about to leave, Krumper called the studio. A PR person at United Artists had read Warren's quote about the James Bond movie and offered to arrange a screening of *Die Another Day* for him at his convenience. Warren grunted contentedly when I told him the news. Everything was easy—except for the fact that he was dying.

A few weeks later Bruce Springsteen flew to Hollywood on a day off from his tour. It was an incredible gesture that required Springsteen to fly back and forth from the Northwest on a private plane that he paid for. Like all of the other guests Bruce worked for free and made sure his record company signed all of the requisite releases. Warren originally expected him to sing harmonies, but Bruce turned "Disorder in the House" into a full-blown duet and played a sizzling lead guitar part on it as well.

Brigette called me at one point nearly in tears to complain that VH1 was overreaching. They had wanted to go with him to his doctor's office, and wanted to interview Warren's daughter. Ariel was shy and had always avoided any kind of spotlight. "We let them in the control room with Springsteen," Brigette shouted. "That ought to be enough." When I called Moll, he backed off, but Read somehow convinced Warren to let him shoot thirty seconds in the doctor's office, which ended up being one the most powerful moments in the film.

During this period Zevon stayed utterly in character: gruff, sarcastic, blunt, and emotionally honest. The cancer was originally thought to be in both his lungs and his liver. "The doctors aren't so sure about my liver now," he said to me on the phone one day. "You think everybody's gonna be mad if I don't kick off right away?" He told Carl Hiaasen he was "living out this low-budget Elvis twilight." When VH1 filmmaker Read asked him how the rest of his life was going, Warren grinned and replied with brio, "Schopenhauer says that when we buy a book we tell ourselves that we are also buying the time to read it. Ain't that grand?" He called our mutual friend, film music supervisor Debbie Gold, for the first time in years and asked, "How do you feel about sex with the terminally ill?"

When the album was almost finished, the sessions suddenly came to a grinding halt. I was worried that the end was near, but Jordan later explained to me that the problem was that Warren's medical need for painkillers had trumped his AA discipline and left him without the inner compass he had carefully nurtured over the last two decades. "By Christmastime things really went to shit," Jordan said. "He was drinking and taking every pill you could get as well as liquid morphine. He was totally isolated, living off of groceries delivered to his doorstep." Jordan rang his doorbell for over an hour one day till his dad answered the door. "He was in really bad shape—looked like a zombie."

Having been a notoriously inattentive dad when Jordan was growing up, Warren had spent years making up for lost time. They called each other "Johnny Son" and "Johnny Pop" and bantered in a profane mock macho language that, Jordan felt, was "like getting a big hug." Jordan was an accomplished musician and composer in his own right but had worked as a publicist at Arista to make a living. He had often thought it might make sense for him to manage his dad's career the way Tony Bennett's son did with his dad. But Warren had always resisted any professional relationship. He had a long history of demonizing businesspeople, whom he often referred to as "turd handlers," telling Jordan honestly, "You can't be my manager. I need someone I can yell at." In these final months, however, there was no one other than Jordan he could trust. Jordan helped him reduce his drug intake, hired a Jamaican woman to read the Bible to him, made final decisions about photos and the like, and he and Jorge got Warren to do his final vocal on the last song he wrote, "Keep Me in Your Heart."

Suddenly Brigette was all over us about getting the album ready to release so it could come out while he was still alive. On June 12 Ariel gave birth to the twin boys. Warren told me that the twins had fallen asleep on his chest and "it was just heaven."

Jordan did many of the prerelease interviews, since Warren was too weak to do them with the kind of brio he expected of himself. When I mentioned the intelligence of Jordan's quotes in the press about the album, Warren said, "I'm so proud. He's such a good kid."

Just as the album was about to be released, Brigette had a falling-out with Azoff. Most likely it was simply that she wasn't bringing in any money. When she left she wanted Warren to "go with her," but to her shock Warren wanted to stay with Azoff. Warren told me, "I appreciate what Brigette did for me, but I want to be represented by Irving." It wasn't that Irving personally could do much for him, but to the end he wanted a more big-time image. Brigette was disconsolate, but she made the terrible mistake of bad-mouthing Jordan, which distanced her during the last month of Warren's life.

I called Warren after the first reviews were coming in, and to my amazement he called back. "Yeah, the nurse went out and I was able to get a message myself for a change," he growled. He asked about the reviews in considerable detail and seemed pleased but also sounded weak and exhausted.

As Warren had anticipated, several Triple A and rock radio stations who had avoided his music in recent years played "Knockin' on Heaven's Door." Don Imus premiered the entire album on his national talk show. The VH1 special aired on August 25 and the album was in the stores the next day. Warren's prior album, *My Ride's Here,* had sold around 30,000 copies, and retailers typically based their orders on what they had sold on an artist's previous effort. With all of the publicity around this album and the impending VH1 special and guest appearances from Springsteen et al, we hounded our distributor. Daniel and I personally called all of the major retail chains and were able to get advance orders for 76,000 pieces. Within a few days the orders were up to 150,000 and we had the sweetest of all crises—stock problems, which were alleviated with a few frantic calls to manufacturers. *The Wind* SoundScanned 48,000 the first week and debuted at number fourteen. The only time an album of his had attained a higher chart position was when *Excitable Boy* had gone to number eight, twenty-five years earlier.

On Thursday, September 4, I called Warren with the news and told him the album would soon be gold. Three days later, as Rosemary and I were putting the kids to bed, the phone rang; it was Jorge. He was sitting in Warren's apartment waiting for the hearse from Forest Lawn to come. Warren had passed away a few hours earlier, around four-thirty L.A. time. Jorge told me that Warren's friend Ryan Rayston had been with him at the last moments and said that he was smiling.

"At some point," Jackson had said to knowing laughter near the end of his remarks at Warren's funeral, "every one of his friends had a falling-out with Warren." Afterward it seemed like everyone wanted to describe the time when Warren had turned on them. Jorge wondered why Warren had made *My Ride's Here* without him. Michael Wolff, the jazz pianist and former music director of the Arsenio Hall TV show, was cut off for more than a year because of some misunderstanding over a piece of borrowed equipment. As someone who met and worked with Warren only in the last few years of his life, I had gotten off pretty easily. But Jackson had endured the unique resentment of a debtor. "It wasn't really fair to him that he was known as my protégé," Jackson explained. Not only could Warren never really repay him, but he had to endure the fact that Jackson was perennially a bigger star. Warren morosely observed on more than one occasion that Jackson had "perfect hair." His retribution had been to find petty reasons to keep Jackson at a distance. It was a weapon that could only be effective on someone who loved Warren as much as Jackson did but was somewhat mitigated by Jackson's awareness that in the cosmic scheme of things, Zevon reciprocated his affection.

Neil Portnow, who ran NARAS, the organization that gave out the Grammy Awards, had given Warren a President's Committee Award, a certificate of some kind, when he got sick, but I wanted a real Grammy. I figured he would be nominated for Contemporary Folk, which had become the catch-all for singer-songwriters. Two artists I had signed at Mercury, Lucinda Williams and Shelby Lynne, had won that award in successive years, and I knew that Contemporary Folk was one of dozens of awards (along with the classical, jazz, polka, and spoken-word categories) that were given out in a pretelevised ceremony attended by artists, significant others, and a few people in the business who worked with the artists. Nontelevised awards didn't have much of an impact on record sales. We wanted nominations for awards that would be given out on TV.

I got a few well-intentioned calls from various people involved in the album wanting to know what we were "doing" to maximize his nominations. Even my own executives hypothesized about some sort of "campaign." When I managed Bonnie I had never gotten the impression that Capitol had any particular campaign to target NARAS members. They seemed as surprised as we were when she got nominated for Album of the Year and as shocked as we were when she won. At Mercury we were similarly surprised when Joan Osborne got nominated for so many awards. (I was president of the company at the time and I knew for sure that there was no campaign.) But now the Grammy rules had changed and there was some committee system that produced the nominations. Artemis was an independent label with a staff that was down to thirty people, none of whom, as far as I knew, were voting members of NARAS. The big companies had a few thousand each, many of whom were members. My confidence in the theory that "it either happens or it doesn't" was sufficiently shaken that I called Portnow. He firmly advised me, "Don't do anything," implying that any campaign could only backfire. "Warren has plenty of fans here," he assured me.

It was good advice. *The Wind* got four nominations: Contemporary Folk (for the album), Rock Duet (with Springsteen for "Disorder in the House," which was also nominated for Best Rock Song), and, amazingly, Song of the Year (for "Keep Me in Your Heart"). But musical performances sold as many records as winning awards on TV did, sometimes even more. It was a long shot, but I decided to pitch the idea of a musical tribute to Warren in lieu of a performance.

The Grammy TV show had long been produced by Ken Ehrlich, a veteran of dozens of award shows and a real music lover. Ehrlich's favorite story was about getting Aretha Franklin to replace Luciano Pavarotti at the last minute when the legendary tenor got a sore throat as he was about to sing *Nessun dorma*. I knew from experience with Ehrlich that he always looked for something unique so that the show would have some must-see moments. Most of the details of the show were left to coproducer Tisha Fein. Tisha's father, Irving Fein, was a legendary show business figure, having been the personal manager of Jack Benny and George Burns, but Tisha's career had been all about rock and roll. I had known her since the seventies, when she booked the pre-MTV late-night rock show *Midnight Special*. For decades it seemed like every award show hired Tisha to organize the performances. I pitched the idea of a tribute performance by Warren's friends and dropped the names of Springsteen, Petty, Henley, and Jackson Browne.

Ehrlich made it clear that without a superstar the idea was a nonstarter. The previous year Springsteen had been nominated for several Grammys, attended the telecast, and come up empty-handed. Even though he and Landau knew that the producers of the show didn't decide who had won, Bruce was not inclined to shlep across the country to do the show. And he had certainly done his thing for Warren in the recording and on the VH1 special. Henley had to be somewhere else, and Petty's management said that Tom hadn't really known Warren that well. I reported these disappointments to Tisha, figuring we were dead, but to my surprise she said that if I could get Jackson Browne she could still probably sell Ken on the idea.

The problem was that Jackson wasn't into it. The Grammys weren't a culture that related to an artist like Warren. The poet Paul Muldoon would later write a poem about Warren called "Sillyhow Stride," in which he described watching the Grammys with "all those bling-it-ons in their bulletproof broughams," adding that Warren's spirit was, to the poet, "as incongruous / there as John Donne at a Junior Prom." That was more or less what Jackson felt. When I tried to defend the eclectic nature of the award show, Jackson upped the ante by adding sharply that "Keep Me in Your Heart" was "not a song that lends itself to four-part harmony." I was certainly out of my depths discussing musical arrangements and Jackson knew it. I played my only **275** remaining card: "Jackson, I don't have the knowledge or talent to talk to you about music. I'm just trying to keep my company going. I need this to sell more records." It was kind of creepy of me. Jackson bowed to no one in his views on music, but he was susceptible to a guilt trip. After a pregnant pause Jackson sighed and said, "I understand. Of course I'll do it."

But the next day he balked again, this time trumping my need with his own vulnerability. "I'm not a good harmony singer. You need Don, not me. And if I do sing, I'll be mixed out and no one will hear me." Although I knew I had no chance of getting Henley, I told Jackson I was working on it, hung up, and called Jorge, who was as invested in the Grammy performance as I was.

Jorge somehow got Jackson to relent and at the show he, Billy Bob Thornton, Tim Schmit, Jorge, Jordan, Ariel, and Emmylou Harris sang muted harmonies on the chorus of "Keep Me in Your Heart" on a dimly lit stage while on TV the picture primarily consisted of Warren's own performance from the VH1 special. Over the end of it they included a scroll of other artists who had died that year. I was amazed that the Grammy TV show had given us, in essence, a commercial for our album. Backstage I asked Tisha how it had happened. This was the opposite of the kind of unique programming Ehrlich had always demanded. And Johnny Cash, a Grammy staple, a far larger superstar than Warren, had died the same year! Tisha looked at me and shrugged. "I kept having all these dreams the last few weeks in which Warren was talking to me. I just had to do it."

Warren won two Grammys, Contemporary Folk and Best Rock Duet, the latter of which was indeed televised. Jordan accepted for him and thanked me and Artemis on national TV. The album went gold the next week.

We had a party afterward at McCabe's Guitar Shop. Jackson and his band had learned and played ten Zevon songs, a repertoire Jackson had never done before and hasn't since. "You are in the right place at the right time," Jackson told the audience of a few hundred as the band commenced their labor of love. "His name," Jackson said, "will come to be as well-known for how he faced and dealt with death as for his music." Although I had made it clear I would pay any rehearsal or cartage costs, Jackson never charged Artemis a penny.

Over the next few months we worked on the tribute record. Jorge produced several of the tracks. Jackson did "Poor Poor Pitiful Me," with harmonies by Bonnie Raitt. Jordan found a version of "Mutineer," sung by Dylan, that was on Napster. I e-mailed the recording to Dylan's manager, Jeff Rosen, and within a couple of days he sent me permission to release it—for free. Jorge produced Don Henley singing "Searching for a Heart." ("They say that love conquers all, / You can't start it like a car, / You can't stop it with a gun.") Jordan sang the previously un-released "Studebaker." We also got songs from the Pixies, the Wallflowers, and Pete Yorn. Jorge plaintively sang "Keep Me in Your Heart" and Billy Bob Thornton did a great job on the pre-viously unrecorded song "The Wind," which had not appeared on Warren's album.

I'd gotten the rights to a version of "Werewolves of Lon-don" by the Grateful Dead, but Jorge called with big news from Waddy Wachtel, who had cowritten and produced War-ren's original version of "Werewolves." Wachtel had spoken to Adam Sandler about recording a version of the song and Sandler had agreed. As unlikely as this seemed to me, I called Sandler's longtime manager, Sandy Wernick, who confirmed the news. "He liked Warren and he loves Waddy," Sandy said to me, and inquired, "I assume there is no money in this. Is this a charity album?" I gulped. "The only charity is to keep Artemis in business," I said. Wernick laughed and said that was fine.

"This means a lot to Waddy," Jorge told me, "because War-ren and Waddy weren't speaking for the last year." Having written his biggest hit with Warren, having been mentioned by name in Warren's song "Things to Do in Denver When You're

277

Dead," he had one of the ultimate "falling-outs" that Jackson had spoken about at the funeral.

Yet there was Waddy in the studio with Adam Sandler, wanting to pay tribute to Warren one last time, have a musical reconciliation with him, manically explaining to me that on the original track he and Warren had enlisted the help of Mick Fleetwood to play the drum part because it was too quirky for any of the regular session guys to play. For the Sandler session Waddy found and used that same rhythm track. Jordan came to the session and Sandler told him that his own father had recently died and played him a song he had written about his own dad. From the grave Warren had again combined laughter and tears and, for Waddy, a reconnection.

I had wanted to call the album *Werewolves of London,* but luckily Jordan put his foot down and insisted on *Enjoy Every Sandwich*. I had fantasized about having a pop hit with Sandler, but radio stations didn't take it seriously. I tried to get Waddy to talk Sandler into making a video to no avail. I couldn't fault him for that. Sandler was one of the most famous movie stars in the world and unless the song was acting like a hit at radio, it would be silly for him to risk looking like he had a flop. There was no chicken and no egg. In general tribute albums didn't do very well because there was no artist to focus on promoting it. *Enjoy Every Sandwich* netted out at around seventy-five thousand but it remains one of my favorite albums that I was ever involved with.

Like Bob Dylan, Bruce Springsteen performed some of Warren's songs in concert when Warren got sick. He gave us a version he did of "My Ride's Here" the day after Warren died. Bruce's voice singing the lyrics Warren wrote with Paul Muldoon still choke me up:

> *Shelley and Keats were out in the street*
> *And even Lord Byron was leaving for Greece*
> *While back at the Hilton, last but not least*

Milton was holding his sides
Saying, "You bravos had better be
ready to fight
Or we'll never get out of East Texas tonight
The trail is long and the river is wide
And my ride's here"

Around the time Zevon was finishing *The Wind*, I sold control of Artemis to pay its bills and a year later the investment bankers who had bought the company merged it into some other labels. I got a nonmusic job as CEO of Air America Radio, which had a political purpose I loved but which had been, and would be, hampered by underfunding that I could not remedy. In the summer of 2006 I started a new management company called Gold Village Entertainment. Steve Earle and his wife, singer-songwriter Allison Moorer, were my first clients.

While I was running Artemis, we had released three of Steve's albums, *Transcendental Blues, Jerusalem,* and *The Revolution Starts . . . Now.* Steve's music and temperament were a perfect match for the sensibilities of many music journalists, and a long series of publicists had their reputations enhanced by their association with him. His recording career had accelerated in the 1980s because of support from rock critics like Robert Hillburn and Dave Marsh and from a few Triple A stations such as WXRT in Chicago. Like many "adult" rock artists he made the most of his living on the road, at least half of it in Europe.

The last two Artemis releases were openly political collections of songs written in reaction to the Iraq war. The song "John Walker's Blues," on *Jerusalem,* was a mournful meditation on the personality of John Walker Lindh, an American who had been arrested because he was a member of the Taliban. It was obvious to music critics and to his fans that the song was in the long tradition of folk songs about prisoners and criminals, but a right-wing talk-radio host in Nashville absurdly accused Steve of "supporting" the Taliban and there was a flurry of efforts in the tabloid press to demonize Steve as had been done to the Dixie Chicks. We made a documentary of his tour following the controversy called *Just an American Boy. The Revolution Starts . . . Now* won Steve a Grammy Award in the Contemporary Folk category. It was his first award after having been nominated eight previous times.

Steve is at least as sophisticated about the business as I am, and he is a true renaissance man. Having had a well-publicized drug problem in his younger years, he was a man with a work ethic that made it seem as if he was making up for lost time. While on Artemis, in addition to the three albums of original material in five years, he released a "live" album and *Side-tracks,* a collection of songs he had written for compilations and soundtracks. During the same period he had written and produced a play (*Karla*) and a book of short stories (*Doghouse Roses*), and was finishing a novel. As an actor he played a recurring role in the HBO series *The Wire.* As I was finishing this book he was in the middle of a worldwide tour, but during his off time he produced a new Joan Baez album. Steve was also a dedicated political activist who focused particularly on the abolition of the death penalty and antiwar work. On those rare occasions when he was not immersed in one of his vocations he took on projects such as the writing of a

haiku every day for a year. Having never graduated from high school, Steve was a classic autodidact and was one of the best-read people I knew.

Near the end of the Artemis period Steve married Allison and rented a place in Greenwich Village around the corner from where my family lived. I got him a new record deal with indie New West Records and he recorded *Washington Square Serenade,* a group of songs expressing his love for Allison, for New York City, and for the legacy of the Greenwich Village folk scene. "Rock and roll became art because of what happened here," he would often say as he looked down Jones Street at the locale of the photo Bob Dylan had taken for the cover of *The Freewheelin' Bob Dylan.* In 2008 *Washington Square Serenade* earned Steve his second Grammy Award, also in the Contemporary Folk category.

Gold Village Entertainment added the Hives, Tom Morello, Ben Lee, the Old 97's, Rhett Miller, and Ian Hunter as clients. I also created a small imprint called Ammal Records, which released some early Warren Zevon demos and a new album by Ray Davies, and created a partnership with Ryan Gentles, manager of the Strokes, to handle clients together.

In the previous several years the music business had undergone enormous changes. By early 2008 the recording side of the business was in a downward spiral. An increasing proportion of the music audience was getting recordings for free on the Internet. Billions of dollars vanished from major record companies, along with almost all of the jobs that related to long-term development and career building. Overall CD sales had declined by more than half in the preceding decade and uncertainty about the future had depressed the asset value of catalogs. The Warner Music Group had been sold to an investor group headed by Edgar Bronfman and then had gone public. In the year 2007, during which Warner Music actually increased its market share, its stock price dropped more than 70 percent, a reflection of the huge decline of the value of recordings.

iTunes had emerged as one of the largest record retailers, but the big money was not made by artists or the people who worked with them but by Apple, who made billions selling the iPods while more or less breaking even selling recordings. A company called Media Defender charged major media companies millions per year to make it harder for fans to find illegal files of superstars on peer-to-peer networks, but the effort merely slowed the decline of sales.

With the staff and marketing support declining at the majors for most artists, many established stars opted to release their own records, including Jackson Browne, the Eagles, and Nine Inch Nails. Radiohead got worldwide publicity when they invited fans to pay whatever they wanted for their record *In Rainbows*. Like the previous several Radiohead albums it did extremely well, but it seemed to me that this was a reflection of the genius of the band's music, the intensity of their following, and the cleverness of their managers, rather than a model that other artists could profitably follow.

Other music media were affected by the Internet as well. Many of the most passionate new music fans began plugging their iPods into car stereos, leaving radio stations with an even more passive and unadventurous audience to sell to advertisers. MTV and VH1 got their ratings from reality shows and played fewer music videos than ever. Teenagers were as likely to find out about a new song from their friends on Facebook or MySpace as from the old media. Meanwhile, many artists still relied on the support of journalists both in print and on the Web to bond them with cult fans.

Some rock artists, such as John Mellencamp, found that licensing their music to TV commercials, which in previous decades had been a sign of inauthenticity, was the best way of exposing their music. Steve Earle explained, "Michelangelo didn't love the pope's politics. He just needed a ceiling to paint. Artists will do what they have to do to make a living and get their art out there."

As record companies scaled down their marketing efforts, other business entities, such as Starbucks, vied to be the driver of careers, along with a handful of music publishing companies such as Primary Wave, which had bought an interest in the copyrights of Kurt Cobain and Steve Earle.

Meanwhile, the concert business was booming. Computers could not deliver the social experience of a live show, and it was not difficult to find musclebound security guards to make sure fans couldn't get in without a ticket. It turned out that there was an enormous value in building a long-term image of integrity. Artists such as Iggy Pop, Sonic Youth, and Wilco, none of whom had histories of radio hits, did better business on the road than ever. When fans loved an artist they would pay high ticket prices. The giant concert promoter Live Nation bought up several merchandising companies and made a long-term deal with Madonna, U2, Jay-Z and several other artists, in which they would be responsible for all aspects of their careers including recordings. The William Morris Agency was becoming more aggressive in structuring multimedia deals that included records.

Ahmet Ertegun died at the age of eighty-two at the end of 2006, the result of a nasty fall he had taken backstage at a Rolling Stones concert. At his memorial service the following year I was one of a couple thousand friends, acquaintances, elite of the music business, and wannabes who crowded into the Lincoln Center jazz space in the Time Warner Center to hear music from Eric Clapton, Stevie Nicks, Crosby, Stills, Nash and Young, and Bette Midler and talks from New York mayor Michael Bloomberg, Henry Kissinger, Oscar de la Renta, and Mick Jagger.

A month earlier, at a shabby alcove of St. Mark's Church on the Lower East Side, I had attended a less glamorous but equally moving memorial for Paul Nelson, the pioneering journalist who had died at the age of sixty-nine, apparently from malnutrition. Paul had gotten a severe case of writer's block

285

during the last decade of his life. He worked at the Evergreen Video store in Greenwich Village a few blocks from my home, and I visited him from time to time to get his gloomy but trenchant insights about reissues of cinema noir classics and compare notes about the latest work of rock poets like Leonard Cohen.

David Johansen, Warren Zevon's ex-wife Crystal, Jon Landau, and Bob Dylan's manager Jeff Rosen joined with dozens of rock writers to honor Paul's elegant prose and passionate advocacy of music he loved. (The very week of the memorial Bob Dylan's album *Modern Times* had reached number one on the album sales charts, his first number-one album in thirty years. This feat was accomplished in part through an ingenious strategy that included promotions with iPod and Starbucks.)

Nirvana biographer Michael Azerrad noted that "when Paul started you couldn't make a living writing about rock music. There were no commercial editors' jobs or best sellers to be written about rock. You wrote about it only because you loved it." Danny Fields, choking with emotion, said that he hired Nelson at the short-lived sixties magazine *Hullabaloo* because "he was someone who liked rock and roll. There's so much not to like—there is so little *to* like. And when Paul liked something, he got other people to like it."

Rock and roll refused to die. Amid the pop wave driven by the TV show *American Idol,* the continued vitality of hiphop, movies like *School of Rock,* and video games like "Guitar Hero" and "Imagine Rock Star," millions of teenagers bonded with rock and roll.

Millions of older rock fans maintained great loyalty to their favorite artists. Promoters estimated that a new Led Zeppelin tour could gross more than a billion dollars. Jimmy Page had played brilliantly at the Led Zeppelin reunion concert in London. The middle-aged audience who had flown in from more than fifty countries were rewarded with a two-hour set filled with energy and creativity. I joined a sea of aging rock-

and-rollers in an audience that had the feel of a high school reunion. I felt a retroactive validation when, immediately prior to the band's entrance, they showed a minute-long video consisting in its entirety of news footage from the 1973 Tampa Stadium show in which some long-forgotten local newsman breathlessly explained that Led Zeppelin had "broken the Beatles' record."

Krist Novoselic worked assiduously as a political activist in Washington State and wrote a book that Robert Greenwald and I published on our RDV imprint called *Of Grunge and Government.*

Patti Smith was inducted into the Rock and Roll Hall of Fame in 2007. Zack de la Rocha of Rage Against the Machine gave the induction speech. Patti dedicated her award to the memory of her late husband, Fred Smith, who had played guitar for the MC5. The couple's song "People Have the Power" was used for the big celebrity jam that always ends the Hall of Fame program. Among those onstage with her were Eddie Vedder, Stephen Stills, Keith Richards, and members of cohonoree R.E.M.

Patti played at the Santa Monica Pier that summer, and I watched the show with Rosemary, who had been her attorney for more than a decade, and our son Max. Standing on the side of the stage as a crowd of ten thousand awaited Patti's performance, Lenny Kaye recalled the journalist who had written about us in *The Sydney Morning Herald* in 1970 and had died of asthma three years later. "If only Lillian Roxon were alive to see this. She would have loved it," he said with a wistful smile.

Patti wore her trademark black jacket and slacks with a white T-shirt that had a hand-painted peace sign and the word LOVE written underneath it. Her graying hair flying, her body bouncing with the energy of a teenager's, Patti grooved joyously with Flea, the bass player of the Red Hot Chili Peppers, as they played the Stones classic "Gimme Shelter." At the end of an impassioned version of Jefferson Airplane's "White Rabbit" Patti **287** exhorted the audience to remember "you can do anything. You can go anywhere. Imagination is king."

As the show drew to a close Patti mused, "Forty years ago I was in my shitty apartment in south Jersey and forty years later—things have improved." Then she broke the sky open with a version of Jimi Hendrix's "Are You Experienced," ending with Hendrix's cosmic observation of rock and roll reality: "Not necessarily stoned but beautiful."

ABOUT THE AUTHOR

Danny Goldberg has been in the music business since the 1960s as a journalist, PR person, personal manager whose clients included Nirvana and Bonnie Raitt, and as president of three major record companies—Atlantic Records, Warner Bros. Records, and Mercury Records. Goldberg currently runs Gold Village Entertainment, a personal management company. He is the author of the book *How the Left Lost Teen Spirit* and lives in New York with his wife, Rosemary Carroll, and their children, Katie and Max.

INDEX

293